ISBN: 9781314901207

Published by:
HardPress Publishing
8345 NW 66TH ST #2561
MIAMI FL 33166-2626

Email: info@hardpress.net
Web: http://www.hardpress.net

BOOK OF PRAISE

FOR THE SUNDAY SCHOOL,

WITH HYMNS AND TUNES APPROPRIATE FOR THE PRAYER MEETING

AND THE HOME CIRCLE.

EDITED BY

GEORGE A. BELL and HUBERT P. MAIN.

New York and Chicago:

BIGLOW & MAIN, PUBLISHERS.

For Sale by Booksellers and Music Dealers.

PREFACE.

THE hymns in this Collection have been arranged in order under the following subjects :—

The "BOOK OF PRAISE" like its predecessor "Christian Songs" is a compilation of old and new hymns and tunes. It is mainly the result of a judgement formed during an active superintendence of large city schools in which singing has been a leading feature. Compositions which have been tested by time and proved to be of substantial merit have been inserted ; and new music and new hymns have been selected from recent publications, including "Brightest and Best."

Simplicity has neither been aimed at nor avoided. We have not worked on the belief that only the highest class of music and the *standard* hymns (as they are called) should be used in our schools, nor yet have we failed to introduce such compositions freely. We have endeavored to elevate the taste, and yet not destroy the fervor of worship.

Our thanks are due to many authors and to owners of copyright for their kind permission to use valuable contributions. And here it is necessary that we should say that nearly all the pieces, both WORDS and MUSIC, being Copyright Property, permission must be obtained from the owners for their use in any form.

Many improvements pointed out by that excellent guide, experience, have been introduced, and indeed every effort has been put forth to make this a satisfactory and useful book not only for the Sunday School but also for the Prayer Meeting and for the Home Circle.

GEORGE A. BELL, } *Editors.*
HUBERT P. MAIN,

BOOK OF PRAISE

FOR THE

SUNDAY SCHOOL.

REVIVE US AGAIN.

Dr. W. P. MACKAY, 1866.

From "New Praises of Jesus," by per.

1. We praise Thee, O God! for the Son of Thy love, For   Je - sus who died, and is now gone a - bove.
2. We praise Thee, O God! for Thy Spir-it   of light, Who has shown us our Saviour, and scattered our night.
3. All glo - ry and praise, to the Lamb that was slain, Who has borne all our sins, and has cleansed every stain.

CHORUS.

{ Hal - le - lu - jah! Thine the glo - ry,   Hal-le - lu - jah! A - men. }
{ Hal - le - lu - jah! Thine the glo - ry,   [Omit......................] } Re-vive us a - gain.

(PRAISE.)

4

ST. GEORGE.

DEAN ALFORD.   Sir G. J. ELVEY.

1, Come, ye thankful peo-ple, come, Raise the song of Har-vest-Home! All   is safe-ly gathered in,
2. What   is earth but God's own field, Fruit un-to His praise to yield? Wheat and tares therein are sown,
3. For   we know that Thou wilt come, And   wilt take Thy peo-ple home ; From Thy field wilt purge a - way

Ere the winter storms begin ; God our Maker, doth provide,   For our wants to be supplied; Come to God's own
Un-to joy or sorrow grown; Ripening with a wondrous pow'r, Till the fi-nal Harvest-hour: Grant, O Lord of
All that doth offend, that day; And Thine angels charge at last In the fire the tares to cast,   But the fruitful

4.

tem-ple, come; Raise the song of Har-vest Home !
life, that we   Ho - ly grain and pure may be.   A - men.
ears to store In Thy gar-ner ev - er more.

Come then, Lord of mercy, come,
Bid us sing Thy Harvest-Home !
Let Thy saints be gathered in,
Free from sorrow, free from sin ;
All upon the golden floor
Praising Thee for evermore ;
Come, with thousand angels, come ;
Bid us sing Thy Harvest-Home ! Amen.

(PRAISE.)

TO GOD BE THE GLORY.

FANNY J. CROSBY. 1875.

From "Brightest and Best." W. H. DOANE.

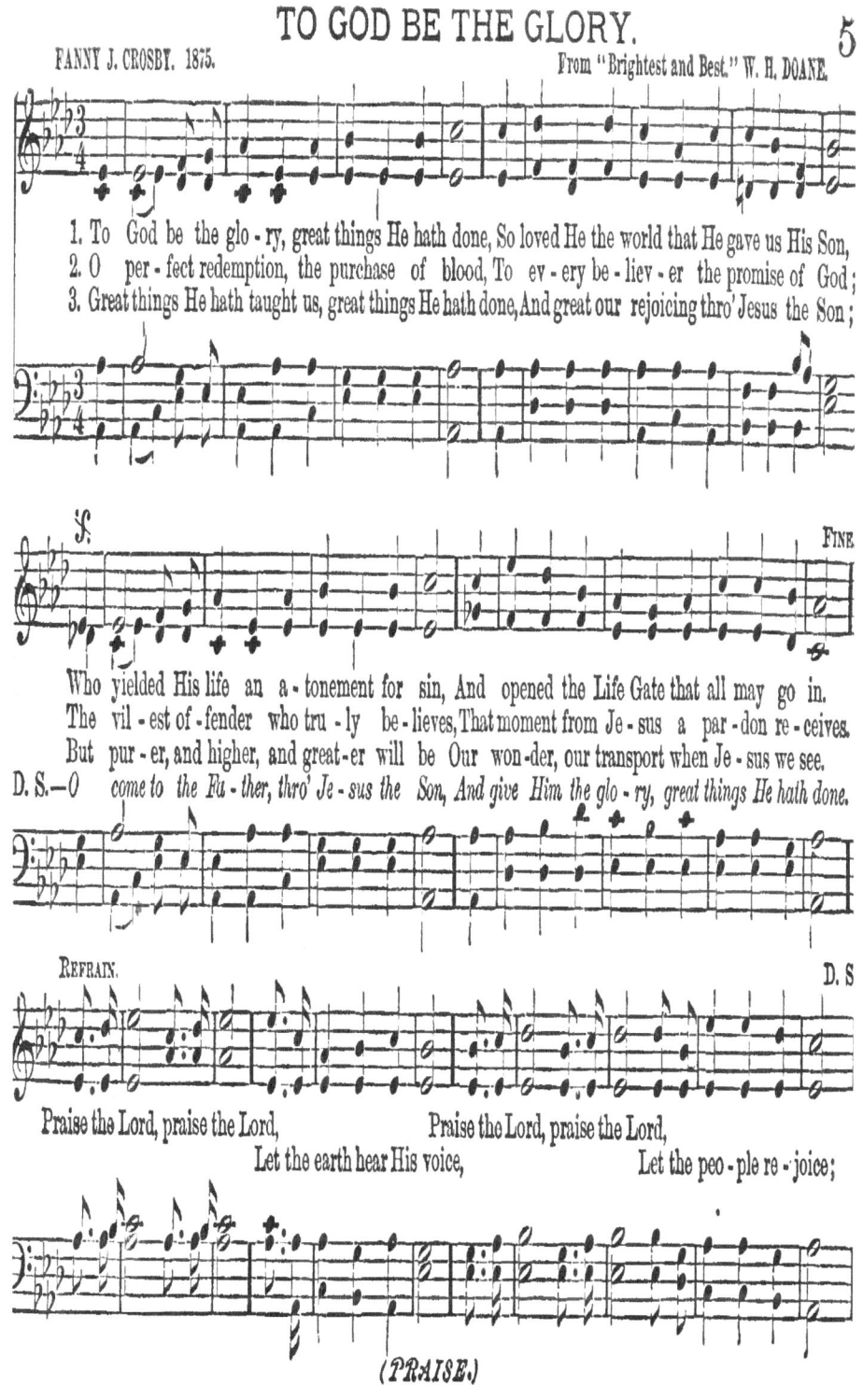

1. To God be the glo - ry, great things He hath done, So loved He the world that He gave us His Son,
2. O per - fect redemption, the purchase of blood, To ev - ery be - liev - er the promise of God;
3. Great things He hath taught us, great things He hath done, And great our rejoicing thro' Jesus the Son;

Who yielded His life an a - tonement for sin, And opened the Life Gate that all may go in.
The vil - est of - fender who tru - ly be - lieves, That moment from Je - sus a par - don re - ceives.
But pur - er, and higher, and great - er will be Our won - der, our transport when Je - sus we see.

D. S.—O come to the Fa - ther, thro' Je - sus the Son, And give Him the glo - ry, great things He hath done.

REFRAIN.

D. S

Praise the Lord, praise the Lord,   Praise the Lord, praise the Lord,
Let the earth hear His voice,   Let the peo - ple re - joice;

(PRAISE.)

JESUS SHALL REIGN. L. M.

ISAAC WATTS. 1719.

KARL WILHELM, Arr.

1. Je - sus shall reign where'er the sun Does his suc - cessive journeys run; His kingdom spread from shore to
2. To Him shall endless prayer be made And endless praises crown His head; His name like sweet perfume shall

shore, Till moons shall wax and wane no more. From north to south the princes meet, To pay their homage
rise With ev - ery morning sac - ri - fice. Peo - ple and realms of ev - ery tongue Dwell on His love with

at His feet; While western em - pires own their Lord, And sav - age tribes at - tend His word.
sweetest song, And in - fant voic - es shall pro - claim Their ear - ly bless - ings on His Name.

SECOND HYMN.

THE NEW SONG.

Miss M. Elsie Thalheimer.

1.

Thro' the new heav'n what voices ring
In praise triumphant to our King?
Like many waters, hark, they pour
Their tide along the golden shore!
"All blessing, honor, power divine,
All might and majesty be Thine!
Holy and true are all Thy words,
Thou King of kings and Lord of lords!"

2.

These from the martyr's bed of flame,
These from the gloomy dungeon came,
These, on the dreadful battle-field,
Stood firm till death and would not yield.
All voices in that faithful throng,
Swell clear and true the glorious song;
"Holy and just are all Thy words,
Thou King of kings and Lord of lords,"

3.

These bore Thy banner o'er the sea,
Exiled and poor for love of Thee,
And found in danger and distress,
Thy presence in the wilderness.
No storm could shake, no ill could harm
So strong was Thy protecting arm,
"Holy and true are all Thy words,
Thou King of kings and Lord of lords!"

(PRAISE.)

EASTER HYMN.

R. W. Raymond.

1 Ye fainting souls, lift up your eyes
  To where the morning lights the skies!
    The awful shadows flee away
    Before the swift advancing day.
‖: The sun has burst His gloomy pris'n, :‖
‖: Turn ye to meet the Lord; the Lord is risen! :‖

2 The Lord is risen; He could not die;
  He lives for you eternally;
    And by His victory o'er the grave
    His people He will surely save! The sun has, &c.

3 No longer mourn your seeming loss;
  No longer weep before the cross,
    Nor search the darkness of the tomb;
    While overhead the morn is come!
  The sun has burst, &c.

4 Now what shall harm your joyful souls
  While your Redeemer all controls?
    No night shall hide again His face;
    No grave shall be His resting-place.
  The sun has burst, &c.

T. DWIGHT, 1800.

LYMAN. 6s & 4s.

From BEETHOVEN.

1. In Zi-on's sa-cred gates, Let hymns of praise begin, While acts of faith and love In ceaseless beau-ty
2. The promis-es I sing, Which sovereign love hath spoke; Nor will our heav'nly King His words of grace re-
3. The mountains melt away, When once the Judge appears; And sun and moon decay, That measure mortal
4. Rejoice! our Lord is King! Our God and King a-dore; Yea, all give thanks and sing, And triumph ev-er-

shine; In mer-cy there, While God is known, Be-fore His throne With songs ap-pear.
voke; They stand se-cure, And stead-fast still, Nor Zi-on's hill A-bides so sure.
years; But still the same, In ra-diant lines, Thy promise shines Thro'all the flame.
more; Lift up the heart, Lift up the voice, Re-joice a-loud, Let all re-joice.

(PRAISE.)

WITH GLADSOME FEET WE PRESS.

CORBET SINGLETON. 1867.

G. A. McFARREN.

1. With gladsome feet we press To Si-on's holy mount, Where gushes from its deep recess, The cooling fount:

Oh! hap - py, happy hill, The joy of every saint! With sweet Siloam's crystal rill, That cheers the faint.

2 Great City, blest of God!
    Jerusalem the free!
With ceaseless step the path be trod
    That leads to Thee!
The martyr's bleeding feet,
    The saints with woundless breast,
Alike have sought Thy golden seat
    To win their rest.

3 There, calming all alarms,
    Thy Cross of Love is traced,
Outstretching salutary arms,
    To bless the waste ;
The sinner there can plead
    In ever listening ears ;
On hope and Thee, can sweetly feed,
    And dry his tears.

4 So this our festal day
    Celestial joy shall raise,
While lips and hearts, conjoined, essay
    To hymn Thy praise !
The very stones shall ring,
    Resound each holy wall, [Spring,
With Thee, Thyself the Rock, the
    Our Heaven, our All !

CROWN HIM WITH MANY CROWNS.

MATTHEW BRIDGES. 1848.

Dr. J. G. ELVEY.

1. Crown Him with many crowns, The Lamb upon His throne; Hark, how the heavenly anthem drowns All music but its own:
2. Crown Him the Lord of love: Be-hold His hands and side, Rich Wounds yet visible a - bove, In beau-ty glo - ri - fied:

(PRAISE.)

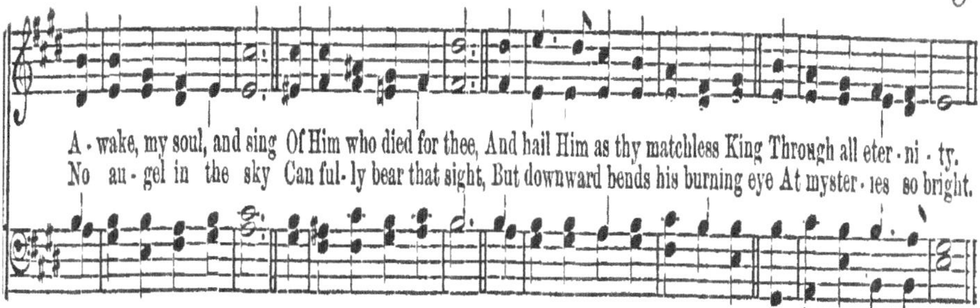

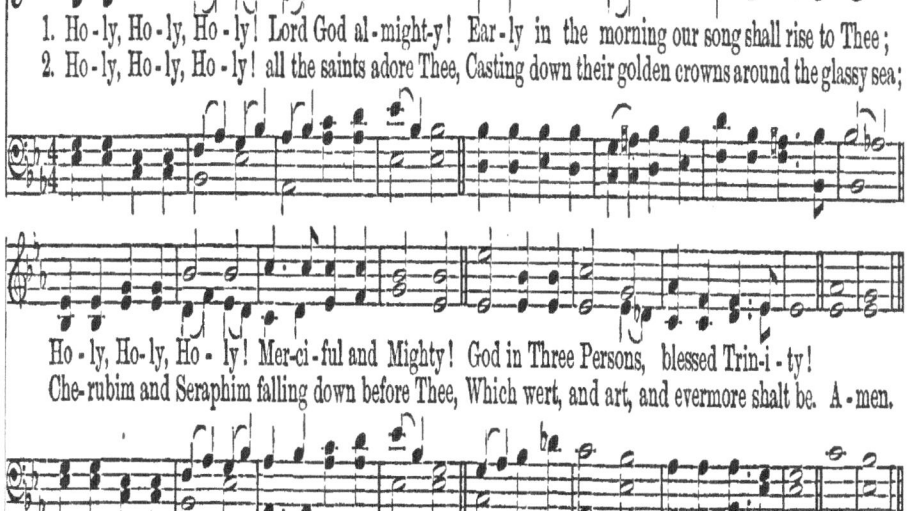

A - wake, my soul, and sing Of Him who died for thee, And hail Him as thy matchless King Through all eter - ni - ty.
No au - gel in the sky Can ful - ly bear that sight, But downward bends his burning eye At myster - ies so bright.

3 Crown Him the Lord of peace:
Whose power a sceptre sways
From pole to pole, that wars may cease,
And all be prayer and praise:
His reign shall know no end,
And round His pierced feet

Fair flowers of Paradise extend
Their fragrance ever sweet.

4 Crown Him the Lord of years,
The Potentate of time,

Creator of the rolling spheres,
Ineffably sublime.
All hail, Redeemer, hail!
For Thou hast died for me;
Thy praise shall never, never fail
Throughout eternity.

HOLY, HOLY! LORD GOD ALMIGHTY!

Bp. REGINALD HEBER. 1827.

Rev. J. B. DYKES. 1861.

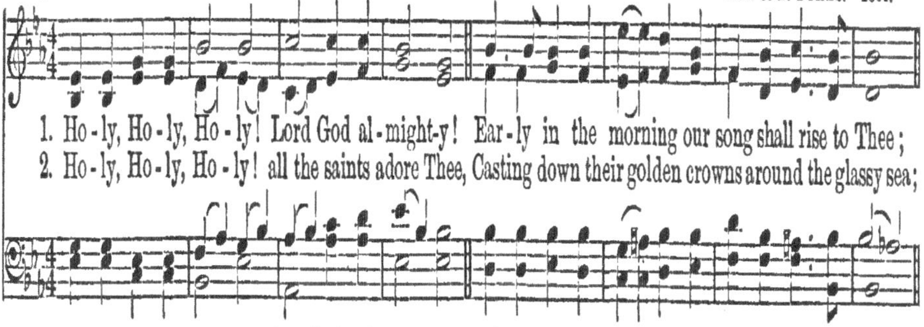

1. Ho - ly, Ho - ly, Ho - ly! Lord God al - might - y! Ear - ly in the morning our song shall rise to Thee;
2. Ho - ly, Ho - ly, Ho - ly! all the saints adore Thee, Casting down their golden crowns around the glassy sea;

Ho - ly, Ho - ly, Ho - ly! Mer - ci - ful and Mighty! God in Three Persons, blessed Trin - i - ty!
Che - rubim and Seraphim falling down before Thee, Which wert, and art, and evermore shalt be. A - men.

3 Holy, Holy, Holy! though the darkness hide Thee,
Though the eye of sinful man Thy glory may not see,
Only Thou art Holy, there is none beside Thee
Perfect in power, in love, and purity.

4 Holy, Holy, Holy! Lord God Almighty! [sea;
All Thy works shall praise Thy Name in earth, and sky, and
Holy, Holy, Holy! Merciful and Mighty!
God in Three Persons, blessed Trinity! Amen.

(PRAISE.)

(PRAISE.)

COME, SING WITH HOLY GLADNESS.

J. J. DANIELL.

Ancient Melody.

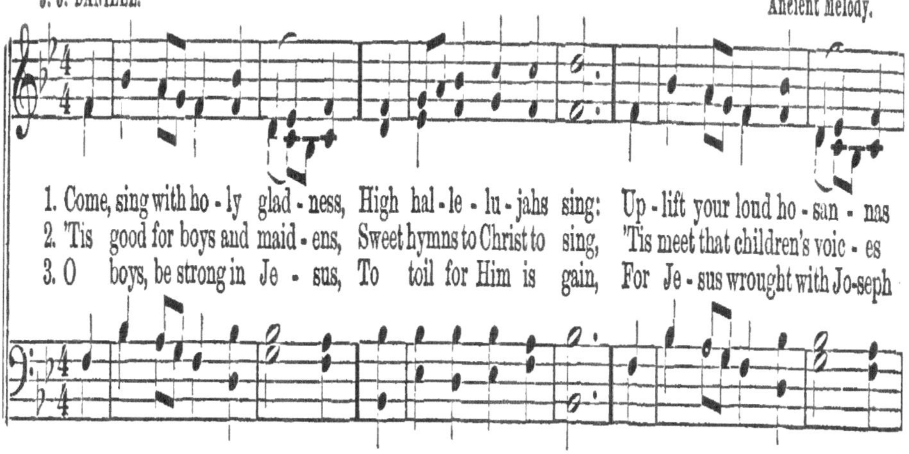

1. Come, sing with ho - ly glad - ness, High hal - le - lu - jahs sing: Up - lift your loud ho - san - nas
2. 'Tis good for boys and maid - ens, Sweet hymns to Christ to sing, 'Tis meet that children's voic - es
3. O boys, be strong in Je - sus, To toil for Him is gain, For Je - sus wrought with Jo - seph

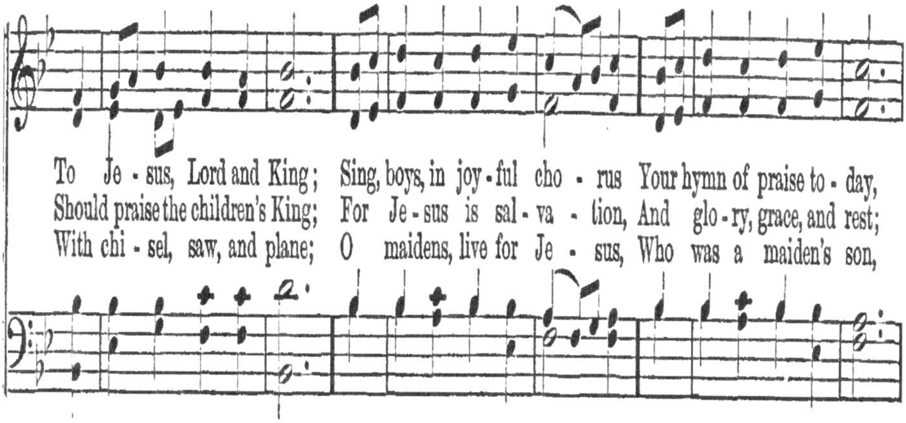

To Je - sus, Lord and King; Sing, boys, in joy - ful cho - rus Your hymn of praise to - day,
Should praise the children's King; For Je - sus is sal - va - tion, And glo - ry, grace, and rest;
With chi - sel, saw, and plane; O maidens, live for Je - sus, Who was a maiden's son,

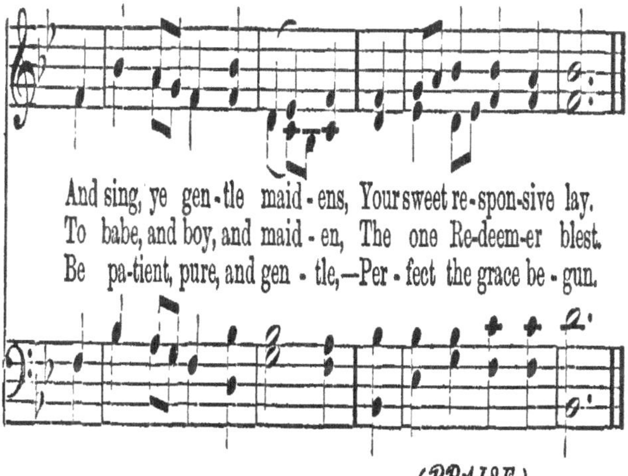

And sing, ye gen - tle maid - ens, Your sweet re - spon - sive lay.
To babe, and boy, and maid - en, The one Re - deem - er blest.
Be pa - tient, pure, and gen - tle, — Per - fect the grace be - gun.

4.
Soon in the golden city
The boys and girls shall stand,
And through the dazzling mansions
Rejoice, a ransomed band ;
O Christ, prepare Thy children
With that triumphant throng
To pass the burnished portals,
And sing th'eternal song.

(PRAISE.)

FANNY J. CROSBY. 1875.

HUBERT P. MAIN, 1874, by per.

1. Praise the Rock of our sal-va-tion, Praise the might-y God a-bove; Come be-fore His sa-cred
2. Je-sus' blood so free-ly of-fered, Je-sus' blood a-vails for sin; Je-sus at the door of
3. Praise the Rock of our sal-va-tion; Catch from yon-der ra-diant clime, Strains by ev-er-last-ing

CHORUS.

pres-ence With a grate-ful song of love. Hal-le-lu-jah! Hal-le-lu-jah! He is
mer-cy, Waits to let the wanderer in.
a-ges, Ech-oed back in tones sublime.

God, and He a-lone; Wake the song of ad-or-a-tion, Come with joy be-fore His throne.

(PRAISE.)

WAKE THE SONG.

SECOND HYMN.

Fanny J. Crosby, 1874.

1 Like the sound of many waters
　　Rolling on through ages long ;
In a tide of rapture breaking,—
　　Hark ! the mighty choral song !
Cho.—Hallelujah ! Hallelujah !
　　　Let the heavenly portals ring !
　　Christ is born, the Prince of glory !
　　　Christ the Lord, our mighty King !

2 Lo ! the Morning Star appeareth,
　　O'er the world His beams are cast ;

He the Alpha and Omega,
　　He, the Great, the First, the Last.

3 Clap your hands with exultation !
　　Sing aloud, rejoice with mirth,
Peace her silver wing hath folded :—
　　Lo ! she comes to dwell on earth !

4 Saviour, not with costly treasure,
　　Do we gather at Thy throne,
All we have, our hearts we give Thee,—
　　Consecrate them Thine alone.

PRAISE AND PRAYER.

R. W. RAYMOND.

Arr. by J. R. HOWARD.

1. Wake, children, wake ! wake, children, wake ! For His care in the night passed by, Praise God ; For His
2. Strive, children, strive ! strive, children, strive ! For a pure and earn-est mind, Pray God ; If you
3. Sleep, children, sleep ! sleep, children, sleep ! For life, and la-bor, and rest, Praise God ; And, with

grace and His par-don to-day, Pray God For Je-sus' sake when-e'er you wake.
strive while you pray, you will find, Praise God, His grace He'll give to all who strive.
heav-en's own peace in your breast, Pray God Your souls to keep, in death or sleep.

(PRAISE.)

THE CHORUS OF PRAISE.

R. W. RAYMOND.

J. C. LOWRY, 1820, arr.

1. O what can you tell, lit-tle pebble, lit-tle pebble, O what can you tell, lit-tle pebble, by the sea! The
Ref.—It is the love of God in heav'n, The God who made both you and me, And

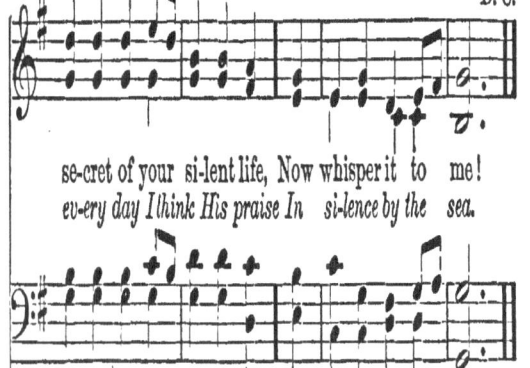

D. C.

se-cret of your si-lent life, Now whisper it to me!
ev-ery day I think His praise In si-lence by the sea.

2 O what can you tell, little flower, little flower,
  O what can you tell, little flower on the lea!
    The secret of your sweet perfume,
    Now whisper it to me.

Ref.—It is the love of God in heav'n,
    The God who made both you and me,
    And every day I breathe His praise
    In fragrance on the lea.

3 O what can you tell, little bird, little bird,
  O what can you tell, little bird upon the tree!
    The secret of your joyous song,
    Now whisper it to me!

Ref.—It is the love of God in heav'n,
    The God who made both you and me,
    And every day I sing His praise
    Upon the summer tree.

4 O what can you tell, little child, little child,
  O what can you tell, little child upon my knee!
    The secret of your happy smile,
    Now whisper it to me!

Ref.—It is the love of God in heav'n,
    The God who made both you and me,
    And every day I seek His praise
    Upon my bended knee!

Full Cho.—Thus to the love of God in heav'n,
    The God who made both you and me,

The praise of all things here is giv'n,
And evermore shall be!

(PRAISE.)

Rev. HORATIUS BONAR.

J. BAPTISTE CALKIN.

1. Upward where the stars are burning, Si - lent, si - lent in their turning, Round the nev - er changing pole ;

ritenuto.

Upward where the sky is bright-est, Upward where the blue is light - est, — Lift I now my long - ing soul.

ritenuto.

2.	3.	4.
Far beyond that arch of gladness,	Where the Lamb on high is seated,	Blessing, honor, without measure,
Far beyond these clouds of sadness,	By ten thousand voices greeted :	Heav'nly riches, earthly treasure,
Are the many mansions fair.	Lord of lords, and King of kings.	Lay we at His blessed feet.
Far from pain and sin and folly,	Son of man, they crown, they crown Him,	Poor the praise that now we render,
In that palace of the holy—	Son of God, they own, they own Him,	Loud shall be our voices yonder,
I would find my mansion there.	With His name the palace rings.	When before His Throne we meet.

(PRAISE.)

Rev. J. H. H.

Rev. JOHN H. HOPKINS, by per.

Trio. 1. We three Kings of O - ri - ent are; Bear-ing gifts, we traverse a - far Field and fountain, Moor and

D. C.—Hal - le - lu - jah, A - - men. Hal-le-lu-jah, A - - men. Hal-le-lu-jah, Hal-le-

FINE. CHORUS.

mountain, Following yon-der Star. O Star of won-der, Star of Night; Star with roy-al beau-ty bright;

lu - jah, A - - - - - men.

D. C.

Westward leading, Still pro-ceed-ing, Guide us to Thy per-fect light.

*Solo :—*GASPARD.

2 Born a King on Bethlehem plain,
  Gold I bring to crown Him again
  King for ever ; Ceasing never
  Over us all to reign.—

*Solo :—*MELCHIOR.

3 FRANKINCENSE to offer have I,
  Incense owns a Deity nigh :
  Prayer and praising, All men raising,
  Worship Him, God on high.—

*Solo :—*BALTHAZAR.

4 MYRRH is mine ; its bitter perfume
  Breathes a life of gathering gloom ;—
  Sorrowing, sighing, Bleeding, dying,
  Sealed in the stone-cold tomb.—

Trio.

5 Glorious now behold Him arise,
  King, and God, and Sacrifice ;
  Hallelujah, Hallelujah !
  Heaven and earth replies.—

(PRAISE.)

FLEMMING. 11, 11, 11 & 5.

(18) Page 188, Key A♮.

1 Praise ye the Father! for His loving kindness,
Tenderly cares He for His erring children,
Praise Him, ye angels, Praise Him in the heavens,
Praise ye Jehovah!

2 Praise ye the Saviour! great is His compassion,
Graciously cares He for His chosen people:
Young men and maidens, ye old men and children,
Praise ye the Saviour!

3 Praise ye the Spirit! comforter of Israel,
Sent of the Father, and the Son to bless us;
Praise ye the Father, Son, and Holy Spirit,
Praise ye the Triune God!

HALE. 11, & 10.

(19) Victory, page 282. Key B♮.

1 Brightest and best of the sons of the morning!
Dawn on our darkness, and lend us thine aid;
Star of the East! the horizon adorning,—
Guide where our infant Redeemer is laid.

2 Cold on His cradle, the dew-drops are shining;
Low lies His head with the beasts of the stall;
Angels adore Him in slumber reclining—
Maker, and Monarch, and Saviour of all.

3 Say, shall we yield Him, in costly devotion,
Odors of Edom, and offerings divine,
Gems of the mountain, and pearls of the ocean,
Myrrh from the forest, or gold from the mine?

4 Vainly we offer each ample oblation,
Vainly with gold would His favor secure;
Richer, by far, is the heart's adoration,—
Dearer to God are the prayers of the poor.

5 Brightest and best of the sons of the morning!
Dawn on our darkness, and lend us thine aid;
Star of the East!—the horizon adorning,—
Guide where our infant Redeemer is laid.

LYONS. 10, & 11.

(20) Victory, page 257. Key B♮.

1 Oh! praise ye the Lord; prepare your glad voice,
His praise in the great assembly to sing:
In their great Creator let all rejoice,
And heirs of salvation be glad in their King.

2 Let them His great name, devoutly adore,
In loud-swelling strains His praises express,
Who graciously opens His bountiful store,
Their wants to relieve, and His children to bless.

3 With glory adorned, His people shall sing
To God, who defence and plenty supplies;
Their loud acclamations to Him, their great King,
Through earth shall be sounded, and reach to the skies

4 Ye angels above! His glories who've sung,
In loftiest notes, now publish His praise:
We mortals, delighted, would borrow your tongue—
Would join in your numbers, and chant to your lays.

HAIL TO THE BRIGHTNESS. 11, 10.

(21) Victory, page 282. Key B♮.

1 Hail to the brightness of Zion's glad morning!
Joy to the lands that in darkness have lain!
Hushed be the accents of sorrow and mourning!
Zion in triumph begins her mild reign.

2 Hail to the brightness of Zion's glad morning,
Long by the prophets of Israel foretold;
Hail to the millions from bondage returning!
Gentiles and Jews the blest vision behold.

3 Lo! in the desert rich flowers are springing,
Streams ever copious are gliding along,
Loud from the mountain-top, echoes are ringing,
Wastes rise in verdure, and mingle in song.

4 See! from all lands, from the isles of the ocean,
Praise to Jehovah ascending on high;
Fallen are the engines of war and commotion,
Shouts of salvation are rending the sky.

O SAVIOUR, PRECIOUS SAVIOUR.

FRANCES RIDLEY HAVERGAL. 1870.

Arr. from W. F. SHERWIN.

1. O Sav-iour, pre-cious Sav-iour, Whom, yet un-seen, we love, O Name of might and fa-vor,
2. O Bring-er of sal-va-tion, Who won-drous-ly hast wrought Thyself the rev-e-la-tion,
3. In Thee all ful-ness dwell-eth, All grace and power di-vine; The glo-ry that ex-cell-eth,

CHORUS.

All oth-er names a-bove; We wor-ship Thee, we bless Thee, To Thee a-lone we sing;
Of love be-yond our thought; We wor-ship Thee, we bless Thee, To Thee a-lone we sing;
O Son of God, is Thine; We wor-ship Thee, we bless Thee, To Thee a-lone we sing;

We praise Thee and con-fess Thee Our ho-ly God and King!
We praise Thee and con-fess Thee Our gra-cious Lord and King!
We praise Thee and con-fess Thee Our glo-rious Lord and King!

4.
O grant the consummation
Of this our song above,
In endless adoration
And everlasting love;
We worship Thee, we bless Thee,
To Thee alone we sing;
We praise Thee and confess Thee
Our gracious Lord and King!

(PRAISE.)

ITALIAN HYMN. 6s & 4s.

(23) Christian Songs, 197. Key G.

1 COME, Thou almighty King,
Help us Thy name to sing,
Help us to praise!
Father all glorious,
O'er all victorious,
Come and reign over us,
Ancient of days.

2 Come, Thou incarnate Word
Gird on Thy mighty sword;
Our prayer attend;
Come, and Thy people bless;
Come, give Thy word success;
Spirit of holiness,
On us descend.

3 Come, holy Comforter,
Thy sacred witness bear,
In this glad hour;
Thou, who almighty art,
Now rule in every heart,
And ne'er from us depart,
Spirit of power.

4 To thee, great One in Three,
The highest praises be,
Hence evermore;
Thy sovereign majesty
May we in glory see,
And to eternity
Love and adore.

OLD HUNDRED. L. M.

(24) Bradbury Trio, 101. Key G.

1 LOUD hallelujahs to the Lord,
From distant worlds where crea-
tures dwell,
Let heaven begin the solemn word,
And sound it dreadful down to hell.

2 Wide as His vast dominion lies,
Make the Creator's name be known
Loud as His thunder, shout His praise,
And sound it lofty as His throne.

3 Jehovah—'t is a glorious word!
O, may it dwell on every tongue!
But saints, who best have known the
Lord,
Are bound to raise the noblest song.

4 Speak of the wonders of that love
Which Gabriel plays on every chord;
From all below, and all above,
Loud hallelujahs to the Lord.

RUTHERFORD. 7s & 6s.

(25) Page 190. Key F.

1 To Thee, our God and Saviour,
Our hearts exulting spring,
Rejoicing in Thy favor,
Thou everlasting King:
We'll celebrate Thy glory,
With all the saints above;
And tell the wondrous story
Of Thy redeeming love.

2 By Thee through life supported,
We pass the dang'rous road,

By heavenly hosts escorted,
Up to their bright abode;
There cast our crowns before Thee,
Our toils and conflicts o'er.
And day and night adore Thee,
Forever, evermore.

CORONATION. C. M.

(26) Bradbury Trio, 179. Key G.

1 ALL hail the power of Jesus' name,
Let angels prostrate fall;
Bring forth the royal diadem,
And crown Him Lord of all.

2 Crown Him, ye morning stars of light,
Who fix'd this floating ball;
Now hail the strength of Israel's
might,
And crown Him Lord of all.

3 Sinners, whose love can ne'er forget
The wormwood and the gall;
Go, spread your trophies at His feet,
And crown Him Lord of all.

4 Let every kindred, every tribe,
On this terrestrial ball,
To Him all majesty ascribe,
And crown Him Lord of all.

5 O that with yonder sacred throng,
We at His feet may fall;
We'll join the everlasting song,
And crown Him Lord of all.

GLORY TO GOD IN THE HIGHEST!

WM. B. BRADBURY.

FANNY J. CROSBY. 1864.

From "Golden Censer," by per.

FULL CHORUS.

1. Glo-ry to God in the high-est! Glo-ry to God! Glo-ry to God! Glo-ry to God in the highest! Shall
2. Glo-ry to God in the high-est! Glo-ry to God! Glo-ry to God! Glo-ry to God in the highest! Shall

SEMI-CHORUS, OR DUET.

be our song to-day; An-oth-er year's rich mercies prove His ceaseless care and boundless love; So
be our song to-day; O, may we, an un-broken band, A-round the throne of Je-sus stand, And

FULL CHORUS.

let our loud-est voi-ces raise Our glad and grate-ful song of praise. Glo-ry to God in the highest!
there with angels and the throng Of his redeemed ones, join the song.

Glo-ry to God in the highest! Glo-ry, glory, glory, glory, Glory be to God on high! God on high!

(PRAISE.)

STRIKE THE HARP.

(28) Christian Songs, 12. Key A.

1 STRIKE the harp of Zion, wake the
   tuneful lay;
Bear the joyful tidings far away;
Lo! the morn is breaking, morn of
   purest love,
Praise forever, praise to God above.
CHO. Glory! glory. hark! the angels
   sing,
   Glory! glory! hear the echo ring!
   Strike the harp of Zion, wake the
     tuneful lay;   [far away,
   Bear the joyful tidings far away,
   Bear the joyful tidings far away.

2 Over distant regions vailed in errors
   night,
See the holy dawn of gospel light;
See! the nations coming at the Sav-
   iour's call,
Coming now to crown Him Lord of all.

3 O, the joyful story, life to every soul!
Like a mighty ocean let it roll,
Bringing home the lost ones from the
   path of sin,
Till the world shall all be gathered in.

ST. THOMAS. S. M.

(29) Bradbury Trio, 224 Key G.

1 COME ye that love the Lord,
   And let your joys be known;
Join in a song with sweet accord,
   And thus surround the throne.

2 Let those refuse to sing,
   That never knew our God;
But favorites of the heavenly King
   May speak their joys abroad.

3 The men of grace have found
   Glory begun below:
Celestial fruits on earthly ground
   From faith and hope may grow.

4 The hill of Zion yields
   A thousand sacred sweets,
Before we reach the heavenly fields,
   Or walk the golden streets.

5 Then let our songs abound,
   And every tear dry;   [ground
We're marching through Immanuel's
   To fairer worlds on high.

ESSEX. 7s.

(30) Christian Songs, 85. Key D.

1 SONGS of praise the angels sang,
Heav'n with hallelujah's rang,
When Jehovah's work begun,
‖: When He spake and it was done.:‖

2 Songs of praise awoke the morn,
When the Prince of Peace was born;
Songs of praise arose, when He,
‖: Captive led captivity. :‖

3 Heav'n and earth must pass away,—
Songs of praise shall crown that day;

God will make new heav'ns and earth,
‖: Songs of praise shall hail their birth.‖

4 Men, redeemed with heart and voice,
Here in songs of praise rejoice;
And amidst eternal joy,
‖: Songs of praise their pow'rs employ.‖

HYMNS OF GRATEFUL LOVE.

(31) Christian Songs, 103. Key B♭.

1 SHALL hymns of grateful love,
   Thro' heaven's high arches ring,
And all the hosts above,
   Their songs of triumph sing;
CHO. And shall not we take up the strain,
   And send the echo back again!
   And ‖: send the echo, *send the echo,*‖
   Send the echo, send the echo back
    again.

2 Shall every ransomed tribe
   Of Adam's scattered race,
To Christ all powers ascribe,
   Who saved them by His grace;

3 Shall they adore the Lord,
   Who bought them with His blood,
And all the love record,
   That led them home to God:

4 Then spread the joyful sound,
   The Saviour's love proclaim,
And publish all around,
   Salvation through His name.

JOY-BELLS.

HENRY TUCKER.

JOSEPHINE POLLARD, 1867.

From "Brightest and Best," by per.

1. Joy-bells ring-ing, Children sing-ing, Fill the air with music sweet; Jocund measure, Guileless pleasure,
2. Joy-bells ring-ing, Children sing-ing, Hark! their voices, loud and clear; Breaking o'er us, Like a cho - rus,
3. Earth seems brighter, Hearts grow lighter, As the jocund mel-o-dy Charms our sadness In-to glad-ness,

CHORUS.

Make the chain of song com - plete. }
From a pur - er, hap - pier sphere. }
Peal - ing, peal - ing, joy - ful - ly.

Joy - bells! joy - bells! Nev - er, nev - er cease your ringing;
Chil - dren! chil - dren! Nev - er, nev - er cease your singing;

Very soft.   Loud.

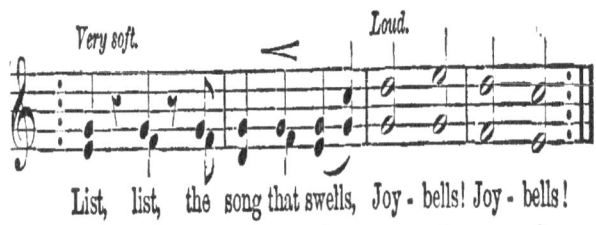

List, list, the song that swells, Joy - bells! Joy - bells!

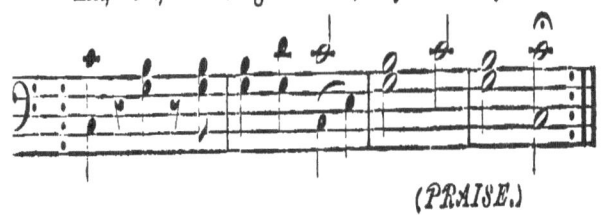

4 Joy-bells nearer
    Sound, and clearer,
When the heart is free from care;
    Skies are cheering,
    And we're hearing
Joy-bells ringing everywhere.
    Joy-bells, etc.

(PRAISE.)

FANNY J. CROSBY. 1873.

S. LASAR, by per.

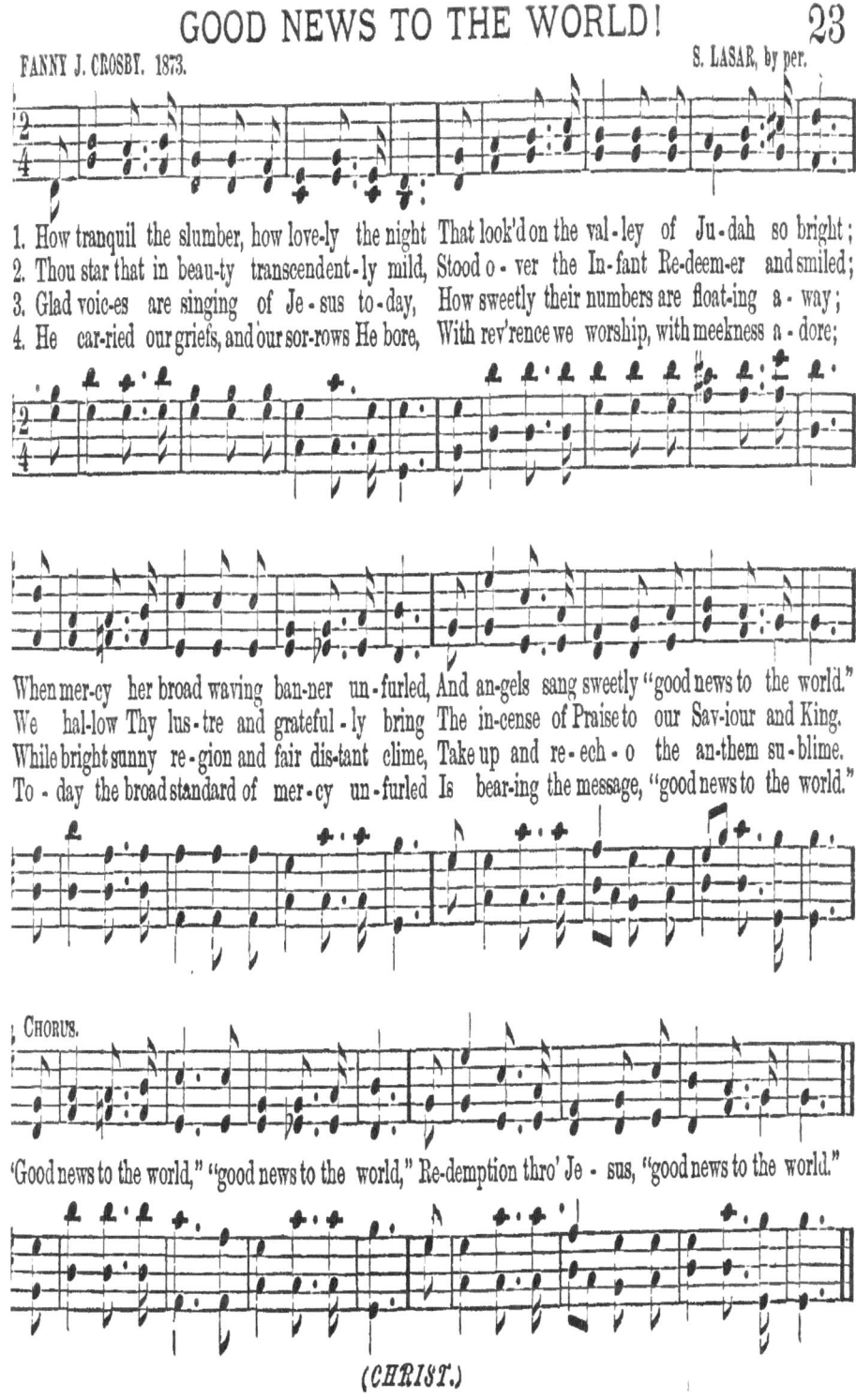

1. How tranquil the slumber, how love-ly the night That look'd on the val-ley of Ju-dah so bright;
2. Thou star that in beau-ty transcendent-ly mild, Stood o-ver the In-fant Re-deem-er and smiled;
3. Glad voic-es are singing of Je-sus to-day, How sweetly their numbers are float-ing a-way;
4. He car-ried our griefs, and our sor-rows He bore, With rev'rence we worship, with meekness a-dore;

When mer-cy her broad waving ban-ner un-furled, And an-gels sang sweetly "good news to the world."
We hal-low Thy lus-tre and grateful-ly bring The in-cense of Praise to our Sav-iour and King.
While bright sunny re-gion and fair dis-tant clime, Take up and re-ech-o the an-them su-blime.
To-day the broad standard of mer-cy un-furled Is bear-ing the message, "good news to the world."

CHORUS.

'Good news to the world," "good news to the world," Re-demption thro' Je-sus, "good news to the world."

(CHRIST.)

STAR, BEAUTIFUL STAR.

R. W. RAYMOND.

FRED. SCHILLING, by per.

SOLO.

1. There's a beauti - ful star, a beau-ti - ful star, The wea - ry travelers have fol - lowed far,
2. In the land of the East, in the sha-dows of night, We saw the glo-ry of thy new light,
3. We have gold for tribute and gifts for pray-er, In - cense of myrrh, and spic - es rare:

CHORUS.

Shin-ing so bright-ly all the way, Till it stood o'er the place where the young child lay. Star, star,
Tell-ing us, in our dis - tant home, The King - Re-deem-er to earth hath come!
All that we have, we hith - er bring, To lay it with joy at the feet of the King.

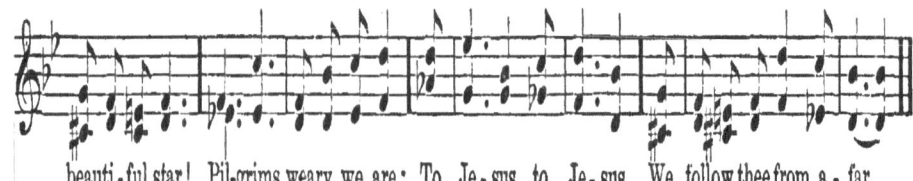

beauti - ful star! Pil-grims weary we are; To Je - sus, to Je - sus, We follow thee from a - far.

(CHRIST.)

HERALD-ANGELS. 7s.

C. WESLEY. 1739.

MENDELSSOHN. Arr.

1. Hark! the her - ald an - gels sing, "Glo - ry to the new-born King; Peace on earth, and mer-cy mild;
2. Hail! the heav'n-born Prince of Peace! Hail! the Sun of righteousness! Light and life to all He brings,

God and sin-ners re - conciled;" Joy-ful all ye na - tions rise, Join the triumph of the skies;
Risen with heal-ing in His wings; Let us then with an - gels sing, "Glo - ry to the new-born King;

With th' angel - ic host proclaim, Christ is born in Beth-le - hem, With th' angel - ic host proclaim,
Peace on earth, and mer - cy mild; God and sin - ners re - conciled, Peace on earth and mer - cy mild;

Christ is born in Beth-le - hem.
God and sin-ners re - con-ciled.

SECOND HYMN. 8s & 7s.

Crown His head with endless blessing
Who, in God the Father's name,
With compassion never ceasing,
Comes, salvation to proclaim;
Lo, Jehovah, we adore Thee—
Thee, our Saviour—Thee our God;
||: From Thy throne let beams of glory
Shine through all the world abroad.:||

2 Jesus Thee our Saviour hailing,
Thee our God in praise we own;
Highest honors, never failing,
Rise eternal round Thy throne;
Now, ye saints, His power confessing,
In your grateful strains adore;
||: For His mercy, never ceasing,
Flows, and flows for evermore.:||

(CHRIST.)

MERRY, MERRY CHRISTMAS!

Mrs. R. S. C. 1876

Mrs. T. J. COOK, by per.

1. Mer - ry, mer - ry Christmas ev - ery where! Cheeri - ly it ring - eth through the air; Christmas bells,
2. Mer - ry, mer - ry Christmas ev - ery where! Cheeri - ly it ring - eth through the air; Christmas bells,

Christmas trees, Christmas o - dors on the breeze. Merry, merry Christmas ev - ery where!
Christmas trees, Christmas o - dors on the breeze. Merry, merry Christmas ev - ery where!

Cheeri - ly it ringeth through the air; Why should we so joy - ful - ly Sing, with grateful mirth?
Cheeri - ly it ringeth through the air; Light for wea - ry wan - der - ers, Com - fort for th' oppressed!

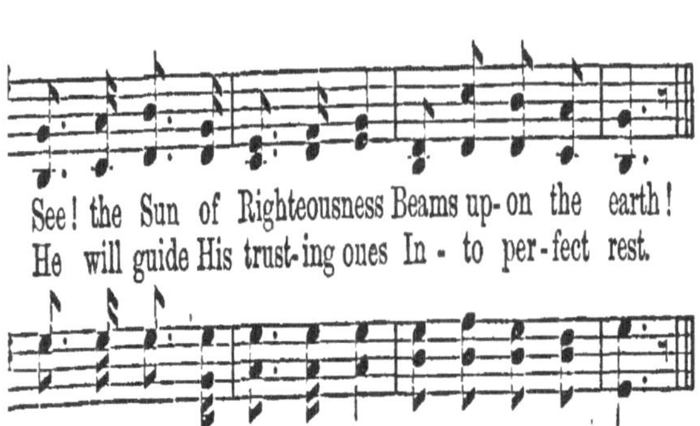

See! the Sun of Righteousness Beams up - on the earth!
He will guide His trust - ing ones In - to per - fect rest.

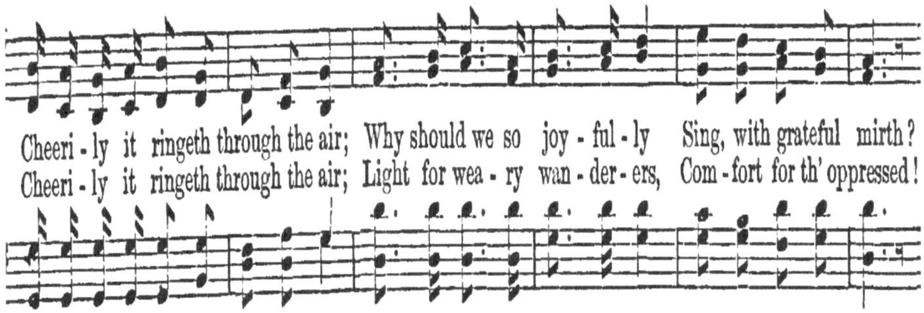

3 Merry, merry Christmas everywhere!
Cheerily it ringeth through the air;
Christmas bells, Christmas trees,
Christmas odors on the breeze:
Merry, merry Christmas everywhere!
Cheerily it ringeth through the air
Deeds of Faith and Charity;
These our off'rings be,
Leading every soul to sing,
Christ was born for me!

(CHRIST.)

Mrs. CECIL FRANCES ALEXANDER, 1867

Dr. GAUNTLETT.

1. {
Once in roy-al Da-vid's Cit-y, Stood a low-ly cat-tle shed,
Where a mother laid her Ba-by, In a manger for His bed:
} Ma-ry was that mother mild,

2. {
He came down to earth from heaven, Who is God and King of all,
And His shel-ter was a sta-ble, And His cra-dle was a stall;
} With the poor, and mean, and lowly,

Je - sus Christ that lit - tle Child.
Lived on earth our Saviour Ho-ly.

3.

Oh, our eyes at last shall see Him,
    Through His own redeeming love,
For that Child so dear and gentle
    Is our God in heaven above ;
And He leads His children on
    To the place where He is gone.

4.

Not in that poor lowly stable,
    With the oxen standing by,
We shall see Him ; but in heaven,
    Set at God's right hand on high ;
When like stars His children crowned
    All in white shall wait around.

SECOND HYMN.

1 "Christ the Lord is risen to-day,"
    Sons of men and angels say :
‖: Raise your joys and triumphs high ;
    Sing, ye heavens, and earth, reply. :‖

2 Love's redeeming work is done,
    Fought the fight, the battle won ;

‖: Death in vain forbids Him rise,
    Christ hath opened Paradise. :‖

3 Soar we now where Christ hath led,
    Following our exalted Head ;
‖: Made like Him, like Him we rise ;
    Ours the cross, the grave, the skies. :‖

(CHRIST.)

RING THE MERRY BELLS.—Carol.

Words and Music by R. R. RAYMOND.

1. Ring the mer - ry bells, the silver-sounding bells, It is the Christmas morn! To

all the world their mer - ry mu - sic tells That Christ the Lord is born.

(CHRIST.)

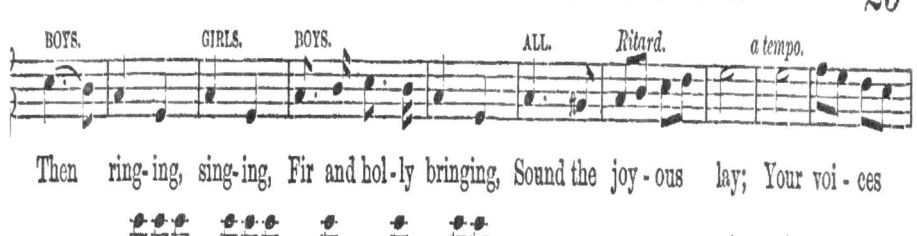

Then ring-ing, sing-ing, Fir and hol-ly bringing, Sound the joy-ous lay; Your voi-ces

raise, to sing the praise, Of the babe that was born to-day!

2 Crowding all the dome of the starry winter sky,
    The heavenly host again
Sing, Glory, glory be to God on high,
    Good will and peace to men!
      Then ringing, &c.

3 Joyfully the shepherds haste to Bethlehem,
    And wise men from afar,
The lowly stable we enter now with them,
    Beneath the guiding Star.
      Then ringing, &c.

4 There the shining angels mingle undefiled
    With oxen in the stall;
The Mother mild bends above the Holy Child,
    And at His feet we fall.
      Then ringing, &c.

5 Glorious Redeemer, on thy baby-brow
    Belongs a royal crown;
The Lord of all the universe art Thou,
    Yet love hath brought Thee down.
      Then ringing, &c.

(CHRIST.)

FANNY J. CROSBY. 1874.

THEO. E. PERKINS, by per.

1. Hark! the mighty tones sublime, Trumpet tongues of olden time—Breathing on the silent air, Shouting glo - ry
2. Mourning captive, cease thy tears; Lo! the promised day appears, Thro' the misty veil of night, Bursting in a
3. Now with healing in her wings, Hark! a white robed angel sings :—"Mortals, from the realms above I have borne my

ev - ery where! Hark! again their joyful sound Rings a - far, the earth a - round; While a vast, a -
flood of light; Oh, what wondrous things are done By the Father, thro' the Son! Oh, the smile of
harp of love; Hal - le - lu - jah! sing with me! Hail your greatest ju - bi - lee! Sing, in pur - est,

D. S.—E - den lost, to

FINE. CHORUS.

D. S.

dor - ing throng Catch the strain and join the song. Un - to us a child is given; Open now the gates of heaven;
pard'ning grace, Beaming in the Saviour's face.
sweetest lays, On this ho - ly day of days."

man restored, Thro' the birth of Christ the Lord.

(CHRIST.)

ONWARD, CHRISTIAN.

1 Onward, Christian, press thy way,
See the light of endless day
Breaks beyond the clouds that rise
Darkly o'er these changeful skies;
Heavenly music greets thine ear,
Jesus calls thee, stay not here;
Onward, Christian, faithful prove,
Haste to purer joys above.

Cho.—On those ever verdant plains,
Where eternal glory reigns,

Thou shalt join the holy throng,
Praising God in joyful song.

2 Onward, Christian, watch and pray,
Hoping, trusting, day by day;
More than Conqueror thou shalt be,
Thro' His love, who died for thee;
Onward, Christian, God is near,
He will comfort, He will cheer;
Constant joy thy heart shall fill,
Onward, Christian, onward still.

3 Upward lift thy longing eyes;
Upward let thy thoughts arise;
Upward on the wings of love
Speed to brighter scenes above;
There the fruits immortal grow;
There the living waters flow;
There thy raptured eye shall see
Christ, whose mercy ransomed thee.

Fanny J. Crosby. 1875.

CHILDS' HYMN TO JESUS.

From the German by R. R. RAYMOND.

Arranged, H.

1. O precious Sav-iour, who on earth, For children stooped to mor-tal birth, That we, from ev-ery
2. Thou Light, sent forth from God's own hand, Into our dark-ling earthly land, A child of heav'n, a
3. Dear Saviour! bless a lit-tle child, And make my spir-it pure and mild, O cleanse my soul from

sin set free, Children of God might tru-ly be.
heav'n-ly glow, To draw our souls from shades be-low.
heav'n a-bove, In the rich fountains of Thy love.

4 That I may like God's angels be,
In Love and in Humility,—
With Thee the crown of joy to wear;—
This, blessed Jesus, is my prayer!

For Christmas, sing this verse first.

This is the blessed Christmas day,
When Jesus in the manger lay,—
To children all, of every clime,
A thankful, happy, holy time.

(CHRIST.)

AVISON.

Wm. A. MUHLENBERG, D. D.

CHAS. AVISON.

CHORUS.

V. 1 & 2. V. 3. ✱

Shout the glad ti-dings, ex-ult-ing-ly sing;........ Je-ru-sa-lem tri-umphs, Mes-si-ah is King! King,

1. Zi - on, the marvellous sto - ry be telling, The Son of the Highest, how lowly His birth, The brightest archangel in
2. Tell how He cometh, from nation to nation, The heart-cheering news let the earth echo round, How free to the faithful He
3. Mor-tals, your homage be gratefully bringing, And sweet let the gladsome hosanna a - rise; Ye an-gels, the full hal-le-

ril.

D. C. for CHORUS. | ✱ After 3rd verse, let Chorus end with this line.

glo-ry ex-cell-ing, He stoops to re-deem thee, He reigns upon earth. Mes-si-ah is King, Mes-si-ah is King!
of-fers sal-vation,—His peo-ple with joy ev-er-last-ing are crowned.
lu-jah be singing, One cho-rus resound thro' the earth and the skies.

(CHRIST.)

Arranged.

S. THALBERG.

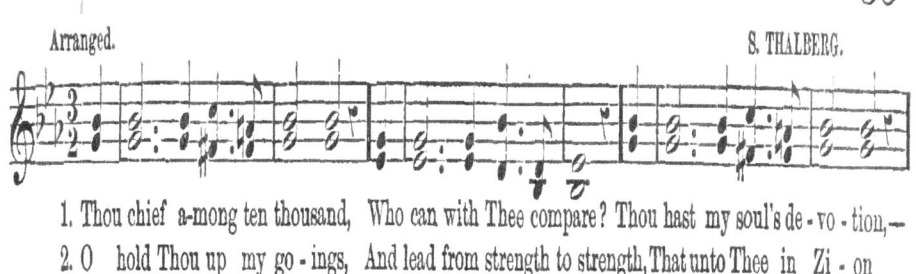

1. Thou chief a-mong ten thousand, Who can with Thee compare? Thou hast my soul's de - vo - tion,—
2. O hold Thou up my go - ings, And lead from strength to strength, That unto Thee in Zi - on

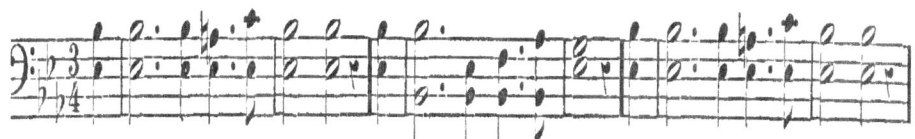

Supreme, Thou reignest there: I know no life di - vid - ed O bless - ed Lord, from Thee; In
I may appear at length: O make my spir-it wor - thy To join the ransomed throng; O

Rit.

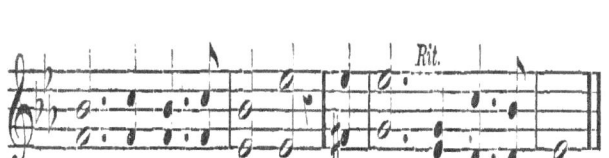

Thee is life pro - vid - ed For all mankind and me.
teach my lips to ut - ter That ev - er - last-ing song.

3 O give that last, best blessing
That even saints can know,
To follow in Thy footsteps
Wherever Thou dost go :
Not wisdom, might, or glory
I ask to win above ;
I ask for Thee, Thee only,
O Thou Eternal Love !

(CHRIST.)

SHEPPARD. 6s & 5s.

After GODFREY THRING.

From FRANZ SCHUBERT.

1. Dear Saviour! our Saviour! Hear, hear as we sing,   Our glad voi - ces raising Loud praise to our King;
2. Still brighter and brighter Come rays from the sun, O'er - shedding with gladness Our work that is done:
3. Bliss! bliss all   ex - celling! When, ransom'd, the soul, Earth's toils all forgetting, Now finds its sought goal;

We bring Thee our tribute, We yield Thee our all; Our hearts now re - joic - ing, Before Thee would fall.
Soon time will   be o - ver, Toil, sorrow, all past; And we, blessed Saviour, At home rest at last.
Then anthems   celes - tial With angels we'll sing, And give all the glo - ry To Jesus, our King.

Our Saviour! dear Saviour! Our strong refuge be; Oh, hear us, our Saviour! We cry un - to Thee!

(CHRIST.)

WAKE THE GLAD STRAIN.

FANNY J. CROSBY. 1874.

HUBERT P. MAIN, by per.

Sprightly.

1. Je - sus from bondage His peo-ple will save, Ris-ing He hal-lows the night of the grave; Ris-ing He

tak-eth transgres-sion a - way, Christ, our Redeem — er, is ris - en to - day.

REFRAIN.

Ser-aph and Cher - u-bim,

wake the glad strain, Je - sus, the cru - ci-fied liv - eth a - gain, Ser-aph and Cherubim, wake the glad strain,

Je - sus, the cru - ci-fied liv - eth a - gain.

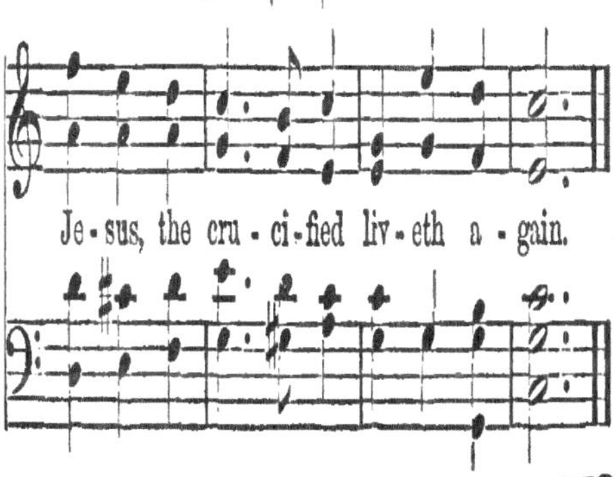

2 Liveth, the sceptre of mercy to wield,
   Light of the faithful, their buckler and shield;
   Him shall all nations and kingdoms obey,
   Him who in glory is risen to-day.

3 Saviour, look down from Thy dwelling above,
   Cover us all with Thy banner of love;
   Thine be the glory, O, Ancient of Days,
   Thou hast redeemed us, and Thine be the praise.

(CHRIST.)

HAIL THE DAY THAT SEES HIM RISE.

C. WESLEY, 1739.   WM. H. MONK. 1860.

1. Hail the day that sees Him rise,   Hal - le - lu - jah!   To His throne above the skies;   Hal - le - lu - jah!

Christ, the Lamb for sinners given,   Hal - le - lu - jah!   En-ters now the highest heaven.   Hal - le - lu - jah!

2.

There for Him high triumph waits;   Hallelujah!
Lift your heads, eternal gates!   Hallelujah!
He hath conquered death and sin,   Hallelujah!
Take the King of Glory in.   Hallelujah!

3.

Lo, the heaven its Lord receives!   Hallelujah!
Yet He loves the earth He leaves;   Hallelujah!
Though returning to His throne,   Hallelujah!
Still He calls mankind His own.   Hallelujah!

4.

Still for us He intercedes,   Hallelujah!
His prevailing death He pleads;   Hallelujah!
Near Himself prepares our place,   Hallelujah!
He, the first-fruits of our race.   Hallelujah!

5.

Lord, though parted from our sight   Hallelujah!
Far above the starry height,   Hallelujah!
Grant our hearts may thither rise,   Hallelujah!
Seeking Thee above the skies.   Hallelujah!

(CHRIST.)

OH, HOW HE LOVES!

Mrs. MARRIANNE NUNN, 1813.   HUBERT P. MAIN, by per.

1. One there is a-bove all others, Oh, how He loves! His is love be-yond a brother's,
2. 'Tis e-ter-nal life to know Him, Oh, how He loves! Think, oh, think how much we owe Him,
3. All your sins shall be forgiv-en, Oh, how He loves! Backward shall your foes be driv-en,

Oh, how He loves! Earth-ly friends may fail or leave us, One day soothe, the
Oh, how He loves! With His pre-cious blood He bought us, In the wil-der-
Oh, how He loves! Best of bless-ings He'll pro-vide you, Nought but good shall

next day grieve us, But this Friend will ne'er de-ceive us, Oh, how He loves!
ness He sought us, To His fold He safe-ly brought us, Oh, how He loves!
e'er be-tide you, Safe to glo-ry He will guide you, Oh, how He loves!

(CHRIST.)

R. W. RAYMOND.

Rev. R. LOWRY, by per.

1. { Our Sav-iour is ris-en from Death's gloomy prison, No long-er He wanders by mountain and sea;
But ere He be-reft us, this promise He left us; "Faint not, where I [Omit......................] }

2. { Yet lov-ing and ten-der, new grace He doth render, Nor waits in His mansion till, wea-ry, we come;
He journeys be-side us, to help us and guide us; Un-seen by our [Omit......................] }

CHORUS.

am, my dis-ci-ples shall be!" We shall see Him one day, when the vail rolls a-way, And Christ who re-
eyes till He greets us at home!

deemed us shall wel-come us then; While we join the glad throng, sing-ing aye the new song, And

(CHRIST.)

shout Hal - le - lu - jah! Hal-le-lu-jah! A-men.

3 Our boat often veering obeys not our steering;
'Tis Jesus' strong arm over ours at the helm!
He knows the hid dangers, to which we are strang-
gers,
And He'll bring us safe to His beautiful realm!

4 Then while the swift river flows onward for ever,
That bears us upon its dark tide to the sea,
We view without sighing the banks swiftly flying,
And joyfully haste with our Master to be!

MORNING RED.

R. W. RAYMOND.

German. Arr. by J. R. HOWARD.

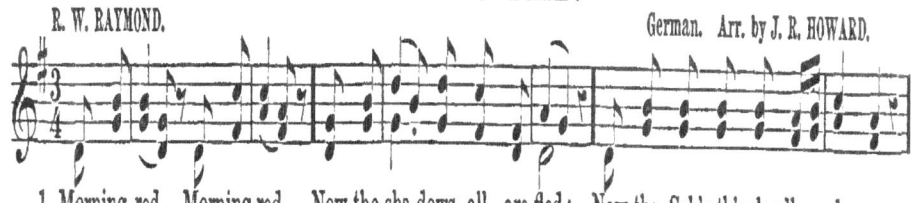

1. Morning red, Morning red, Now the sha-dows all are fled; Now the Sabbath's cloudless glo - ry,
2. All a-round, All a-round, Sol-emn silence reigned profound; When, with blaze and sudden thunder,
3. Forth He came! Forth He came! Robed in white, ce-les - tial flame! Ma - ry, at His emp-ty pri - son,

Tells a-new the wondrous story, Christ is ris - en from the dead.
Angels burst the tomb a-sun-der, And the Sav-iour was un-bound.
Knew not her Redeemer, risen, Till He called her by her name.

4 Morning red! Morning red!
Christ is risen from the dead!
Still He walketh in the garden,
Speaking words of love and pardon,
Though the crown is on His head.

5 Morning red! Morning red!
Thou dost light His crowned head!
Brightest jewel of His glory,
Ever shines that wondrous story,
Christ is risen from the dead.

(CHRIST.)

O SON OF GOD.

Rev. A. C. COXE. 1840.

Arr. from BEETHOVEN.

1. How beauteous were the marks di - vine, That in Thy meekness used to shine,
2. Oh, who like Thee, so calm, so bright, So pure, so made to live in light,—

That lit Thy lone - ly path - way, trod In won - drous love, O Son of God!
Oh, who like Thee did ev - er go So pa - tient through a world of woe?

3 E'en death, which sets the prisoner free
  Was pang and scoff and scorn to Thee;
  Yet love through all Thy torture glowed,
  And mercy with Thy life-blood flowed.

4 Oh, in Thy light be mine to go,
  Illuming all my way of woe!
  And give me ever on the road
  To trace Thy footsteps, Son of God!

LUELLA.

H. N. WHITNEY, by per.

1. Je - sus, ten - der Sav - iour, Hast Thou died for me? Make me ve - ry thankful In my heart to Thee.
2. Now I know Thou lov - est, And dost plead for me; Make me ve - ry thankful, In my pray'rs to Thee.

(CHRIST.)

When the sad, sad sto - ry Of Thy grief I read, Make me ve - ry sor - ry For my sins, in - deed.
Soon, I hope, in glo - ry At Thy side to stand; Make me fit to meet Thee In that hap - py land.

EVENTIDE. 10s.

Rev. HENRY F. LYTE. 1847.

WM. H. MONK.

1. A - bide with me! Fast falls the ev - en - tide; The darkness deep - ens; Lord, with me a - bide!
2. Not a brief glance I beg, a part-ing word; But as thou dwell'st with Thy dis - ci - ples, Lord,

When oth-er help-ers fail, and comforts flee, Help of the helpless, O a - bide with me! A - men.
Fa - mil-iar, con - des - cend-ing, patient, free, Come, not to sojourn, but a - bide with me!

3 Come not in terrors, as the King of kings,
  But kind and good, with healing in Thy wings;
  Tears for all woes, a heart for every plea:
  Come, Friend of sinners, thus abide with me!

4 Thou on my head in early youth didst smile;
  And, though rebellious and perverse meanwhile,
  Thou hast not left me, oft as I left Thee:
  On to the close, O Lord, abide with me!

5 I need Thy presence every passing hour:
  What but Thy grace can foil the tempter's power?
  Who like Thyself my guide and stay can be?
  Through cloud and sunshine, O abide with me!

6 Hold Thou Thy cross before my closing eyes,
  Shine through the gloom, and point me to the skies;
  Heaven's morning breaks, and earth's vain shadows flee;
  In life, in death, O Lord, abide with me! Amen.

(CHRIST.)

BEAUTIFUL MORNING STAR.

Rev. A. A. G.

From "Brightest and Best," by per. Rev. A. A. GRALEY.

1. Beau-ti-ful morning star, Beauti-ful morning star, Be-fore thy fires The night re-tires,
2. Beau-ti-ful morning star, Beauti-ful morning star, Thy glories shine, O Christ di-vine,
3. Beau-ti-ful morning star, Beauti-ful morning star, When fears control My trembling soul,
4. Beau-ti-ful morning star, Beauti-ful morning star, Thy glo-ry bright Shall fill with light,

And gates of morn un-bar.
Like yon bright orb a-far.
Thy beams my com-fort are,
The shin-ing land a-far.

CHORUS.

Beau-ti-ful morn-ing star, Beauti-ful morning star,

ritard.

The pro-phets of old Thy ris-ing fore-told, Beau-ti-ful morn-ing star.

(CHRIST.)

JESUS, SAVIOUR!

ANGELUS, 1660.

Rev. J. B. DYKES.

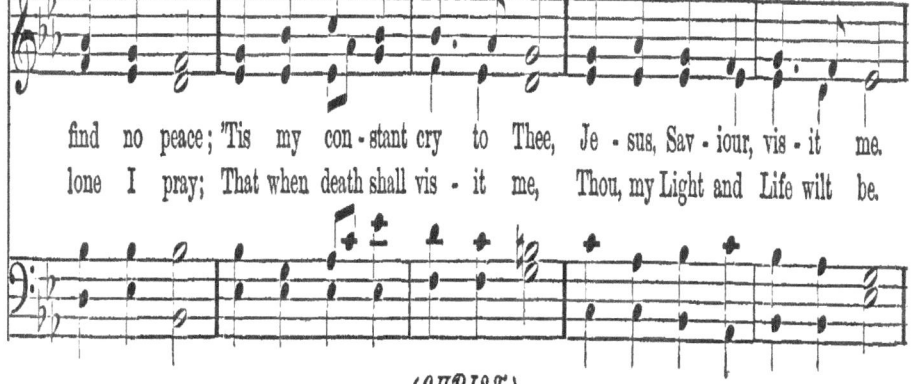

1. Je - sus, Saviour, vis - it me, How my soul longs af - ter Thee! When, my best, my dearest Friend,
2. Thou a - lone, my gracious Lord, Art my shield and great re-ward; All my hope, my Saviour, Thou!

Shall our sep - a - ra - tion end? Lord, my long - ings nev - er cease, With - out Thee I
To Thy sov - reign will I bow; Pa - tient - ly I wait Thy day; For this gift a -

find no peace; 'Tis my con - stant cry to Thee, Je - sus, Sav - iour, vis - it me.
lone I pray; That when death shall vis - it me, Thou, my Light and Life wilt be.

(CHRIST.)

ONLY JESUS FEELS AND KNOWS.

FANNY J. CROSBY, 1874.   From "Brightest and Best," by per. HUBERT P. MAIN.

Gently.

1. On - ly Je - sus feels and knows   All   the weight of hu - man woes; Full and free His
2. On - ly Je - sus looks with - in,   Sees our hearts and all our sin;   On - ly He can
3. On - ly Je - sus an - swers pray'r, Light-er makes the cross we bear; Bids us cast on
4. Safe in Him our souls a - bide,   Safe His hand our steps will guide, Till we sing be -

CHORUS.

mer - cy flows,—Bless-ed, bless-ed Je - sus! O that name we love to hear, Name a -
make us clean; Bless-ed, bless-ed Je - sus!
Him our care; Bless-ed, bless - ed Je - sus!
yond the tide, Bless-ed, bless - ed Je - sus!

bove all oth - ers dear; How it calms our ev - ery fear! Bless - ed, bless - ed Je - sus.

(CHRIST.)

ROTHWELL. L. M.

(58) Christian Songs, 201. Key E♭.

1 HE lives, the great Redeemer lives,
  What joy the blest assurance gives ;
And now, before His Father, God,
  Pleads the full merit of His blood.

2 Repeated crimes awake our fears,
  And justice, armed with frowns, ap-
    pears ;
But in the Saviour's lovely face,
  Sweet mercy smiles, and all is peace.

3 Hence, then, ye black, despairing
    thoughts ;
Above our fears, above our faults,
  His powerful intercessions rise,
And guilt recedes, and terror dies

4 Great Advocate, Almighty Friend !
  On Him our humble hopes depend ;
Our cause can never, never fail,
  For Jesus pleads, and must prevail.

FRANKLIN. C. M.

(59) Christian Songs, 197. Key C.

1 THE head that once was crowned with
    thorns
  Is crowned with glory now ;
A royal diadem adorns
  The mighty Victor's brow.

2 The highest place that heaven affords,
  Is His by sovereign right ;
The King of kings, and Lord of lords,
  He reigns in glory bright ;—

3 The joy of all who dwell above,
  The joy of all below,
To whom He manifests His love,
  And grants His name to know.

4 To them, the cross, with all its shame,
  With all its grace is given ;
Their name, an everlasting name,
  Their joy—the joy of heaven.

BALERMA. C. M.

(60) Bradbury Trio, 123. Key B♭.

1 JESUS, the very thought of Thee,
  With sweetness fills my breast :
But sweeter far Thy face to see,
  And in Thy presence rest.

2 Nor voice can sing, nor heart can frame,
  Nor can the memory find,
A sweeter sound than Thy blest name,
  O Saviour of mankind !

3 O hope of every contrite heart !
  O joy of all the meek !
To those who fall how kind Thou art !
  How good to those who seek !

4 But what to those who find ? Ah ! this,
  Nor tongue, nor pen can show,
The love of Jesus, what it is,
  None but his loved ones know.

MARTYRDOM. C. M.

(61) Christian Songs, 201. Key A♭.

1 I'M not ashamed to own my Lord,
  Nor to defend His cause ;
Maintain the honor of His word,
  The glory of His cross.

(CHRIST.)

2 Jesus, my God ! I know His name ;
  His name is all my trust ;
Nor will He put my soul to shame,
  Nor let my hope be lost.

3 Firm, as His throne, His promise
    stands,
  And He can well secure
What I've committed to His hands,
  Till the decisive hour.

4 Then will he own my worthless name,
  Before His Father's face ;
And in the New Jerusalem
  Appoint my soul a place.

ANTIOCH. C. M.

(62) Christian Songs, 201. Key E♭.

1 Joy to the world, the Lord is come !
  Let earth receive her King ;
Let every heart prepare Him room,
  And heav'n and nature sing.

2 Joy to the world, the Saviour reigns,
  Let men their songs employ ;
While fields and floods, rocks, hills and
    plains,
  Repeat the sounding joy.

3 He rules the world with truth and
    grace,
  And makes the nations prove
The glories of His righteousness,
  And wonders of His love.

ROUND THE LORD IN GLORY SEATED.

Bishop RICHARD MANT, 1837.   Rev. JOHN B. DYKES.

1. Round the Lord in glory seated, Cherubim and Seraphim,   Filled His temple and repeated, Each to each, the alternate hymn:

2. "Lord, Thy glory fills the Heaven, Earth is with its fulness stored; Unto Thee be glory given, Holy! Holy! Holy! Lord!"

3 Heaven is still with glory ringing,
  Earth takes up the angel's cry,
"Holy! Holy! Holy!" singing,
  "Lord of hosts, the Lord most High!"

4 With His seraph-train before Him,
  With His holy Church below,
Thus unite we to adore Him,
  Bid we thus our anthem flow:

5 "Lord, Thy glory fills the Heaven,
  Earth is with its fullness stored;
Unto Thee be glory given,
  Holy! Holy! Holy! Lord!

SECOND HYMN.

1 Praise the Lord! ye heavens adore Him,
  Praise Him, angels, in the height;
Sun and moon, rejoice before Him,
  Praise Him, all ye stars and light.

2 Praise the Lord! for He hath spoken,
  Worlds His mighty voice obeyed;
Laws which never shall be broken,
  For their guidance He hath made.

3 Praise the Lord! for He is glorious,
  Never shall His promise fail;
God hath made His saints victorious,
  Sin and death shall not prevail.

4 Praise the God of our salvation;
  Hosts on high, His power proclaim;
Heaven and earth, and all creation,
  Laud and magnify His name.

Rev. John Kempthorne, 1809.

THIRD HYMN.

1 Hark! a thrilling voice is sounding;
  "Christ is nigh," it seems to say:
"Cast away the dreams of darkness,
  O ye children of the day!"

2 Wakened by the solemn warning,
  Let the earth-bound soul arise;
Christ, her Sun, all ill dispelling,
  Shines upon the morning skies.

3 Lo! the Lamb, so long expected,
  Comes with pardon down from heaven
Let us haste, with tears of gladness,
  One and all to be forgiven.

4 Then when next He comes with glory,
  And the world is wrapped in fear;
With His mercy He will shield us,
  And with words of love draw near.

Anon.

(CHRIST.)

LOVING KINDNESS. L. M.

(66) Christian Songs, 200. Key A.

1 AWAKE, my soul, to joyful lays,
  And sing thy great Redeemer's praise;
  He justly claims a song from me,
  His loving kindness, Oh! how free!

2 He saw me ruined in the fall,
  Yet loved me notwithstanding all:
  He saved me from my lost estate,
  His loving kindness Oh! how great!

3 Though numerous hosts of mighty foes,
  Though earth and hell my way oppose,
  He safely leads my soul along,
  His loving kindness, Oh! how strong!

4 Often I feel my sinful heart,
  Prone from my Jesus to depart;
  But though I have Him oft forgot,
  His loving kindness changes not.

BADEN. L. M.

(67) Christian Songs, 197. Key B♭.

1 OH! the sweet wonders of that cross,
  Where God, the Saviour, loved and
      died;
  Her noblest life my spirit draws
  From His dear wounds, and bleed-
      ing side.

2 I would for ever speak His name,
  In sounds to mortal ears unknown,
  With angels join to praise the Lamb,
  And worship at His Father's throne.

3 All hail! Thou great Immanuel, hail!
  Ten thousand blessings on Thy
      name!
  While thus Thy wondrous love we tell,
  Our bosoms feel the sacred flame.

4 Come, quickly come, Immortal King!
  On earth Thy regal honors raise;
  The full salvation promised bring,
  Then every tongue shall sing Thy
      praise!

MARTYRDOM. C. M.

(68) Christian Songs, 201. Key A♭.

1 ALAS! and did my Saviour bleed?
  And did my sovereign die?
  Would He devote that sacred head
  For such a worm as I?

2 Was it for crimes that I had done
  He groaned upon the tree?
  Amazing pity! grace unknown!
  And love beyond degree!

3 Well might the sun in darkness hide,
  And shut his glories in,
  When Christ, the Lord of glory, died
  For man the creature's sin.

4 Thus might I hide my blushing face
  While his dear cross appears,
  Dissolve my heart in thankfulness,
  And melt mine eyes to tears.

5 But drops of grief can ne'er repay
  The debt of love I owe:
  Here, Lord, I give myself away;
  'Tis all that I can do.

ORTONVILLE. C. M.

(69) Bradbury Trio, 82. Key B♭.

1 MAJESTIC sweetness sits enthroned
  Upon the Saviour's brow;
  His head with radiant glories crown'd,
  His lips with grace o'erflow.

2 He saw me plunged in deep distress,
  And flew to my relief;
  For me He bore the shameful cross,
  And carried all my grief.

3 To Him I owe my life and breath,
  And all the joys I have,
  He makes me triumph over death,
  And saves me from the grave.

4 Since from Thy bounty I receive
  Such proofs of love divine,
  Had I a thousand hearts to give,
  Lord, they should all be Thine.

MARTYRDOM. C. M.

(70) Christian Songs, 201. Key A♭.

1 DEAR Refuge of my weary soul,
  On Thee, when sorrows rise—
  On Thee, when waves of trouble roll,
  My fainting hope relies.

2 To Thee I tell each rising grief,
  For Thou alone canst heal;
  Thy word can bring a sweet relief
  For every pain I feel.

3 But O! when gloomy doubts prevail,
  I fear to call Thee mine;
  The springs of comfort seem to fail,
  And all my hopes decline.

4 Yet, gracious God, where shall I flee!
  Thou art my only trust:
  And still my soul would cleave to
      Thee,
  Though prostrate in the dust.

(CHRIST.)

LOVING WORDS.

FANNY J. CROSBY, 1875.

HUBERT P. MAIN, by per.

1. As the ros - y beams descending Bring a cheerful light to all; So, our lov - ing words of
2. Like the ear - ly dew of morning; Like the balm - y, summer rain; Loving words re - fresh the
3. Lov - ing words are strains of music, Dearly prized and treasured long; Like the echo - ed tones that

REFRAIN.

kind - ness   Scatter smiles where'er they fall. They are trea - sures, gold - en trea - sures, Mak-ing
spir - it,   Fill the heart with joy a - gain.
lin - ger,   When the bird has ceased its song.

bright-er all our pleasures; They are seed whose fruit will grow; Let them fall where'er they go.

(LOVING WORDS.)

WILLIAMS. L. M.

(72) Christian Songs, 201. Key D.

1 WHEN I survey the wondrous cross,
　　On which the Prince of glory died,
My richest gain I count but loss,
　　And pour contempt on all my pride.

2 Forbid it, Lord, that I should boast,
　　Save in the death of Christ, my God;
All the vain things that charm me most,
　　I sacrifice them to His blood.

3 See,from His head,His hands,His feet,
　　Sorrow and love flow mingled down:
Did e'er such love and sorrow meet,
　　Or thorns compose so rich a crown!

4 Were the whole realm of nature mine,
　　That were a present far too small;
Love so amazing, so divine,
　　Demands my soul, my life, my all.

CRUCIFIX. 7s & 6s.

(73) Christian Songs,197. Key Eb.

1 O SACRED Head now wounded,
　　With grief and shame weigh'd down;
Now scornfully surrounded,
　　With thorns Thy only crown;
O sacred Head, what glory,
　　What bliss till now was Thine;
Yet though despised and gory,
　　I joy to call Thee mine.

2 What language shall I borrow,
　　To thank Thee, dearest Friend,
For this Thy dying sorrow,
　　Thy pity without end!
O make me Thine forever,
　　And should I fainting be,
Lord, let me never, never
　　Outlive my love to Thee.

3 If I, a wretch, should leave Thee,
　　O Jesus, leave not me;
In faith may I receive Thee,
　　When death shall set me free.
When strength and comfort languish,
　　And I must hence depart,
Release me then from anguish,
　　By Thine own wounded heart.

4 Be near, when I am dying,
　　O, show Thy cross to me!
And for my succor flying,
　　Come, Lord, to set me free.
These eyes, new faith receiving,
　　From Jesus shall not move;
For he who dies believing,
　　Dies safely—through Thy love.

MARTYN. 7s.

(74) Bradbury Trio, 14. Key F.

1 JESUS, lover of my soul,
　　Let me to Thy bosom fly;
While the billows near me roll,
　　While the tempest still is high.
Hide me, O my Saviour, hide,
　　Till the storm of life be past,
Safe into the haven guide,
　　O receive my soul at last.

2 Other refuge have I none—
　　Hangs my helpless soul on Thee;
Leave, ah! leave me not alone,
　　Still support and comfort me;
All my trust on Thee is stayed,
　　All my help from Thee I bring—
Cover my defenceless head
　　With the shadow of Thy wing.

3 Thou, O Christ, art all I want,
　　More than all in Thee I find,
Raise the fallen, cheer the faint,
　　Heal the sick, and lead the blind.

Just and holy is Thy name,
　　I am all unrighteousness;
Vile and full of sin I am—
　　Thou art full of truth and grace.

4 Plenteous grace with Thee is found—
　　Grace to pardon all my sin;
Let the healing streams abound,
　　Make and keep me pure within;
Thou of life the fountain art,
　　Freely let me take of Thee;
Spring Thou up within my heart,
　　Rise to all eternity.

DENNIS. S. M.

(75) Bradbury Trio, 225. Key F.

1 THE Lord my Shepherd is;
　　I shall be well supplied;
Since He is mine, and I am His
　　What can I want beside?

2 He leads me to the place
　　Where heavenly pasture grows,
Where living waters gently pass,
　　And full salvation flows.

3 If e'er I go astray,
　　He doth my soul reclaim,
And guides me in His own right way,
　　For His most holy name.

4 In sight of all my foes,
　　Thou dost my table spread:
My cup with blessings overflows,
　　And joy exalts my head.

5 The bounties of Thy love
　　Shall crown my future days;
Nor from Thy house will I remove,
　　Nor cease to speak Thy praise.

(CHRIST.)

REST IN THEE.

E. TURNEY, D.D.

R. LOWRY.
From "Royal Diadem," by per.

1. Bless - ed Je - sus, Bless-ed Je - sus, Thou who gav'st Thy - self for me, Leave me not in
2. Hope of all the meek and low-ly, Thou my hope and joy shalt be: Bless - ed Je - sus,
3. Draw me from each sin - ful striv-ing; From my-self, O set me free: Bless - ed Je - sus,
4. High - est, pur - est, sweetest pleasure, Shall Thy ser - vice bring to me: Bless - ed Je - sus,

CHORUS.

sin to wan - der; Bid me come and rest in Thee. Rest in Thee, rest in Thee,
Bless - ed Je - sus, Bid me come and rest in Thee.
Bless - ed Je - sus, Bid me come and rest in Thee.
Bless - ed Je - sus, Bid me come and rest in Thee.

Bid me come and rest in Thee; Rest in Thee, rest in Thee, Bid me come and rest in Thee.

(CHRIST.)

ST. THOMAS. S. M.

(77) Bradbury Trio, 224. Key G.

1 AWAKE, and sing the song
Of Moses and the Lamb;
Wake, every heart, and every tongue,
To praise the Saviour's name.

2 Sing of His dying love,
Sing of His rising power;
Sing how He intercedes above,
For those whose sins He bore.

3 Sing on your heavenly way,
Ye ransomed sinners, sing;
Sing on, rejoicing, every day,
In Christ, the exalted King.

4 Soon shall your raptured tongue
His endless praise proclaim;
And sweeter voices tune the song
Of Moses and the Lamb.

STATE STREET. S. M.

(78) Bradbury Trio, 71. Key B♭.

1 JESUS who knows full well,
The heart of every saint,
Invites us all our griefs to tell,
To pray, and never faint.

2 He bows His gracious ear,
We never plead in vain:
Yet we must wait till He appear,
And pray, and pray again.

3 Jesus, the Lord will hear
His chosen when they cry:
Yes, though He may a while forbear,
He'll help them from on high.

4 Then let us earnest be,
And never faint in prayer;
He loves our importunity,
And makes our cause His care.

———

ORTONVILLE. C. M.

(79) Bradbury Trio, 82. Key B♭.

1 How sweet the name of Jesus sounds
In a believer's ear!
It soothes his sorrows, heals his wounds,
And drives away his fear.

2 It makes the wounded spirit whole,
And calms the troubled breast;
'Tis manna to the hungry soul,
And for the weary, rest.

3 By Thee my prayers acceptance gain,
Although with sin defiled;
Satan accuses me in vain,
And I am owned a child.

4 Jesus! my Shepherd, Guardian, Friend,
My Prophet, Priest, and King;
My Lord, my Life, my Way, my End,
Accept the praise I bring.

———

BADEN. L. M.

(80) Christian Songs, 197. Key B♭.

1 THO' all the world my choice deride,
Yet Jesus shall my portion be;
For I am pleased with none beside;
The fairest of the fair is He.

2 Sweet is the vision of Thy face,
And kindness o'er Thy lips is shed;
Lovely art Thou, and full of grace,
And glory beams around Thy head.

3 Thy sufferings I embrace with Thee,
Thy poverty and shameful cross;
The pleasures of the world I flee,
And deem its treasures only dross.

4 Be daily dearer to my heart,
And ever let me feel Thee near;
Then willingly with all I'd part,
Nor count it worthy of a tear.

———

LENOX. H. M.

(81) Bradbury Trio, 369. Key B♭.

1 COME, every pious heart
That loves the Saviour's name,
Your noblest powers exert
To celebrate His fame:
Tell all above and all below,
The debt of love to Him you owe.

2 He left His starry crown,
And laid His robes aside;
On wings of love came down,
And wept, and bled, and died.
What He endured, O! who can tell?
To save our souls from death and hell.

3 From the dark grave He rose
The mansion of the dead;
And thence His mighty foes
In glorious triumph led:
Up through the sky the conqu'ror rode,
And reigns on high, the Saviour God.

4 Jesus, we ne'er can pay
The debt we owe Thy love;
Yet tell us how we may
Our gratitude approve:
Our hearts—our all to Thee we give:
The gift, tho' small, do Thou receive,

(CHRIST.)

STILL WATER. 10s & 11s.

—KNOX.

Dr. THOS. HASTINGS.

1. The Lord is my Shepherd, He makes me re-pose Where the pas-tures in beauty are grow-
2. He strengthens my spir-it, He shows me the path Where the arms of His love shall en-fold

ing, He leads me a-far from the world and its woes, Where in peace the still waters are flow-ing.
me, And when I walk thro' the dark valley of death, His rod and His staff will up-hold me.

SHEPHERD OF ISRAEL.

SECOND HYMN.

Dr. T. Hastings, 1830.

1 Oh tell me, Thou life and delight of my soul,
    Where the flock of Thy pasture are feeding;
I seek Thy protection, I need Thy control,
    I would go where my Shepherd is leading.

2 Oh tell me the place where Thy flock are at rest,
    Where the noontide will find them reposing?
The tempest now raging, my soul is distressed,
    And the pathway of peace I am losing.

3 Oh why should I stray with the flock of Thy foes,
    'Mid the desert where now they are roving,

Where hunger and thirst, where affliction and woes,
    And temptations their ruin are proving?

4 Oh when shall my foes and my wanderings cease,
    And the follies that fill me with weeping?
Thou Shepherd of Israel, restore me that peace
    Thou dost give to the flock Thou art keeping.

5 A voice from the Shepherd now bids thee return
    By the way where the footprints are lying;
No longer to wander, no longer to mourn,
    Oh fair one, now homeward be flying.

(CHRIST.)

ARIEL. C. P. M

(84) Songs of Devotion, 57. Key E♭.

1 O COULD I speak the matchless worth,
O could I sound the glories forth,
    Which in my Saviour shine!
I'd soar and touch the heavenly strings,
And vie with Gabriel while he sings
    In notes almost divine.

2 I'd sing the precious blood He spilt,
My ransom from the dreadful guilt
    Of sin and wrath divine!
I'd sing His glorious righteousness,
In which all perfect, heavenly dress
    My soul shall ever shine.

3 I'd sing the characters He bears,
And all the forms of love He wears,
    Exalted on His throne:
In loftiest songs of sweetest praise,
I would to everlasting days
    Make all His glories known.

4 Well—the delightful day will come
When my dear Lord will bring me home,
    And I shall see His face:
Then with my Saviour, Brother, Friend,
A blest eternity I'll spend,
    Triumphant in His grace.

HARWELL. 8s & 7s.

(85) Clariona, 61. Key G.

1 HARK, ten thousand harps and voices
Sound the note of praise above;
Jesus reigns, and heaven rejoices;
    Jesus reigns, the God of love.
See! He sits on yonder throne!
Jesus rules the world alone!

2 Jesus, hail! whose glory brightens
    All above and gives it worth:
Lord of love, Thy smile enlightens,
    Cheers and charms Thy saints on earth;
When we think of love like Thine,
Lord, we own it love divine.

3 King of glory, reign forever,
    Thine an everlasting crown;
Nothing from Thy love shall sever
    Those whom Thou hast made Thine own:
Happy objects of Thy grace,
Chosen to behold Thy face.

4 Saviour, hasten Thine appearing;
    Bring, O bring the glorious day!
When, the awful summons hearing,
    Heaven and earth shall pass away!
Then with golden harps we'll sing,
Glory, glory, to our King.

BROWN. C. M.

(86) Bradbury Trio, 97, Key C.

1 O FOR a thousand tongues to sing
    My dear Redeemer's praise—
The glories of my God and King,
    The triumphs of His grace!

2 My gracious Master and my God,
    Assist me to proclaim,
To spread through all the earth abroad,
    The honors of Thy name.

3 Jesus! the name that calms our fears,
    That bids our sorrows cease;
'Tis music in the sinner's ears;
    'T is life, and health, and peace.

4 He breaks the power of reigning sin;
    He sets the prisoner free;
His blood can make the foulest clean;
    His blood availed for me.

ANTIOCH. C. M.

(87) Christian Songs, 201. Key E♭.

1 COME, let us join our cheerful songs
    With angels round the throne;
Ten thousand thousand are their tongues,
    But all their joys are one.

2 "Worthy the Lamb that died," they
    cry,
    "To be exalted thus;"
"Worthy the Lamb," our lips reply,
    "For He was slain for us."

3 Jesus is worthy to receive
    Honor and power divine;
And blessings, more than we can give,
    Be, Lord, for ever Thine.

(CHRIST.)

I'LL THINK OF MY SAVIOUR.

WM. B. BRADBURY.

From "New Golden Shower," by per.

1. I'll think of my Saviour when daylight is breaking A - way from the darkness and gloom of the night,
2. I'll think of my Saviour when daylight is sinking, And blending its beams with the twilight so gray;
3. I'll think of my Saviour when sor - row is flinging Her thick robe of sad - ness a - round the dark tomb;

When, fresh from his slumber, the sun is a - waking, And girding himself with the ar - mor of light.
When bright starry eyes in the azure are winking, And si - lence em - bra - ces the close of the day,
If light from His presence a glo - ry is bringing, 'Twill scat - ter its darkness and hide all its gloom.

CHORUS. GIRLS. BOYS. CHORUS.

I'll think of my Saviour, And trust Him for-ev - er, I'll seek for His fa - vor, And hope, through His love,

FULL CHORUS.

With angels to meet Him, With seraphs to greet Him, And praise Him for-ev - er In mansions a - bove.

(CHRIST.)

STAR OF BETHLEHEM. L. M.

(89) "Bonny Doon," Key G.

1 WHEN marshaled on the nightly plain,
　The glittering host bestud the sky ;
One star alone of all the train
　Can fix the sinner's wandering eye.
Hark ! hark ! to God the chorus breaks
　From every host, from every gem,
But one alone, the Saviour speaks,
　It is the Star of Bethlehem.

2 Once on the raging seas I rode,
　The storm was loud, the night was dark,
The ocean yawned, and wildly blowed
　The wind that tossed my foundering
　　bark.
Deep horror then my vitals froze ;
　Death-struck, I ceased the tide to
　　stem ;
When suddenly a star arose,
　It was the Star of Bethlehem.

3 It was my guide, my light, my all ;
　It bade my dark foreboding cease ;
And thro' the storm and danger's thrall
　It led me to the port of peace.
Now safely moored—my perils o'er—
　I'll sing, first in night's diadem,
For ever and for ever more,
　The Star ! the Star of Bethlehem !

RETREAT. L. M.

(90) Christian Songs, 198. Key B♭.

1 How sweetly flowed the Gospel sound
　From lips of gentleness and grace,
When listening thousands gathered
　round,
And joy and gladness filled the place !

2 From heaven He came, of heaven He
　spoke,
To heaven He led his followers' way ;
Dark clouds of gloomy night He broke,
　Unveiling an immortal day.

3 "Come, wanderers, to my Father's
　home,
Come, all ye weary ones, and rest :"
Yes, sacred Teacher, we will come,
　Obey Thee, love Thee, and be blest.

HAMBURG. L. M.

(91) Coronation, 131. Key E♭.

1 THOU only Sovereign of my heart,
　My Refuge, my almighty Friend—
And can my soul from Thee depart,
　On whom alone my hopes depend !

2 Whither, ah ! whither shall I go,
　A wretched wanderer from my Lord ?
Can this dark world of sin and woe
　One glimpse of happiness afford !

3 Eternal life Thy words impart,
　On these my fainting spirit lives :
Here sweeter comforts cheer my heart,
　Than all the round of nature gives.

4 Low at Thy feet my soul would lie ;
　Here safety dwells, and peace divine ;
Still let me live beneath Thine eye,
　For life, eternal life, is Thine.

SWEET STORY.

(92) Christian Songs, 86. Key F.

1 I think, when I read that sweet story
　of old,
When Jesus was here among men,
How He called little children as lambs
　to His fold, [then.
I should like to have been with them

2 I wish that His hands had been placed
　on my head,—
His arms had been thrown around me,
That I might have seen His kind look
　when He said,
　"Let the little ones come unto me."

3 Yet still to His foot-stool in prayer I
　may go,
And ask for a share in His love ;
And if I thus earnestly seek Him below,
　I shall see Him and hear Him above.

4 In that beautiful place He has gone to
　prepare,
For all who are washed and forgiv'n ;
And many dear children are gather-
　ing there,
For of such is the kingdom of heav'n.

ROCKINGHAM. L. M.

(93) Coronation, 129. Key G.

1 JESUS, thou Joy of loving hearts !
　Thou Fount of Life ! Thou Light of
　　men !
From the best bliss that earth imparts,
　We turn, unfilled, to Thee again.

2 Thy truth unchanged hath ever stood ;
　Thou savest those that on Thee call ;
To them that seek Thee, Thou art good,
　To them that find Thee, All in All !

3 Our restless spirits yearn for Thee,
　Where'er our changeful lot is cast ;
Glad, when Thy gracious smile we see,
　Blest, when our faith can hold Thee
　　fast.

4 O Jesus, ever with us stay ! [bright !
　Make all our moments calm and
Chase the dark night of sin away,
　Shed in our hearts Thy holy light !

LORD, THE MIGHTY WORK IS THINE.

Dr. PHILIP DODDRIDGE.

ALEX. VAN ALSTYNE, 1875, by per.

1. How great the wis - dom, pow'r and grace, Which in re - demption shine ; The heaven-ly host with
2. Be - fore His feet they cast their crowns, Those crowns which Jesus gave, And, with ten thousand
3. They tell the triumphs of His cross, The suff'rings which He bore ; How low He stoop'd, how

CHORUS.—faster.

joy con - fess The work is all di - vine, Lord, the mighty work is Thine, Thine the wisdom,
thousand tongues, Proclaim His pow'r to save.
high He rose,— And rose to stoop no more.

4.
With them let us our voices raise,
And still the song renew ;
Salvation well deserves the praise
Of men and angels too.
Lord, the mighty, &c.

pow'r and grace; Thine the love that came to save Our sin-ful dying race.

(CHRIST.)

BALMY DEW. L. M.

(95) Christian Songs, 114. Key E♭.

1 I KNOW that my Redeemer lives,
　O glory, hallelujah!
What comfort this sweet sentence gives,
　O glory hallelujah!
He lives, He lives who once was dead,
　O glory, hallelujah!
He lives, my ever living Head,
　O glory hallelujah!

2 He lives to bless me with His love,
　He lives to plead for me above,
　He lives my hungry soul to feed,
　He lives to help in time of need.

3 He lives to silence all my fears,
　He lives to wipe away my tears,
　He lives to calm my troubled heart,
　He lives all blessings to impart.

SAVIOUR, LIKE A SHEPHERD LEAD US.

(96) Bradbury Trio, 94. Key E♭.

1 SAVIOUR, like a shepherd lead us,
　Much we need Thy tend'rest care,
　In Thy pleasant pastures feed us,
　For our use Thy folds prepare;
　‖: Blessed Jesus,
　Thou hast bought us, Thine we are :‖

2 We are Thine, do Thou befriend us,
　Be the Guardian of our way;
　Keep Thy flock, from sin defend us,
　Seek us when we go astray;
　‖: Blessed Jesus,
　Hear, O hear us, when we pray. :‖

3 Thou hast promised to receive us,
　Poor and sinful though we be;
　Thou hast mercy to relieve us,
　Grace to cleanse, and power to free;
　‖: Blessed Jesus,
　We will early turn to Thee. :‖

DEAR JESUS. 8s & 6s.

(97) Clariona, 133. Key C.

1 DEAR Jesus ever at my side,
　How loving must Thou be
To leave Thy home in heaven to guard,
　A little child like me.
Thy beautiful and shining face
　I see not though so near;
The sweetness of Thy soft, low voice,
　I am too deaf to hear.

2 I can not feel Thee touch my hand
　With pressure light and mild,
To check me, as my mother did
　When I was but a child.
But I have felt Thee in my thoughts
　Fighting with sin for me;
And when my heart loves God, I know
　The sweetness is from Thee.

3 And when, Dear Saviour! I kneel down,
　Morning and night to prayer,
Something, there is within my heart,
　Which tells me Thou art there.
Yes! when I pray, Thou prayest too—
　Thy prayer is all for me,
But when I sleep, Thou sleepest not,
　But watchest patiently.

THE CHILDREN'S SAVIOUR.

(98) Christian Songs, 121. Key B♭.

1 JESUS is our loving Saviour,
　He, our best, our constant friend;
In His service life is pleasure,
　For He loveth to the end;

‖: Loving Saviour, :‖
‖ Here we at Thy footstool bend.‖

2 Jesus is the children's Saviour!
　"Suffer them," He says, "to come,"
If they seek His face and favor,
　They shall share His Heavenly
　　Home,
　‖: Gracious Saviour! :‖
‖: Never more from Thee to roam. :‖

JESUS LOVES ME.

(99) Bradbury Trio, 194. Key D.

1 JESUS loves me! this I know,
　For the Bible tells me so;
Little ones to Him belong,
　They are weak but He is strong.

CHO.—Yes, Jesus loves me,
　　　Yes, Jesus loves me,
　　　Yes, Jesus loves me,
　　　The Bible tells me so.

2 Jesus loves me! He who died,
　Heaven's gate to open wide;
He will wash away my sin,
　Let His little child come in.

3 Jesus loves me! loves me still,
　Though I'm very weak and ill;
From His shining throne on high,
　Comes to watch me where I lie.

4 Jesus loves me! He will stay,
　Close beside me, all the way;
If I love Him, when I die,
　He will take me home on high.

(CHRIST.)

STAR OF THE MORNING.

R. LOWRY.

Rev. M. A. FOX.

From "Brightest and Best," by per.

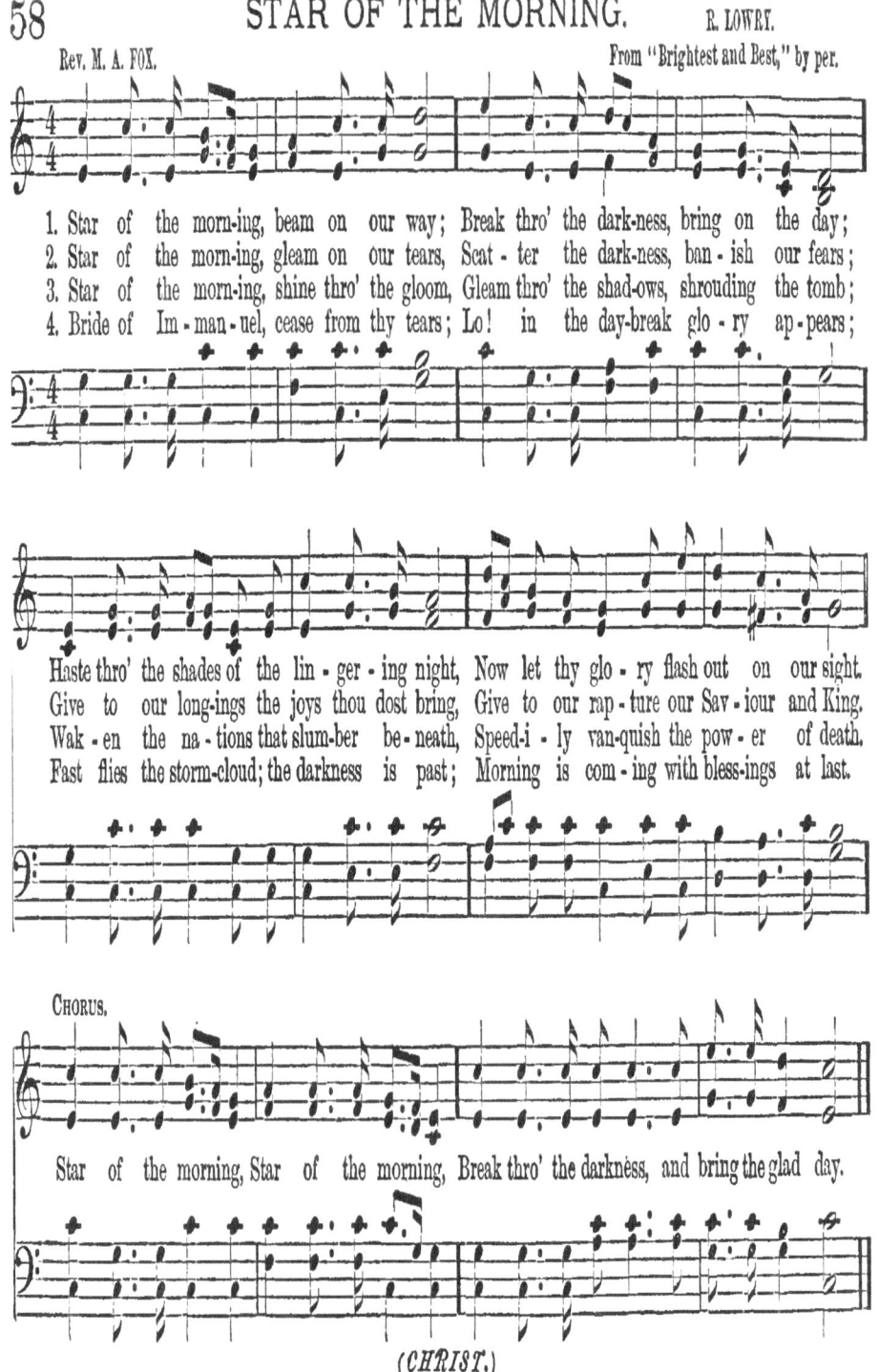

1. Star of the morn-ing, beam on our way; Break thro' the dark-ness, bring on the day;
2. Star of the morn-ing, gleam on our tears, Scat - ter the dark-ness, ban - ish our fears;
3. Star of the morn-ing, shine thro' the gloom, Gleam thro' the shad-ows, shrouding the tomb;
4. Bride of Im - man - uel, cease from thy tears; Lo! in the day-break glo - ry ap - pears;

Haste thro' the shades of the lin - ger - ing night, Now let thy glo - ry flash out on our sight.
Give to our long-ings the joys thou dost bring, Give to our rap - ture our Sav - iour and King.
Wak - en the na - tions that slum-ber be - neath, Speed-i - ly van-quish the pow - er of death.
Fast flies the storm-cloud; the darkness is past; Morning is com - ing with bless-ings at last.

CHORUS.

Star of the morning, Star of the morning, Break thro' the darkness, and bring the glad day.

(CHRIST.)

Mrs. MARY FAWLER MAUDE, 1848.

CHARLES THIRTLE. 1873.

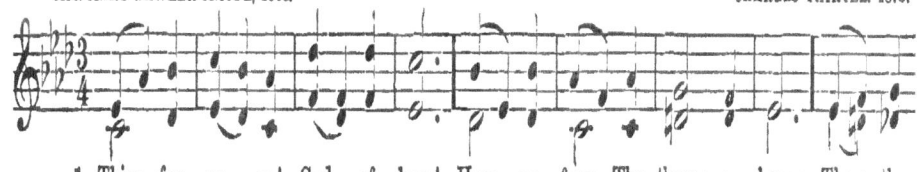

1. Thine for ev - er! God of love! Hear us from Thy throne a - bove; Thou the
2. Thine for ev - er! oh, how blest They who find in Thee their rest; Sav - iour,

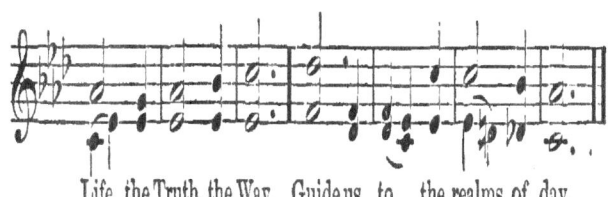

Life, the Truth, the Way, Guide us to the realms of day.
Guardian, Heav'nly Friend, O de - fend us to the end.

3 Thine for ever! Saviour keep
Us, Thy frail and trembling sheep
Safe alone beneath Thy care,
Let us all Thy goodness share.

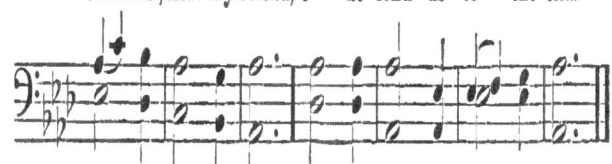

4 Thine for ever! Thou our Guide,
All our wants by Thee supplied ;
All our sins by Thee forgiven,
Lead us, Lord, from earth to heaven

SECOND HYMN.

1 Jesus, grant me this, I pray,
Ever in Thy heart to stay ;
Let me evermore abide
Hidden in Thy wounded side.

2 If the evil one prepare,
Or the world, a tempting snare,
I am safe, when I abide
In Thy heart and wounded side.

3 If the flesh, more dangerous still,
Tempt my soul to deeds of ill,
Naught I fear, when I abide
In Thy heart and wounded side.

4 Death will come one day to me;
Jesus cast me not from Thee·
Dying let me still abide
In Thy heart and wounded side.

Tr: H. W. Baker, 1861.

(JESUS IN DAILY LIFE.)

I NEED THEE EVERY HOUR.

R. LOWRY.

Mrs. A. S. HAWKS.

From "Royal Diadem," by per.

1. I need Thee ev - ery hour, Most gracious Lord; No ten - der voice like Thine Can peace af - ford.
2. I need Thee ev - ery hour, Stay Thou near by; Temp-ta - tions lose their power When Thou art nigh.
3. I need Thee ev - ery hour, In joy or pain; Come quick-ly and a - bide, Or life is vain.
4. I need Thee ev - ery hour, Teach me Thy will; And Thy rich pro-mis - es In me ful - fill.
5. I need Thee ev - ery hour, Most Ho - ly One; Oh, make me Thine in - deed, Thou bless- ed Son.

REFRAIN.

I need Thee; oh! I need Thee; Ev - ery hour I need Thee; O bless me now, my Saviour! I come to Thee.

SAVIOUR, LISTEN TO OUR PRAYER.

E. W. KELLOGG, by per. H. G. ABBEY.

1. Sav - iour, list - en to our prayer, Poor and sin - ful though we are; Guilt con - fess - ing,
2. Strength is Thine; we oft - en stray From the pure and ho - ly way; Wilt Thou guide us,
3. Then may we, when life is o'er, Stand with Thee on yon - der shore; Freed from sin - ning,

(JESUS IN DAILY LIFE.)

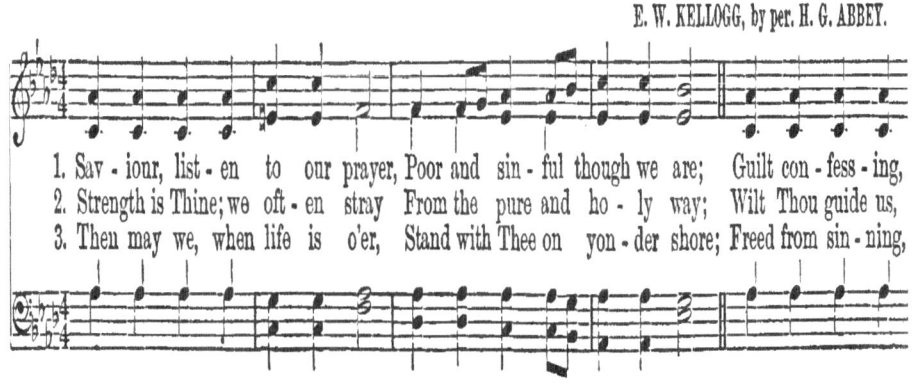

CHORUS.

Give Thy blessing, Grant Thy lov-ing care. O God our Fa-ther, Christ, our King, Now to Thee our
Walk be-side us, Near-er ev-ery day!
Hea-ven winning, Prais-ing ev-er-more!

hearts we bring, Keep them ev-er, Bless-ed Sav-iour, Till in heav'n Thy love we sing.

Rev. WM. A. MUHLENBERG, 1820.   MILWAUKEE. 8s & 7s.   JOHN ZUNDEL, by per.
Rather slow and gentle.

1. Sav-iour, who Thy flock art feed-ing With the Shepherd's kind-est care, All the fee-ble,
2. Now, these lit-tle ones re-ceiv-ing, Fold them in Thy gra-cious arm, There, we know, Thy

f

gent-ly lead-ing, While the lambs Thy bo-som share.
word be-liev-ing, On-ly there, se-cure from harm.

3 Never, from Thy pasture roving,
    Let them be the lion's prey;
    Let Thy tenderness, so loving,
    Keep them thro' life's dangerous way.

4 Then within Thy fold eternal,
    Let them find a resting-place,
    Feed in pastures ever vernal,
    Drink the rivers of Thy grace.

(JESUS IN DAILY LIFE.)

LEAD THOU ME ON.

Rev. JOHN HENRY NEWMAN, D. D., 1833.

Rev. J. B. DYKES.

1. Lead, Kindly Light, a - mid th'en-cir-cling gloom, Lead Thou me on; The night is
2. I was not ev - er thus, nor prayed that Thou Shouldst lead me on; I loved to
3. So long Thy Power hath bless'd me, sure it still Will lead me on O'er moor and

dark, and I am far from home, Lead Thou me on; Keep Thou my feet; I
choose and see my path; but now Lead Thou me on! I loved the gar - ish
fen, o'er crag and tor - rent, till The night is gone; And with the morn those

do not ask to see The dis - tant scene; one step e - nough for me.
day, and spite of fears, Pride ruled my will: re - mem - ber not past years!
an - gel fa - ces smile. Which I have loved long since, and lost a - while!

(JESUS IN DAILY LIFE.)

Miss ADELAIDE A. PROCTER.

ARTHUR BELL.

1. One by one the sands are flow - ing, One by one the moments fall, Some are coming, some are
2. Do not look at life's long sor - row, See how small each moment's pain; God will help thee for to -
3. Do not lin - ger with re - gret - ting, Or for passion's hour despond; Nor, the dai - ly toil for -

go - ing, Do not strive to grasp them all; One by one thy du - ties wait thee, Let thy
mor - row— Ev - ery day be - gin a - gain; Ev - ery hour that fleets so slow - ly, Has its
get - ting, Look too eag - er - ly be - yond; Hours are gold - en links, God's token Reaching

whole strength go to each; Let no fu - ture dreams e - late thee, Learn thou first what those can teach
task to do or bear; Lu - minous the crown, and ho - ly, If thou set each gem with care.
heaven; but, one by one; Take them, lest the chain be broken Ere the pil - grimage be done.

(JESUS IN DAILY LIFE.)

JEWETT. 6s.

Rev. BENJ. SCHMOLKE, 1716

C. M. von WEBER, 1826.

1. My Je - sus as Thou wilt! Oh! may Thy will be mine; In - to T
2. My Je - sus as Thou wilt! All shall be well for me; Each chang-i

hand of love I would my all re - sign; Thro' sor-row, or thro' joy, Con - duct r
fu - ture scene I glad-ly trust with Thee: Straight to my home a - bove I trav - e

as Thine own, And help me still to say, My Lord, Thy will be done!
calm - ly on, And sing, in life or death, My Lord, Thy will be done!

(JESUS IN DAILY LIFE.)

THE LORD WILL PROVIDE.

Mrs. M. A. W. COOK. 1864.

C. S. HARRINGTON, by per.   E. TOURJEE.

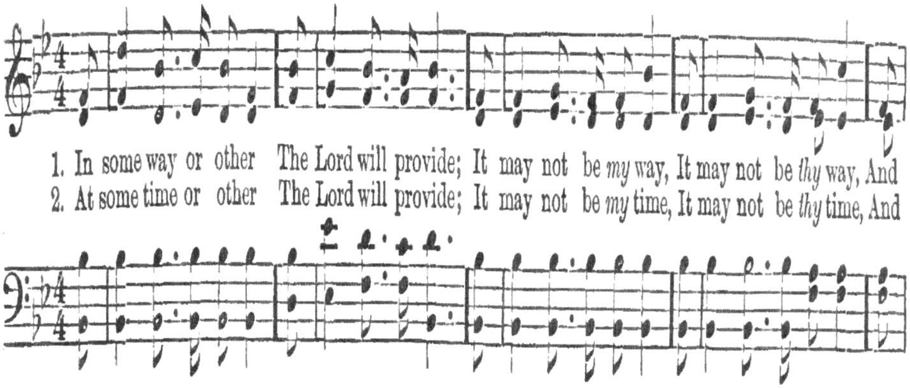

1. In some way or other   The Lord will provide; It may not be *my* way, It may not be *thy* way, And
2. At some time or other   The Lord will provide; It may not be *my* time, It may not be *thy* time, And

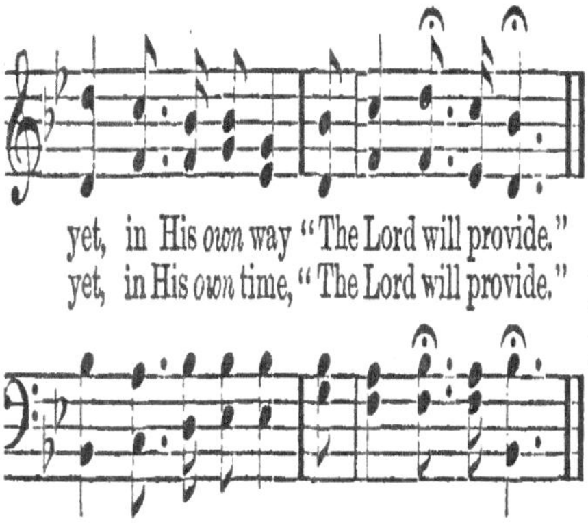

yet, in His *own* way "The Lord will provide."
yet, in His *own* time, "The Lord will provide."

3.
Despond then no longer ;
  The Lord will provide ;
And this be the token—
No word He hath spoken
Was ever yet broken,—
  "The Lord will provide."

4.
March on, then, right boldly ;
  The sea shall divide ;
The pathway made glorious,
With shoutings victorious,
We'll join in the chorus,
  "The Lord will provide."

HARRIETTE B.

I'M A LITTLE PILGRIM.

R. LOWRY, by per.

1. I'm a lit - tle pilgrim, With my staff in hand ; I am journeying onward To a bet - ter land.
2. Per - ils oft   at - tend me, Snares and foes abound ; Wilderness - es round me, Rocks and slippery ground.
3. Of - ten fight I   bravely With some hostile band, Who my steps would hinder To that distant land.
4. Naught can now detain me On these shores of time ; Speed I to that country In the heavenly clime.

(JESUS IN DAILY LIFE.)

65

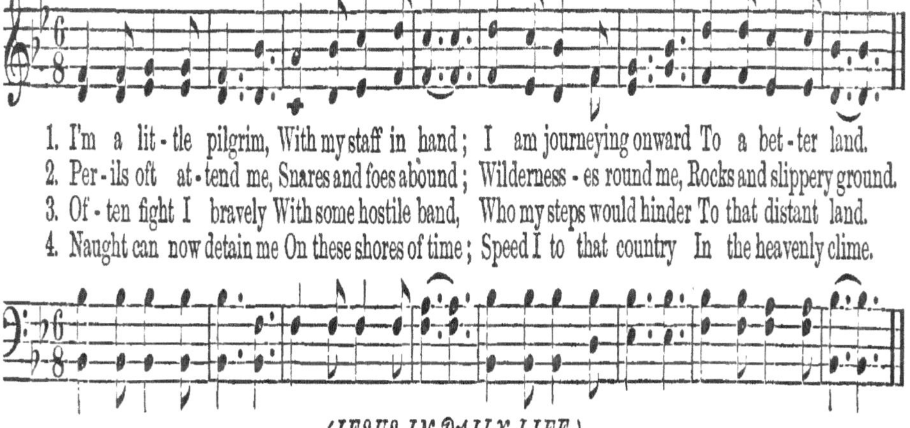

JUST AS GOD LEADS ME.

LAMPERTUS. 1635, arr.

HUBERT P. MAIN, 1866, by per.

1. Just as God leads me, I would go; I do not ask to choose my way; Con-
2. Just as God leads, I am con-tent; I rest me calm-ly in His hands; For
3. Just as God leads, I all re-sign; I trust me to my Fa-ther's will; When

tent with what He will be-stow, Assured He will not let me stray; So as He leads, my
all He has de-creed and sent, I know His will for me commands; I would that He should
rea-son's rays de-cep-tive shine, His coun-sel would I yet ful-fill; That which His love or-

path I make, And step by step I glad-ly take,—A child in Him con-fid-ing.
all ful-fill, That I should do His gra-cious will In liv-ing or in dy-ing.
dained as right, Be-fore He brought me to the light, My all to Him re-sign-ing.

(JESUS IN DAILY LIFE.)

P. P. BLISS.   By per. John Church & Co.   P. P. BLISS.

1. I am so glad that our Fa-ther in heav'n, Tells of His love in the Book He has giv'n;
   Wonder-ful things in the Bi-ble I see, This is the dear-est, that Je-sus loves me.
2. Tho' I for-get Him and wander a-way, Kind-ly He follows where-ev-er I stray;
   Back to His dear lov-ing arms would I flee When I re-member that Je-sus loves me.

CHORUS.

I am so glad that Je-sus loves me, Je-sus loves me, Je-sus loves me; I am so glad that

Je-sus loves me, Je-sus loves e-ven me.

3.
Oh, if there's only one song I can sing,
When in His beauty I see the great King,
This shall my song in eternity be,
Oh, what a wonder that Jesus loves me.
    I am so glad, &c.

(JESUS IN DAILY LIFE.)

THY WAY, NOT MINE, O LORD.

HORATIUS BONAR, D. D. 1856.   HUBERT P. MAIN, by per.

1. Thy way, not mine, O Lord, How-ev-er dark it be! Lead me by Thine own hand;

2. The king-dom that I seek Is Thine: so let the way That leads to it be Thine;

Choose out the path for me: I dare not choose my lot; I would not if I might,

Else I must sure-ly stray: Take Thou my cup, and it With joy or sor-row fill,

Choose Thou for me, my God, So shall I walk a-right.

As best to Thee may seem, Choose Thou my good and ill.

3 Choose Thou for me my friends,
My sickness, or my health,
Choose Thou my cares for me,
My poverty or wealth:
Not mine, not mine the choice,
In things, or great, or small;
Be Thou my Guide, my Strength,
My Wisdom, and my All.

(JESUS IN DAILY LIFE.)

VIOLET. 8s & 7s.

(112) Bradbury Trio, 73. Key A.

1 JESUS, I my cross have taken,
   All to leave and follow Thee;
Naked, poor, despised, forsaken,
   Thou, from hence, my all shalt be.
Perish every fond ambition,
   All I've sougbt, and hoped, and known;
Yet how rich is my condition!
   God and heaven are still my own!

2 Let the world despise and leave me,
   They have left my Saviour, too;
Human hearts and looks deceive me,
   Thou art not, like man untrue;
And while Thou shalt smile upon me,
   God of wisdom, love, and might,
Foes may hate, and friends may shun me;
   Show Thy face, and all is bright.

3 Know, my soul thy full salvation,
   Rise o'er sin, and fear, and care;
Joy to find in every station
   Something still to do or bear.
Think what Spirit dwells within thee;
   What a Father's smile is thine;
What a Saviour died to win thee;
   Child of heaven, shouldst thou repine?

———

CHRISTMAS. C. M.

(113)   Christian Songs, 200. Key E♭.

1 AM I a soldier of the cross—
   A follower of the Lamb—
And shall I fear to own His cause,
   Or blush to speak His name?

2 Must I be carried to the skies
   On flowery beds of ease,
While others fought to win the prize,
   And sailed through bloody seas?

3 Are there no foes for me to face?
   Must I not stem the flood?
Is this vile world a friend to grace?
   To help me on to God?

4 Since I must fight if I would reign,
   Increase my courage, Lord;
I'll bear the toil, endure the pain,
   Supported by Thy word.

———

NAOMI. C. M.

(114) Bradbury Trio, 145. Key D.

1 LORD it belongs not to my care,
   Whether I die, or live;
To love and serve Thee is my share,
   And this Thy grace must give.

2 If life be long I will be glad,
   That I may long obey;
If short, yet why should I be sad
   To soar to endless day?

                              [rooms
3 Christ leads me through no darker
   Than He went through before;
He that into God's kingdom comes,
   Must enter by this door.

                              [meet
4 Come Lord when grace has made me
   Thy blessed face to see;
For if Thy work on earth be sweet
   What will Thy glory be?

(JESUS IN DAILY LIFE.)

5 Then I shall end my sad complaints,
   And weary sinful days;
And join with the triumphant saints
   To sing Jehovah's praise.
6 My knowledge of that life is small,
   The eye of faith is dim:
But 'tis enough that Christ knows all,
   And I shall be with Him.

———

THE SAVIOUR'S PRAISE.

(115) Christian Songs, 145. Key A.

1 HERE we throng to praise the Saviour,
   Cheerfully our voices raise;
He who died for our Redemption,
   Says He will accept our praise.
Hinder not the young from coming,
   "For of such," the Saviour said,
"Is composed My heavenly kingdom;"
   'Tis a rapturous thought indeed.

2 Let us love Him and adore Him,
   In our days of early youth;
May we ever walk before Him,
   In the glorious paths of truth.
Let us never grieve the Saviour,
   Who has died our souls to win;
Let us ever seek His favor,
   Shunning all the paths of sin.

3 If our sins are all forgiven,
   We may read our title clear,
To eternal joy in heaven,
   Far beyond this earthly sphere.
In that blest abode of glory,
   We may join the angel throng;
Jesus' love shall be the story
   Of our never ending song.

GUIDANCE 8s & 7s.

Rev. WM. WILLIAMS, 1773.

From FRED. von FLOTOW. arr. H,

1. { Guide me, O Thou great Je-ho-vah, Pilgrim thro' this bar-ren land, }
   { I am weak, but Thou art mighty, [Omit......................] } Hold me with Thy pow'rful hand.

2. { Feed me with the heav'nly man-na, In this bar-ren wil-der-ness; }
   { Be my sword, and shield, and banner, [Omit......................] } Be the Lord my Righteousness.

O - pen now the crys-tal foun-tain, Whence the liv-ing wa - ters flow, Let the fie - ry
When I tread the verge of Jor-dan, Bid my anx-ious fears sub-side; Death of death, and

cloud - y pil - lar, Lead me all my jour-ney thro', Lead me all my jour-ney thro'.
hell's de-struc-tion, Land me safe on Ca-naan's side, Land me safe on Ca-naan's side.

(JESUS IN DAILY LIFE.)

LOVE AT HOME.

(118) Christian Songs, 120. Key A♭.

1 THERE is beauty all around,
  When there's love at home;
There is joy in every sound,
  When there's love at home.
Peace and plenty here abide,
Smiling sweet on every side,
Time doth softly, sweetly glide,
  When there's love at home.

CHO. Love at home, love at home;
  Time doth softly, sweetly glide,
    When there's love at home.

2 Kindly heaven smiles above,
  When there's love at home;
All the earth is filled with love,
  When there's love at home.
Sweeter sings the brooklet by,
Brighter beams the azure sky;
Oh, there's One who smiles on high
  When there's love at home.

3 Jesus make me wholly Thine
  Then there's love at home;
May Thy sacrifice be mine,
  Then there's love at home.
Safely from all harm I'll rest
With no sinful care distressed,
Through Thy tender mercy blest,
  With Thy love at home.

AUTUMN.

(119) Christian Songs, 184. Key A♭.

1 HOLY Father. Thou hast taught me
  I should live to Thee alone;
Year by year, Thy hand hath brought me
  On through dangers oft unknown.

When I wandered, Thou hast found me,
  When I doubted, sent me light,
Still Thine arm has been around me,
  All my paths were in Thy sight.

2 In the world will foes assail me,
  Craftier, stronger far than I;
And the strife may never fail me,
  Well, I know, before I die.
Therefore, Lord, I come, believing
  Thou canst give the power I need;
Through the prayer of faith receiving
  Strength—the Spirit's strength indeed.

3 I would trust in Thy protecting,
  Wholly rest upon Thine arm;
Follow wholly, Thy directing,
  Thou, mine only guard from harm;
Keep me from mine own undoing,
  Help me turn to Thee when tried,
Still my footsteps, Father, viewing,
  Keep me ever at Thy side!

WE ARE NEARER HOME.

(120) Bradbury Trio, 156. Key G.

1 WE know not what's before us,
    What trials are to come:
But each day passing o'er us,
    Brings us still nearer home.

CHO. We're nearer, nearer home,
  Our blessed, happy home,
  Where grief and sin can never come,
  We're nearer, nearer home.

REF. Nearer home, Nearer home,
  Nearer to my happy home,
  Nearer home, Nearer home,
  Our blessed, happy home.

(JESUS IN DAILY LIFE.)

2 Though dark our path, and lonely,
    And clouds our sky o'ercast,
  Let us remember only,
    That it will soon be past.

3 What e'er of gloom or anguish
    Life to our hearts may bring,
  In doubt we will not languish,
    But cheerfully we'll sing.

I AM COMING, LORD.

(121) Gospel H. & S. S., 63. Key E♭.

1 I HEAR Thy welcome voice
    That calls me, Lord, to Thee
  For cleansing in Thy precious blood
    That flowed on Calvary.

CHO. I am coming Lord!
    Coming now to Thee!
  Wash me, cleanse me in the blood
    That flowed on Calvary.

2 Though coming weak and vile,
    Thou dost my strength assure;
  Thou dost my vileness fully cleanse,
    Till spotless all and pure.

3 'Tis Jesus calls me on
    To perfect faith and love;
  To perfect hope, and peace, and trust,
    For earth and heaven above.

4 'Tis Jesus who confirms
    The blessed work within,
  By adding grace to welcomed grace,
    Where reigned the power of sin.

5 All hail, atoning blood!
    All hail, redeeming grace!
  All hail, the Gift of Christ, our Lord,
    Our Strength and Righteousness!

KEEP THOU MY WAY, O LORD.

FANNY J. CROSBY, 1869.
From "Bright Jewels," by per. HUBERT P. MAIN.

Andante, with expression.

1. Keep Thou my way, O Lord; My-self I can-not guide; Nor dare I trust my
2. For ev-ery act of faith, And ev-ery pure de-sign,— For all of good my
3. O speak, and I will hear; Command, and I o-bey, My will-ing feet with

err-ing steps One mo-ment from Thy side; I can-not think a-right, Un-less in
soul can know, The glo-ry, Lord, be Thine; Free grace my par-don seals, Thro' Thy a-
joy shall haste To run the heavenly way; Keep Thou my wand'ring heart, And bid it

spired by Thee; My heart would fail with-out Thy aid, Choose Thou my thoughts for me.
ton-ing blood; Free grace the full as-sur-ance brings, Of peace with Thee my God.
cease to roam; O bear me safe o'er death's cold wave To heaven, my bliss-ful home.

(JESUS IN DAILY LIFE.)

FANNY J. CROSBY, 1868.

From "Songs of Devotion," by per. W. H. DOANE.

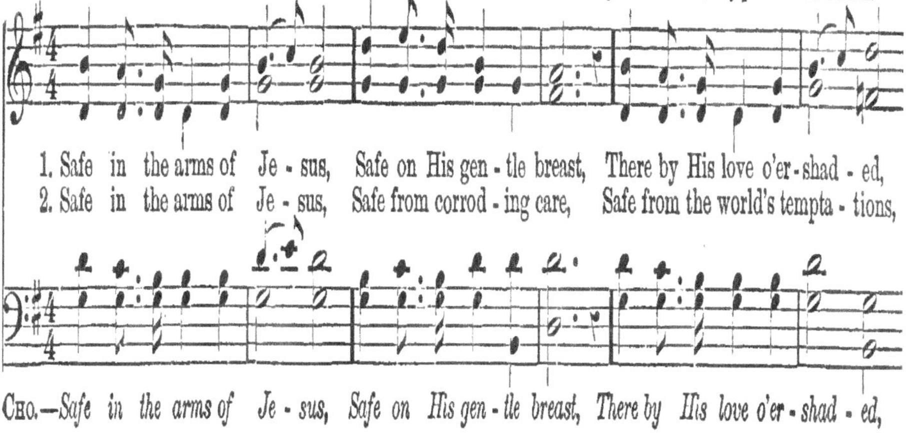

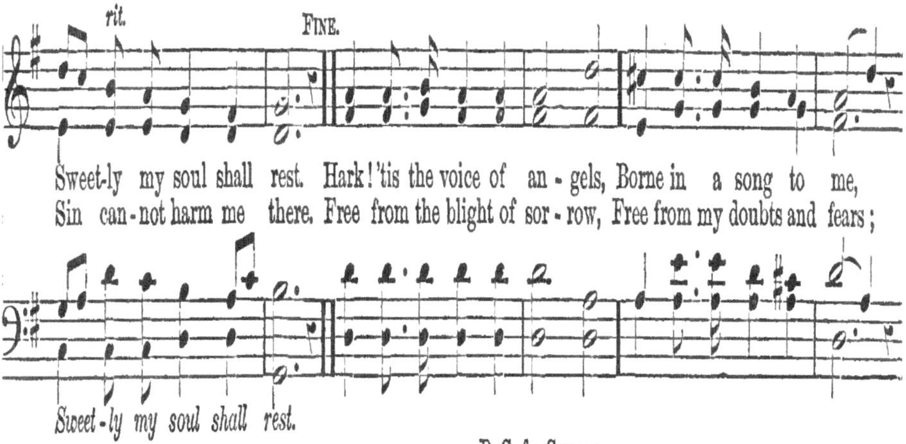

1. Safe in the arms of Je - sus, Safe on His gen - tle breast, There by His love o'er - shad - ed,
2. Safe in the arms of Je - sus, Safe from corrod - ing care, Safe from the world's tempta - tions,

CHO.—*Safe in the arms of Je - sus, Safe on His gen - tle breast, There by His love o'er - shad - ed,*

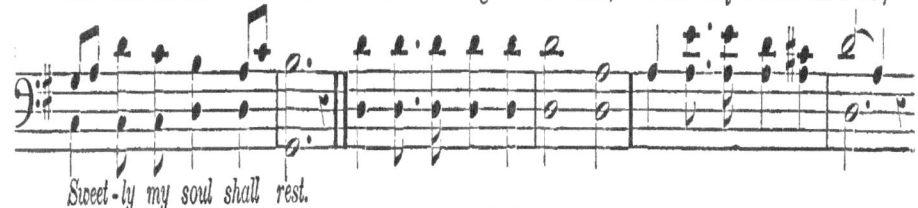

Sweet-ly my soul shall rest. Hark! 'tis the voice of an - gels, Borne in a song to me,
Sin can-not harm me there. Free from the blight of sor - row, Free from my doubts and fears;

Sweet-ly my soul shall rest.

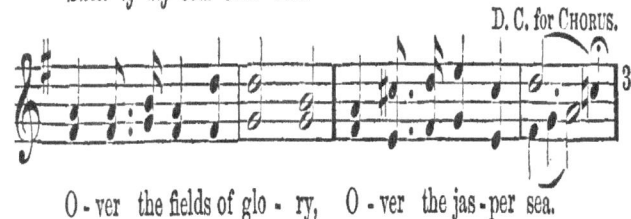

O - ver the fields of glo - ry, O - ver the jas - per sea.
On-ly a few more tri - als, On-ly a few more tears!

3 Jesus, my heart's dear refuge,
Jesus has died for me ;
Firm on the Rock of Ages,
Ever my trust shall be.
Here let me wait with patience,
Wait till the night is o'er ;
Wait till I see the morning
Break on the golden shore.
CHO.—Safe in the arms, &c.

(EXPERIENCE.)

LIKE THE SNOW-FLAKES.

Mrs. G. A. HULSE McLEOD.

HARRY SANDERS, by per.

With expression.

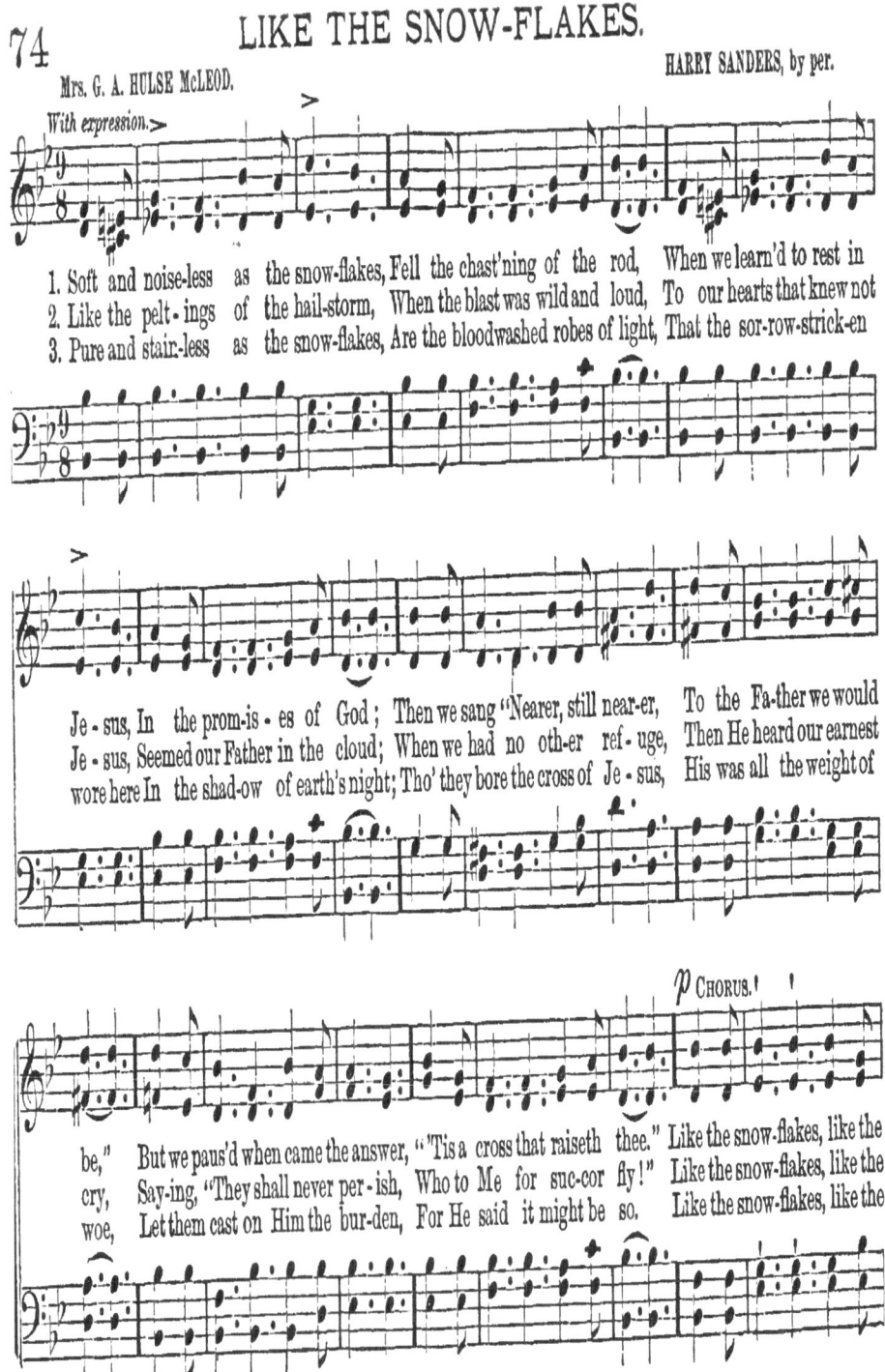

1. Soft and noise-less as the snow-flakes, Fell the chast'ning of the rod, When we learn'd to rest in
2. Like the pelt-ings of the hail-storm, When the blast was wild and loud, To our hearts that knew not
3. Pure and stair-less as the snow-flakes, Are the bloodwashed robes of light, That the sor-row-strick-en

Je - sus, In the prom-is - es of God; Then we sang "Nearer, still near-er, To the Fa-ther we would
Je - sus, Seemed our Father in the cloud; When we had no oth-er ref - uge, Then He heard our earnest
wore here In the shad-ow of earth's night; Tho' they bore the cross of Je - sus, His was all the weight of

p CHORUS.

be," But we paus'd when came the answer, "'Tis a cross that raiseth thee." Like the snow-flakes, like the
cry, Say-ing, "They shall never per - ish, Who to Me for suc-cor fly!" Like the snow-flakes, like the
woe, Let them cast on Him the bur-den, For He said it might be so. Like the snow-flakes, like the

(EXPERIENCE.)

snow-flakes, In their pure and glist'ning sheen, Falls the rod, when His dear promise, Comes so softly in be-tween.
snow-flakes, In the gold-en, &c.
snow-flakes, In the gold-en,   glist'ning sheen, Is the valley where no shadow Comes, our souls and God between.

LORD, ABIDE WITH ME.

FANNY J. CROSBY. 1864.

SYLVESTER MAIN, 1864.

1. Je - sus, Saviour! hear my call, Sin - ful tho' my heart may be; Thou, my life, my hope, my all, Lord, a-bide with me.

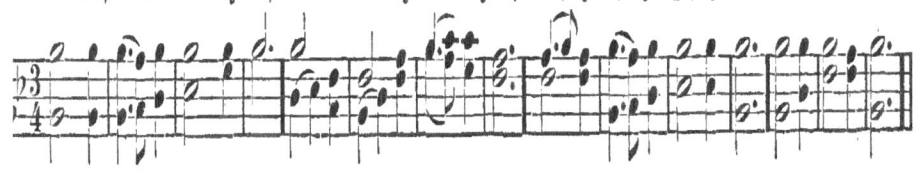

2 Thou hast died the lost to save,
    Died to set the captive free ;
  Thou didst triumph o'er the grave,
    Lord, abide with me.

3 Fill me with Thy love divine,
    Consecrate my life to Thee ;
  Bend my stubborn will to Thine,
    Lord, abide with me.

4 When the shades of death prevail,
    Father, let me cling to Thee ;
  When I pass the gloomy vale,
    Lord, abide with me.

5 Then, oh ! then, my raptured soul
    Heaven's eternal rest shall see ;
  There, while endless ages roll,
    Live and reign with me.

(EXPERIENCE.)

JESUS IS MINE.

JANE C. BONAR, 1843.

THEO. E. PERKINS, 1858, by per.

FINE.

1. Fade, fade each earthly joy, Je - sus is mine : Break, every tender tie, Je - sus is mine : Dark is the

D. S.—Je - sus alone can bless: Je - sus is mine.

D. S.

wilderness ; Earth has no resting place ;

2 Tempt not my soul,
   Jesus is mine :
Here would I ever stay,
   Jesus is mine :
Perishing things of clay,
Born but for one brief day,
Pass from my heart away :
   Jesus is mine.

3 Farewell, ye dreams of night,
   Jesus is mine :
Mine is a dawning bright,
   Jesus is mine :
All that my soul has tried,
Left but a dismal void,—
Jesus has satisfied :
   Jesus is mine.

THINE, LORD, FOREVER.

W. BENNETT, 1868.

HUBERT P, MAIN, by per.

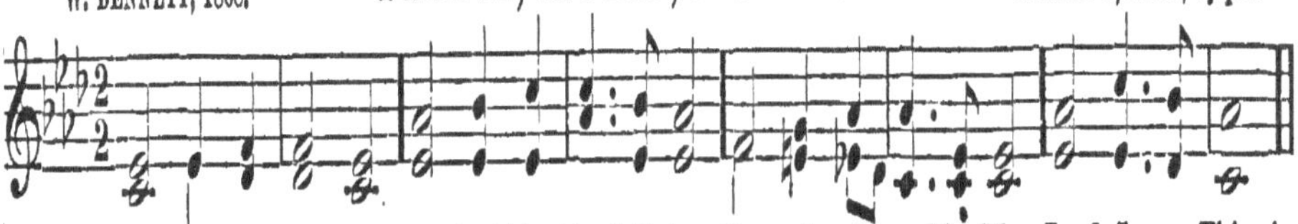

1. Thine, Lord, for - ev - er ! Purchas'd by blood divine, Rescued and saved by Thee, Lord, I am Thine !
2. Thine, Lord, for - ev - er ! Thro' storm and tempest wild, Trusting confid-ing - ly, I am Thy child.
3. Thine, Lord, for - ev-er ! Cheer'd by Thy gracious word, Thro' darkness, doubts, and fears, Thine, thine O Lord!
4. Thine, Lord, for - ev - er ! Tho' death shall lay me low, E'en in that dreadful hour Thine, Lord, I know.
5. Thine, Lord, for - ev - er ! When safe before Thy throne I stand, for - ev - ermore Thine, thine a - lone !

(EXPERIENCE.)

WHEN THE COMFORTER CAME.

WILLIAM MOORE.

R. LOWRY. **77**

From "Brightest and Best," by per.

1. My heart that was heav-y and sad, Was made to re-joice and be glad, And peace without measure I
2. To sin and to e-vil in-clined, With darkness pervad-ing my mind, No rest I could a-ny-where
3. The voice of thanksgiving I raised, The Lord my Re-deem-er I praised; I was at His mer-cy a-

REFRAIN.

had, . When the Comfort-er came. Peace, sweet peace, Peace when the Comforter came! My heart, that was
find, Till the Comfort-er came.
maz'd, When the Comfort-er came.

Rit.

heavy and sad, Was made to rejoice and be glad, And peace without measure I had, When the Comforter came.

(EXPERIENCE.)

OH, NOBODY KNOWS BUT JESUS.

Arr. by M. E. T.

Slave Songs.

1. Oh, no-bod-y knows the trouble I have, Nobod-y knows but Je-sus! No-bod-y knows the
2. Oh, no-bod-y knows the comfort I have, Nobod-y knows but Je-sus! No-bod-y knows the

FINE.

trouble I have, None but dearest Je-sus! When I am plunged in floods of grief, Thou see'st Lord;
comfort I have, None but dearest Je-sus! I cast my load of sin and grief, On Thee Lord;

D. C. AL FINE.

And Thou dost fly to my re-lief, Thou dear Lord.
And joy is mine, for I am Thine, Thou dear Lord.

3 Oh, nobody knows the trouble I have,
    Nobody knows but Jesus;
Nobody knows the comfort I have,
    None but dearest Jesus!
I take my care to Him in prayer,
    Oh, dear Lord!
And He doth bear my load of care,
    Yes, dear Lord!

(EXPERIENCE.)

LEANING ON THEE! L. M.

CHARLOTTE ELLIOTT, 1836.   J. BLOCKLEY

1. Lean-ing on Thee, my Guide and Friend, My gra-cious Sav-iour, I am blest; Tho' wea-ry Thou dost

con-des-cend, Tho' wea-ry, Thou dost con-des-cend, To be my Rest! To be my Rest!

2 Leaning on Thee with child-like faith,
  To Thee the future I confide,
|: Each step of life's untrodden path, :|
  |: Thy love shall guide. :|

3 Leaning on Thee, tho' faint and weak,
  Too weak another voice to hear,
|: Thy heavenly accents comfort speak; :|
  |: "Be of good cheer." :|

4 Leaning on Thee, no fear alarms,
  Altho' I stand on death's dark brink,
|: I'll feel the everlasting arms, :|
  |: I will not sink. :|

GUIDE US TO THEE.

W. F. SHERWIN, by per.

1. Father, Thou art great and holy, Hear us when we bend the knee; Make us humble, meek and lowly, Guide us to Thee.
2. Saints and angels fall before Thee, Where the soul is ever free; Humbly still we would adore Thee, Guide us to Thee.
3. By   Thy love and pow'r defended, May we ever faithful be, And when life's short day is ended, Guide us to Thee.

(EXPERIENCE.)

SUN OF MY SOUL.

JOHN KEBLE, 1827.

WM. F. SHERWIN, by per.

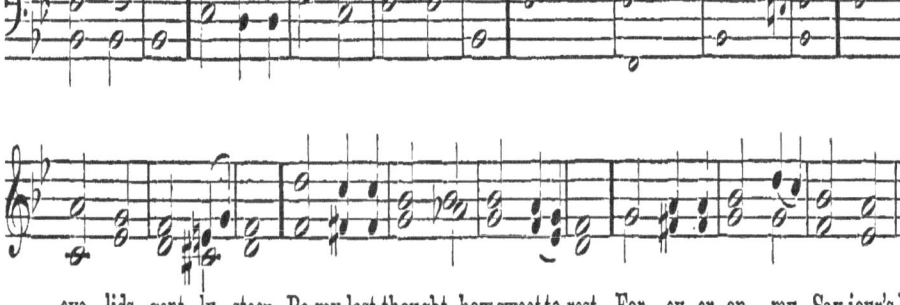

1. Sun of my soul, my Sav-iour dear, It is not night if Thou be near; Oh, let no earth
2. A - bide with me from morn till eve, For without Thee I can - not live; A - bide with me
3. Watch by the sick, en - rich the poor, With blessings from Thy boundless store; Be ev-ery mou

cloud a - rise, To hide Thee from Thy servant's eyes; When the soft dews of kind-ly sleep, My we
night is nigh, For without Thee I dare not die; If some poor wandering child of Thine, Has spurne
sleep to - night, Like infant's slumbers, pure and light; Come near and bless us when we wake, Ere thr

eye - lids gent-ly steep, Be my last thought, how sweet to rest For ev-er on my Sav-iour's b
day Thy voice di - vine, Now, Lord, the gracious work be - gin, Let him no more lie down in s
world our way we take, Till, in the o - cean of Thy love, We rest ourselves in Heaven a - b

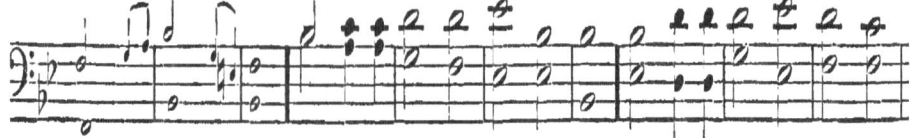

(EXPERIENCE.)

FREDERICK WHITFIELD, 1855.

S. S. WESLEY, Arr.

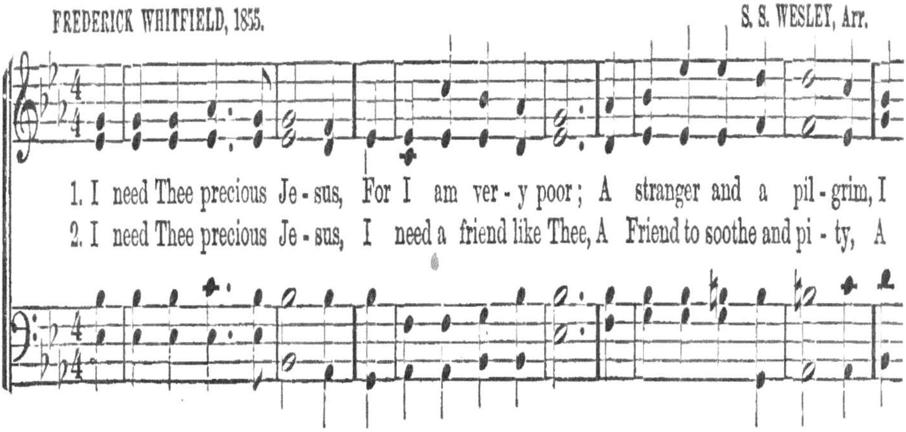

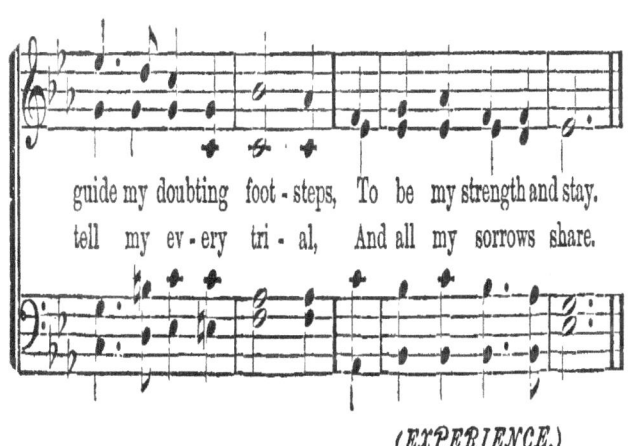

1. I need Thee precious Je - sus, For I am ver - y poor; A stranger and a pil - grim, I
2. I need Thee precious Je - sus, I need a friend like Thee, A Friend to soothe and pi - ty, A

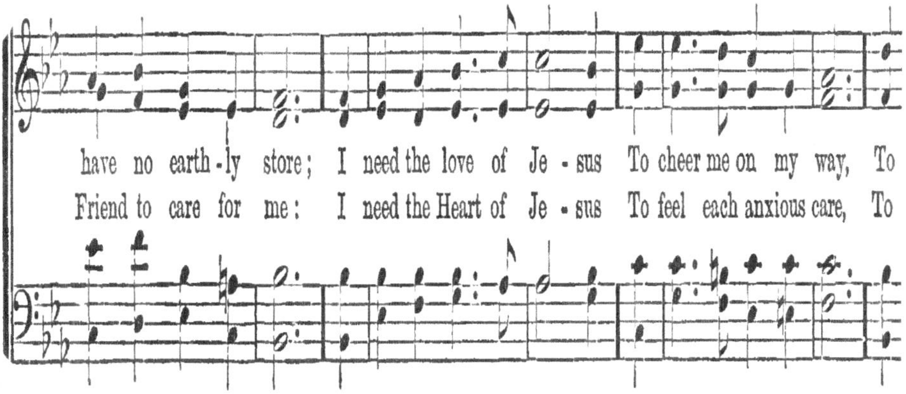

have no earth - ly store; I need the love of Je - sus To cheer me on my way, To
Friend to care for me: I need the Heart of Je - sus To feel each anxious care, To

guide my doubting foot - steps, To be my strength and stay.
tell my ev - ery tri - al, And all my sorrows share.

3 I need Thee, precious Jesus,
I need Thee day by day,
To fill me with Thy fullness,
To lead me on my way:
I need Thy Holy Spirit
To teach me what I am,
To show me more of Jesus,
To point me to the Lamb.

(EXPERIENCE.)

THE TREE OF LIFE.

FANNY J. CROSBY. 1869.   CHESTER G. ALLEN, by per.

1. Our Fa-ther has planted a beau-ti-ful tree, Whose ev-er-green branches His chil-dren be-hold:
2. Be-side the pure riv-er of crys-tal it grows, And yieldeth its fruit ev-ery month, we are told:
3. The hand of the Sav-iour will wipe ev-ery tear, And ban-ish for-ev-er the dark-ness of night

They walk 'neath its shade in the Cit-y a-bove, Whose gates are of pearl and whose streets are of gold.
Its leaves for the heal-ing of na-tions designed, The na-tions who dwell in that Cit-y of gold.
Sweet anthems e-ter-nal that re-gion shall fill, The Lord is its glo-ry, the Lord is its light.

CHORUS.

We may eat of that beau-ti-ful tree of life, That stands in the midst of the Cit-y so fair; We may

eat of its fruit and be healed with its leaves; No hun-ger, nor sick-ness, no sor-row is there.

(EXPERIENCE.)

Mrs. C. F. ALEXANDER, 1848.   RICHARD STORRS WILLIS. 1860.

1. There is a green hill far a-way, With-out a cit-y wall, Where the dear Lord was
2. He died that we might be for-given, He died to make us good, That we might go at
3. O dear-ly, dear-ly has He loved, And we must love Him too, And trust in His re-

cru-ci-fied, Who died to save us all. We may not know, we can-not tell, What
last to heav'n, Saved by His pre-cious blood. There was no oth-er good e-nough, To
deem-ing blood. And try His works to do. For there's a green hill far a-way, With-

pain He had to bear, But we be-lieve it was for us, He hung and suf-fered there.
pay the price of sin, He on-ly could un-lock the gate Of Heav'n, and let us in.
out a cit-y wall, Where the dear Lord was cru-ci-fied, Who died to save us all.

(EXPERIENCE.)

WE ARE BUT LITTLE CHILDREN WEAK.

Mrs. C. F. ALEXANDER.

C. E. WILLING.

1. We are but lit-tle children weak, Nor born in a-ny high es-tate; What can we do for
2. Oh, day by day, each Christian child Has much to do, without, with-in; A death to die for

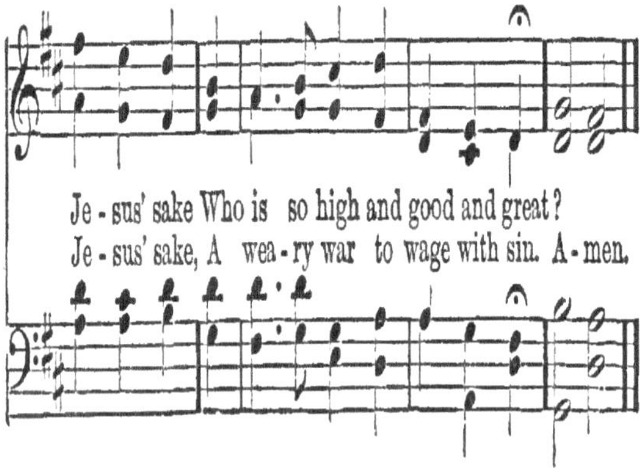

Je-sus' sake Who is so high and good and great?
Je-sus' sake, A wea-ry war to wage with sin. A-men.

3 Now we may stay the angry blow,
  Now we may check the hasty word,
  Give gentle answers back again,
  And fight a battle for our Lord.

4 With smiles of peace, and looks of love,
  Light in our dwellings we may make,
  Bid kind good humor brighten there,
  And do all still for Jesus' sake.   Amen.

OUR SHEPHERD.

HUGH STOWELL, 1846.

SYLVESTER MAIN, 1864, by per.

Earnestly.

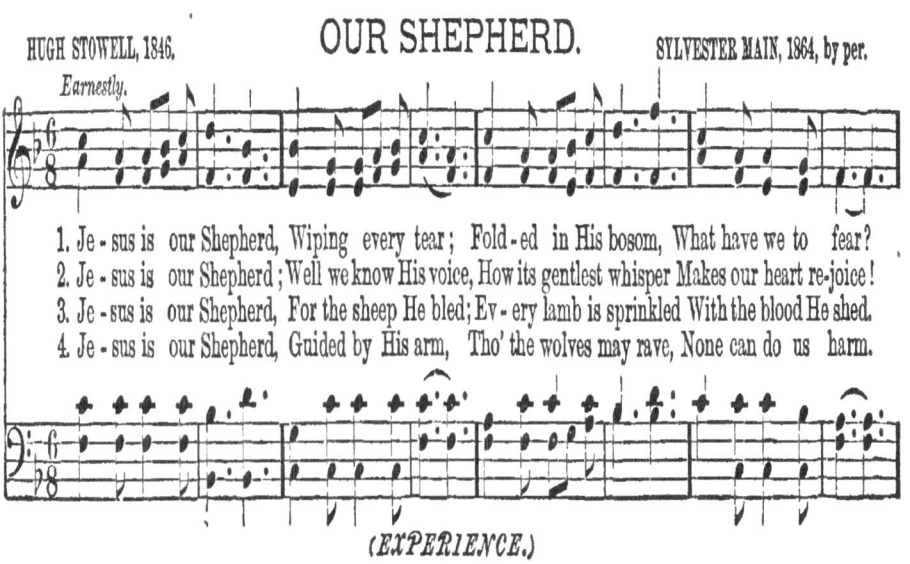

1. Je-sus is our Shepherd, Wiping every tear; Fold-ed in His bosom, What have we to fear?
2. Je-sus is our Shepherd; Well we know His voice, How its gentlest whisper Makes our heart re-joice!
3. Je-sus is our Shepherd, For the sheep He bled; Ev-ery lamb is sprinkled With the blood He shed.
4. Je-sus is our Shepherd, Guided by His arm, Tho' the wolves may rave, None can do us harm.

(EXPERIENCE.)

On - ly let us fol - low Whither He doth lead, To the thirsty des - ert, Or the dew - y mead.
E - ven when He chideth Ten - der is His tone, None but He shall guide us, We are His a - lone.
Then on each He setteth His own se - cret sign: "They that have my Spirit, These," said He, "are mine."
When we tread death's valley, Dark with fearful gloom, We will fear no e - vil, Victors o'er the tomb.

HUGH WHITE, 1841.

COME UNTO ME. Chant.

Wm. B. BRADBURY, 1853.

1 With tearful eyes I look around,
    Life seems a dark and | stormy | sea :
Yet, 'midst the gloom I hear a sound,
    A heavenly | whisper, | Come to | Me.

2 It tells me of a place of rest—
    It tells me where my | soul may | flee ;
Oh ! to the weary, faint, opprest,
    How sweet the | bidding, | Come to | Me.

3 When nature shudders, loth to part
    From all I love, en- | joy, and see,

When a faint chill steals o'er my heart,
    A sweet voice | utters, | Come to | Me.

4 Come, for all else must faint and die,
    Earth is no resting | place for | thee ;
Heavenward direct thy weeping eye,
    I am thy | portion, | Come to | Me.

5 O voice of mercy ! voice of love !
    In conflict, grief, and | ago- | ny,
Support me, cheer me from above !
    And gently | whisper, | Come to | Me.

(EXPERIENCE.)

HYMN ANTHEM.

ISAAC B. WOODBURY.
DUET, SOPRANO AND ALTO.

JOHN ZUNDEL, by per.

Inst

1. Christian, the morn breaks sweetly o'er thee, And all the mid-night shadows flee, Tinged are the dis - tant

To first verse of Chorus. Arise, &c. FEMALE VOICES.

skies with glo - ry, A bea - con light hung out for thee. 2. Tossed on time's rude, re -

lent - less sur - ges, Calmly composed and dauntless stand, For lo ! beyond those scenes emer - ges The

To second verse of Chorus. Behold, &c. *f* MALE VOICES.

dolce.

light that bounds the promised land. 3. Cheer up ! cheer up ! the day breaks o'er thee, Bright as the summer's

(EXPERIENCE.)

noon-tide ray; The star-gem'd crowns and realms of glo - ry In - vite thy hap-py soul a - way.

To third verse of Chorus. Away, &c.

CHORUS.

1st Cho. A - rise, arise! the light breaks o'er thee, Thy name is grav-en on the throne; Thy home is in the
2d Cho. Behold, behold, the land is nearing, Where the wild sea-storm's rage is o'er; Hark! how the heavenly
3d Cho. A - way, away! leave all for glo - ry, Thy name is grav-en on the throne; Thy home is in that

world of glo - ry, Where thy Redeem - er reigns a - lone, Where thy Redeem - er reigns a - lone.
host are cheering, See in what throngs they range the shore! See in what throngs they range the shore.
world of glo - ry, Where thy Redeem - er reigns a - lone, Where thy Redeem - er reigns a - lone.

(EXPERIENCE.)

MY SHEPHERD.

Miss M. ELSIE THALHEIMER.

J. CRAMER.

1. Thou art my shepherd, Car-ing m ev-ery need, Thy lit-tle lamb to feed, Trusting Thee still;
2. Or if my way lie Where death o'erhanging nigh, My soul would ter-ri-fy With sud-den chill,—

In the green pas-tures low, Where liv-ing wa-ters flow, Safe by Thy side I go, Fear-ing no ill.
Yet I am not a-fraid; While soft-ly on my head Thy ten-der hand is laid, I fear no ill.

SECOND HYMN.

1 Lord, do not leave me!
   I'm but an erring child,
   Weak, poor, and sin defiled,
      Afraid, alone;
   But Thou art strong and wise
   No ill can Thee surprise;
   Beneath Thy loving eyes
      Danger is none.

2 If Thou wilt guide me,
   Gladly I'll go with Thee;—
   No harm can come to me.
      Holding Thy hand;
   And soon my weary feet,
   Safe in the golden street,
   Where all who love Thee meet,
      Redeemed shall stand.

M. E. T.

(EXPERIENCE.)

IN HEAVENLY LOVE.

(143) Tune Rutherford, 190. Key F.

1 IN heavenly love abiding,
   No change my heart shall fear,
And safe is such confiding,
   For nothing changes here:
The storm may roar without me,
   My heart may low be laid,
But God is round about me,
   And can I be dismayed?

2 Wherever He may guide me,
   No want shall turn me back,
My Shepherd is beside me,
   And nothing can I lack:
His wisdom ever waketh,
   His sight is never dim;
He knows the way He taketh,
   And I will walk with Him.

3 Green pastures are before me,
   Which yet I have not seen;
Bright skies will soon be o'er me,
   Where darkest clouds have been:
My hope I cannot measure,
   My path to life is free;
My Saviour has my treasure,
   And He will walk with me.

PARK STREET. L. M.

(144) "Coronation," 128. Key A♭.

1 FOUNTAIN of grace, rich, full, and free,
What need I, that is not in Thee?
Full pardon, strength to meet the day,
And peace which none can take away.

2 Doth sickness fill the heart with fear?
'Tis sweet to know that Thou art near;
Am I with dread of justice tried?
'Tis sweet to feel that Christ hath died.

3 In life, Thy promises of aid
Forbid my heart to be afraid;
In death, peace gently veils the eyes;
Christ rose, and I shall surely rise.

4 O, all-sufficient Saviour! be
This all-sufficiency to me;
Nor pain, nor sin, nor death can harm
The weakest, shielded by Thine arm.

SHIRLAND. S. M.

(145) "Coronation," 178. Key G.

1 AND are we yet alive,
   And see each others face?
Glory and praise to Jesus give,
   For His redeeming grace.

2 What troubles have we seen!
   What conflicts have we past!
Fightings without, and fears within,
   Since we assembled last!

3 But out of all, the Lord
   Hath brought us by His love;
And still He doth His help afford,
   And hides our life above.

4 Then let us make our boast
   Of His redeeming power,
Which saves us to the uttermost,
   Till we can sin no more.

(EXPERIENCE.)

ARLINGTON. C. M.

(146) Songs of Devotion, 13. Key G.

1 O GOD of Bethel! by whose hand
   Thy people still are fed;
Who through this weary pilgrimage
   Hast all our fathers led!

2 Through each perplexing path of life
   Our wandering footsteps guide,
Give us each day our daily bread
   And raiment fit provide.

3 O spread Thy covering wings around,
   Till all our wanderings cease,
And, at our Father's loved abode,
   Our souls arrive in peace.

PETERBOROUGH. C. M.

(147) Bradbury Trio, 77. Key G.

1 To heaven we lift our waiting eyes;
   There all our hopes are laid;
The Lord that built the earth and skies
   Is our perpetual aid.

2 Their feet shall never slide nor fall
   Whom He designs to keep;
His ear attends the softest call·
   His eyes can never sleep.

3 He will sustain our weakest powers
   With His almighty arm,
And watch our most unguarded hours
   Against surprising harm.

4 Israel, rejoice, and rest secure;
   Thy keeper is the Lord;
His wakeful eyes employ His power
   For thine eternal guard.

GREENWOOD. S. M.

P. GERHARDT.

JOS. E. SWEETSER. 1849.

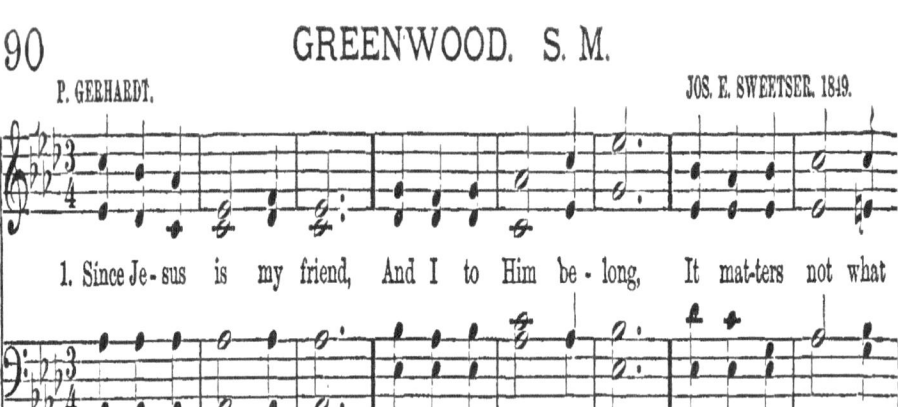

1. Since Je-sus is my friend, And I to Him be-long, It mat-ters not what

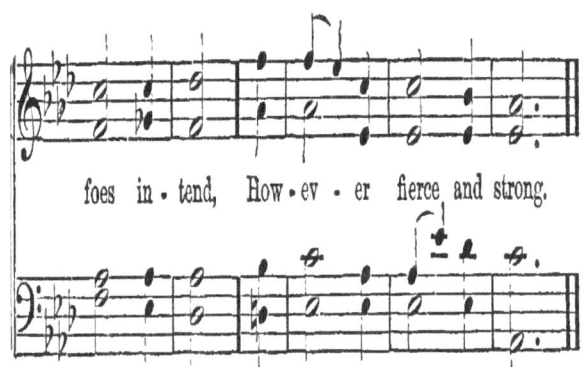

foes in - tend, How-ev-er fierce and strong.

2 He whispers in my breast
  Sweet words of holy cheer,
How they who seek in God their rest,
  Shall ever find Him near.

3 Oh, I would fix mine eyes
  On Christ, the Lord I love ;
And sing for joy of that which lies
  Stored up for me above.

WM. H. FURNESS, D. D., (1808—) 1836.

DEPENDENCE. 7s.

HUBERT P. MAIN, 1867, by per.

Graceful.

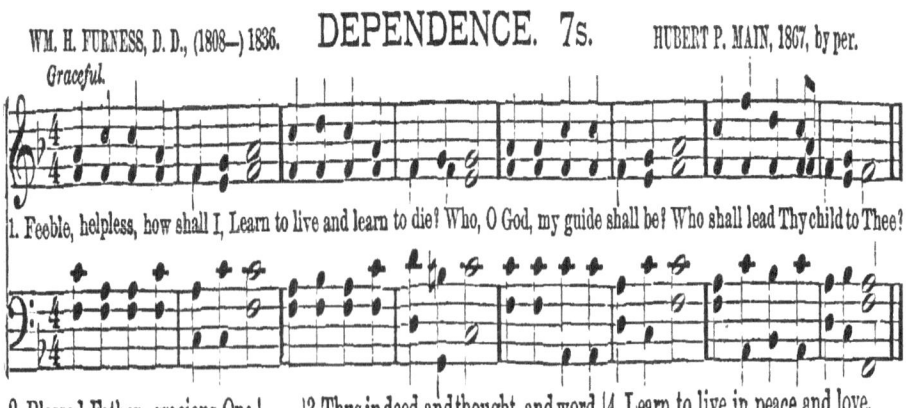

1. Feeble, helpless, how shall I, Learn to live and learn to die? Who, O God, my guide shall be? Who shall lead Thy child to Thee?

2 Blessed Father, gracious One !
  Thou hast sent Thy holy Son,
  He will give the light I need,
  He my trembling steps shall lead.

3 Thus indeed, and thought, and word,
  Led by Jesus Christ, the Lord,
  In my meekness, thus shall I
  Learn to live and learn to die.

4 Learn to live in peace and love,
  Like the perfect ones above ;
  Learn to die without a fear,
  Feeling Thee, my Saviour, near.

(EXPERIENCE.)

HE LEADETH ME.

(151) Christian Songs, 148. Key

1 HE leadeth me! O, blessed thought,
  O, words with heavenly comfort
    fraught,
  What e'er I do, where e'er I be,
  Still 'tis God's hand that leadeth me.
CHO.
  He leadeth me! He leadeth me
  By His own hand He leadeth me;
  His faithful follower I would be,
  For by His hand He leadeth me.

2 Lord, I would clasp Thy hand in mine,
  Nor ever murmur nor repine—
  Content, what ever lot I see.
  Since 'tis my God that leadeth me.

; And when my task on earth is done,
  When, by Thy grace, the victory's won,
  E'en death's cold wave I will not flee,
  Since God thro' Jordan leadeth me.

A LIGHT IN THE WINDOW.

(152) Christian Songs, 52. Key A♭.

1 THERE's a light in the window for thee,
  brother,
  There's a light in the window for thee;
  A dear one has moved to the mansions
    above,
  There's a light in the window for thee.
CHO.
‖:A mansion in heaven we see,
  And a light in the window for thee:‖

2 There's a crown and a robe, and a palm,
  brother,   [free;
  When from toil and from care you are
    [home,
  The Saviour has gone to prepare you a
  With a light in the window for thee.

3 O watch, and be faithful, and pray,
  brother,
  All your journey o'er life's troubled sea,
  Though afflictions assail you, and storms
    beat severe,
  There's a light in the window for thee.

4 Then on, perseveringly on, brother,
  Till from conflict and suffering free,
  Bright angels now beckon you over the
    stream,
  There's a light in the window for thee.

I AM WAITING BY THE RIVER. 8s & 7s.

(153) Christian Songs, 83. Key C.

1 I am waiting by the river,
  And my heart has waited long;
  Now I think I hear the chorus
  Of the angels welcome song,
  Oh, I see the dawn is breaking
  On the hill-tops of the blest, [ling,
  "Where the wicked cease from troub-
  And the weary be at rest."

2 Far away beyond the shadows
  Of this weary vale of tears,
  There the tide of bliss is sweeping
  Through the bright and changeless
    years
  O! I long to be with Jesus,
  In the mansions of the blest, [ling,
  "Where the wicked cease from troub-
  And the weary be at rest."

3 They are launching on the river,
  From the calm and quiet shore,
  And they soon will bear my spirit
  Where the weary sigh no more;

For the tide is swiftly flowing,
  And I long to greet the blest, [ling,
  "Where the wicked cease from troub-
  And the weary be at rest."

DE FLEURY. 8s.

(154) Chapel Mel., 166. Key G.

1 How tedious and tasteless the hours,
  When Jesus no longer I see!
  Sweet prospects, sweet birds, and sweet
    flowers,
  Have lost all their sweetness with me.

2 The mid-summer sun shines but dim,
  The fields strive in vain to look gay;
  But when I am happy in Him
  December's as pleasant as May.

3 His name yields the richest perfume,
  And sweeter than music His voice;
  His presence disperses my gloom,
  And makes all within me rejoice.

4 I should, were He always thus nigh,
  Have nothing to wish or to fear;
  No mortal so happy as I—
  My summer would last all the year.

5 Dear Lord, if indeed I am Thine,
  If Thou art my sun and my song,
  Say, why do I languish and pine,
  And why are my winters so long?

6 O drive these dark clouds from my sky,
  Thy soul-cheering presence restore;
  Or bid me soar upward on high,
  Where winter and clouds are no
    more.

(EXPERIENCE.)

92 ROCK OF AGES.

A. M. TOPLADY.   FRANZ ABT.

GIRLS.   BOYS.

1. Rock of A - ges, cleft for me, Let me hide   my-self in Thee! Let the wa - ter and the
2. Not the la - bors of my hands Can ful - fil   Thy law's de-mands: Could my zeal no re - spite
3. Noth-ing in   my hand I   bring: Sim-ply to   Thy cross I   cling; Nak - ed, come to Thee for
4. While I   draw this fleet-ing breath, When my eye - lids close in death, When I   soar to worlds un-

GIRLS.

blood, From Thy riv-en side which flow'd, Be   of sin   the double cure, Cleanse me from its guilt and pow'r.
know, Could my tears for ev - er   flow, All for sin could not a-tone: Thou must save, and Thou alone.
dress, Helpless, look to Thee for grace; Foul, I   to   Thy fountain fly; Wash me, Sav-iour, or I   die.
known, See Thee on Thy judgment throne, Rock of A - ges, cleft for me Let   me hide myself in Thee.

WHOLE SCHOOL.   rit.

Rock of A - ges, cleft   for me, Let   me hide my-self in Thee; Let   me hide my-self   in Thee.

(EXPERIENCE.)

WEBB. 7s & 6s.

(**156**) Bradbury Trio, 104. Key B♭.

1 WE bring no glittering treasures,
  No gems from earth's deep mine;
We come with simple measures,
  To chant Thy love divine.
We all, Thy favors sharing,
  Our voice of thanks would raise;
Father, accept our offering,
  Our song of grateful praise.

2 The dearest gift of Heaven,
  Love's precious word of Truth,
To sinners Thou hast given,
  To guide their steps in youth;
To tell the wondrous story,
  The tale of Calvary;
To tell of homes in glory,
  From sin and sorrow free.

3 Redeemer, grant Thy blessing;
  Oh, teach us how to pray!
That we, Thy love possessing
  May tread life's devious way;
Till where the pure are dwelling
  By grace we meet again,
And, sweeter numbers swelling,
  Forever praise Thy name.

AMSTERDAM. 7s & 6s.

(**157**) Christian Songs, 199. Key G.

1 RISE, my soul, and stretch thy wings,
  Thy better portion trace;
Rise, from transitory things,
  Toward heaven, thy native place:

Sun, and moon, and stars decay,
  Time shall soon this earth remove;
Rise, my soul, and haste away
  To seats prepared above.

2 Rivers to the ocean run,
  Nor stay in all their course;
Fire ascending, seeks the sun,
  Both speed them to their source;
So a soul that's born of God,
  Pants to see His glorious face,
Upward tends to His abode,
  To rest in His embrace.

3 Cease, ye pilgrims, cease to mourn,
  Press onward to the prize;
Soon our Saviour will return
  Triumphant in the skies;
There we'll join the heavenly train,
  Welcomed to partake the bliss;
Fly from sorrow and from pain,
  To realms of endless peace.

———

BETHANY. 6s & 4s.

(**158**) Bradbury Trio, 77. Key G.

1 NEARER, my God, to Thee,
  Nearer to Thee!
E'en though it be a cross
  That raiseth me;
Still all my song shall be—
Nearer, my God, to Thee!
  Nearer to Thee!

(*EXPERIENCE.*)

2 Though, like the wanderer,
  The sun gone down,
Darkness be over me,
  My rest a stone;
Yet in my dreams I'd be—
Nearer, my God, to Thee!
  Nearer to Thee!

3 There let the way appear,
  Steps unto heaven;
All that Thou sendest me,
  In mercy given;
Angels to beckon me
Nearer, my God, to Thee—
  Nearer to Thee!

4 Then with my waking thoughts,
  Bright with Thy praise,
Out of my stony griefs,
  Bethel I'll raise;
So by my woes to be
Nearer, my God, to Thee!
  Nearer to Thee!

5 Or if on joyful wing,
  Cleaving the sky,
Sun, moon, and stars forgot,
  Upward I fly;
Still all my song shall be—
Nearer, my God, to Thee!
  Nearer to Thee!

SAVIOUR, WALK BESIDE US.

Mrs. MARY A. KIDDER. 1875.   HUBERT P. MAIN, by per.

1. Saviour, walk Thou still beside us; Weak and way-ward are our feet; Safe-ly thro' the ma - zes
2. Ten - der are Thy words of blessing, Cheering us as on we go; All our sins to Thee con-
3. Lord, impart Thy great sal-va - tion, Flowing full and free to all; Short will be our earth-pro-

guide us Till we reach Thy mer-cy seat. Precious Saviour, Precious Saviour, Give us
fess - ing, Wash our souls as white as snow. Precious Saviour, Precious Saviour, Make us
ba - tion; Fit us for the heavenly call. Precious Saviour, Precious Saviour, Be to

|1st.| |2nd.|

of Thy bread to eat,   of Thy bread to eat.
Thine while here be - low, Thine while here be - low.
us our all in all,   us our all in all.

4.
By and by when death shall find us,
And we lay our burdens down,
We shall leave the cross behind us,
And take up the shining crown.
Precious Saviour,
Precious Saviour,
Take from Thee the shining crown.

(EXPERIENCE.)

HOMEWARD BOUND.

(160) Christian Songs, 199. Key A♭.

1 OUT on an ocean all boundless we ride,
 We're homeward bound;
Tossed on the waves of a rough, restless tide,
 We're homeward bound;
Far from the safe, quiet harbor we rode,
Seeking our Father's celestial abode,
Promise of which on us each He bestowed,
 We're homeward bound.

2 Wildly the storm sweeps us on as it roars;
 We're homeward bound;
Look! yonder lie the bright heavenly shores,
 We're homeward bound;
Steady! O pilot! stand firm at the wheel,
Steady, we soon shall outweather the gale,
Oh! how we fly 'neath the loud-creaking sail,
 We're homeward bound.

3 We'll tell the world as we journey along,
 We're homeward bound;
Try to persuade them to enter our throng,
 We're homeward bound;
Come, trembling sinner, forlorn and oppressed,
Join in our number, O come and be blest;
Journey with us to the mansions of rest,
 We're homeward bound.

4 Into the harbor of heaven now we glide,
 We're home at last;
Softly we drift on its bright silver tide,
 We're home at last;
Glory to God! all our dangers are o'er;
We stand secure on the glorified shore,
Glory to God! we will shout evermore,
 We're home at last.

FREDERICK. IIS.

(161) Coronation, 249. Key F.

1 I WOULD not live alway: I ask not to stay
 Where storm after storm rises dark o'er the way;
 The few lurid mornings that dawn on us here
 Are enough for life's woes, full enough for its cheer.

2 I would not live alway, thus fettered by sin,
 Temptation without, and corruption within;
 E'en the rapture of pardon is mingled with fears,
 And the cup of thanksgiving with penitent tears.

3 I would not live alway; no, welcome the tomb;
 Since Jesus hath lain there, I dread not its gloom:
 There sweet be my rest till He bid me arise,
 To hail Him in triumph descending the skies.

4 Who, who would live alway, away from his God—
 Away from yon heaven, that blissful abode,
 Where the rivers of pleasure flow o'er the bright plains
 And the noontide of glory eternally reigns?

5 Where the saints of all ages in harmony meet,
 Their Saviour and brethren transported to greet;
 While the anthems of rapture unceasingly roll,
 And the smile of the Lord is the feast of the soul!

———

(162) MEAR. C. M.

Coronation, 158. Key F.

1 WHEN waves of trouble round me swell,
 My soul is not dismay'd;
I hear a voice I know full well,—
 "'T is I; be not afraid."

2 There is a gulf that must be cross'd;
 Saviour, be near to aid!
Whisper, when my frail bark is toss'd,
 "'T is I; be not afraid."

(EXPERIENCE.)

SOMETIMES A LIGHT SURPRISES.

WILLIAM COWPER, 1779   JOHN HULLAH, 1867.

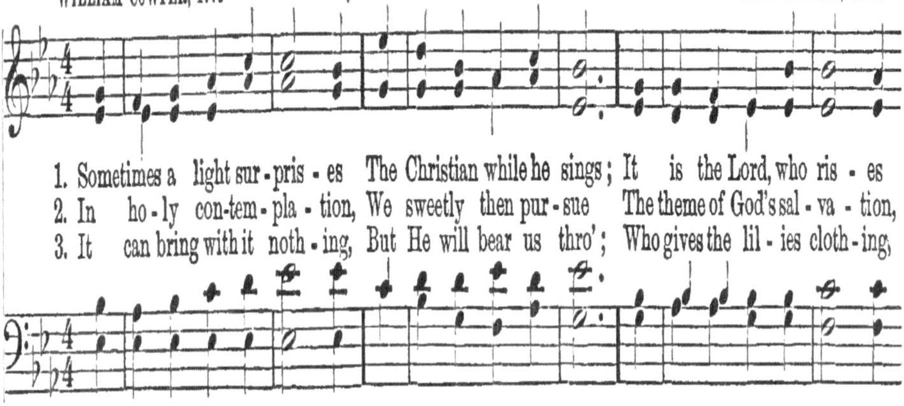

1. Sometimes a light sur-pris - es The Christian while he sings; It is the Lord, who ris - es
2. In ho - ly con-tem - pla - tion, We sweetly then pur - sue The theme of God's sal - va - tion,
3. It can bring with it noth - ing, But He will bear us thro'; Who gives the lil - ies cloth-ing,

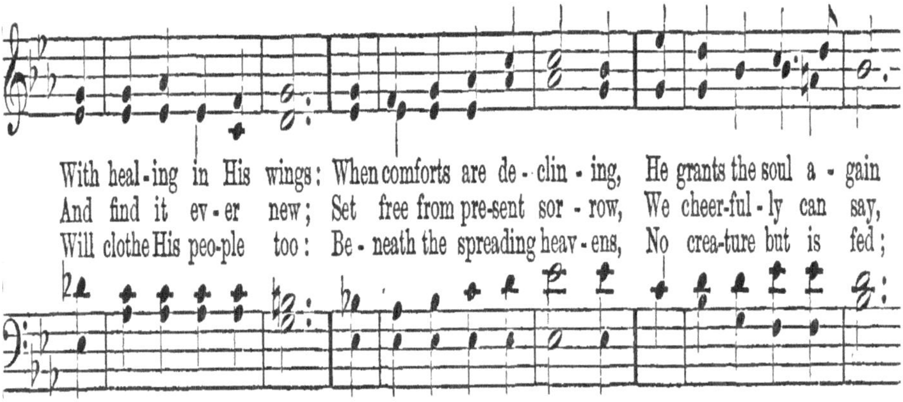

With heal - ing in His wings: When comforts are de - clin - ing, He grants the soul a - gain
And find it ev - er new; Set free from pre-sent sor - row, We cheer-ful - ly can say,
Will clothe His peo-ple too: Be - neath the spreading heav - ens, No crea-ture but is fed;

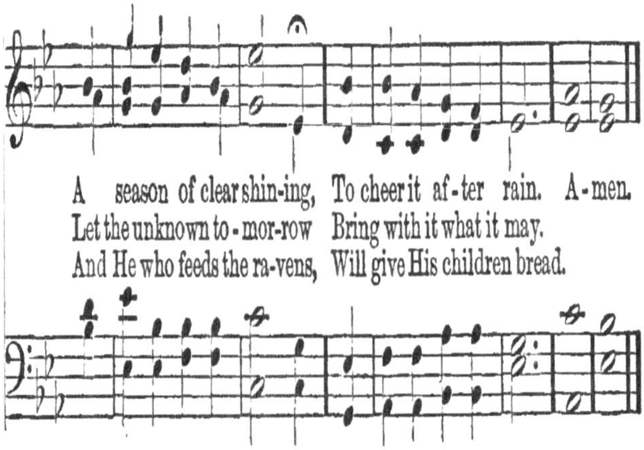

A season of clear shin-ing, To cheer it af - ter rain. A - men.
Let the unknown to - mor-row Bring with it what it may.
And He who feeds the ra - vens, Will give His children bread.

4.
Though vine nor fig-tree neither
Their wonted fruit should bear,
Though all the fields should wither,
Nor flocks nor herds be there ;
Yet God the same abiding,
His praise shall tune my voice,
For while in Him confiding,
I cannot but rejoice. Amen.

(EXPERIENCE.)

JOYFULLY. 10S.

163)   Songs of Devotion, III. Key G.

1 JOYFULLY, joyfully onward I move,
  Bound to the land of bright spirits above
  Angelic choristers sing as I come,
  Joyfully, joyfully haste to thy home;
  Soon with my pilgrimage ended below,
  Home to that land of delight will I go;
  Pilgrim and stranger no more shall I roam,
  Joyfully, joyfully resting at home.

2 Friends, fondly cherished, have passed on before;
  Waiting, they watch me approaching the shore;
  Singing, to cheer me thro' death's chilling gloom,
  Joyfully, joyfully haste to thy home.
  Sounds of sweet melody fall on my ear;
  Harps of the blessed your voices I hear;
  Rings with the harmony heaven's high dome,—
  Joyfully, joyfully haste to thy home.

3 Death, with thy weapons of war lay me low,
  Strike, king of terrors! I fear not the blow;
  Jesus hath broken the bars of the tomb!
  Joyfully, joyfully will I go home;
  Bright will the morn of eternity dawn,
  Death shall be banished, his scepter be gone;
  Joyfully, then, shall I witness his doom,
  Joyfully, joyfully, safely at home.

PEACE BE STILL.

(164)

1 FIERCE raged the tempest o'er the deep,
  Watch did Thine anxious servants keep,
  But Thou wast wrapped in guileless sleep,
     Calm and still.

2 "Save, Lord, we perish," was their cry,
  "O save us in our agony!"
  Thy word above the storm rose high,
     "Peace be still."

3 The wild winds hushed, the angry deep
  Sank, like a little child to sleep;

The sullen billows cease to leap,
     At Thy will.

4 So when our life is clouded o'er,
  And storm-winds drift us from the shore,—
  Say, (lest we sink to rise no more,)
     "Peace be still!"

PORTUGUESE HYMN.

(165)   Christian Songs, 199. Key A.

1 How firm a foundation, ye saints of the Lord,
  Is laid for your faith in His excellent word;
  What more can He say, than to you He hath said—
  Who unto the Saviour for refuge have fled.

2 Fear not, I am with thee, oh! be not dismayed,
  For I am thy God, and will still give thee aid:
  I'll strengthen thee, help thee, and cause thee to stand,
  Upheld by My righteous, omnipotent hand.

3 When through the deep waters I call thee to go,
  The rivers of sorrow shall not overflow;
  For I will be with thee thy trials to bless,
  And sanctify to thee thy deepest distress.

4 When through fiery trials thy pathway shall lie,
  My grace, all-sufficient, shall be thy supply;
  The flame shall not hurt thee, I only design
  Thy dross to consume, and thy gold to refine.

5 E'en down to old age all My people shall prove
  My sovereign, eternal, unchangeable love;
  And then, when grey hairs shall their temples adorn,
  Like lambs they shall still in My bosom be borne.

6 The soul that on Jesus hath leaned for repose,
  I will not—I will not desert to his foes:
  That soul—though all hell should endeavor to shake,
  I'll never—no never—no never forsake!

(EXPERIENCE.)

NEVER ALONE.

R. W. RAYMOND.

FERD. SILCHER.

1. Far out on the des-o-late bil-low, The sail-or sails the sea, A-lone with the night and the
2. Far down in the earth's dark bo-som, The min-er mines the ore; Death lurks in the dark be-
3. Forth in-to the dread-ful bat-tle The stead-fast sol-dier goes, No friend, when he lies a
4. Lord, grant as we sail life's o-cean, Or delve in its mines of woe; Or fight in its ter-ri-ble

CHORUS.

temp-est, Where countless dan-gers be. Yet, nev-er a-lone is the Christ-ian, Who
hind him, And hides in the rock be-fore. Yet, &c.
dy-ing His eyes to kiss and close. Yet, &c.
con-flict, This com-fort all to know, That, &c.

lives by faith and prayer; For God is a Friend un-fail-ing, And God is every-where.

(EXPERIENCE.)

SUNDAY-SCHOOL WAR-CRY.

W. H. DOANE. **99**

W. BENNETT.
Spirited.

From "Royal Diadem," by per.

1. On to the conflict, soldiers for the right, Arm you with the Spirit's sword, and march to the fight;
2. Fierce-ly it ra-ges, dead-ly is the strife, But the prize that you shall win will be end-less life;
3. Val-iant and cheerful, marching right a-long, Ev-ery foe shall quit the field, tho' haughty and strong;
4. Soon shall the war-fare and the con-flict cease, Soon shall dawn the welcome day of rest-ing and peace;

Truth be your watchword, sound the ring-ing cry, Vic-to-ry, vic-to-ry, vic-to-ry!
Je-sus will crown you, your re-ward shall be Vic-to-ry, vic-to-ry, vic-to-ry!
Fear shall oppress them, truth shall make them flee; Vic-to-ry, vic-to-ry, vic-to-ry!
Foes all subdued, we'll raise to heaven the cry, Vic-to-ry, vic-to-ry, vic-to-ry!

CHORUS.

Ev-er this the war-cry, Vic-to-ry, vic-to-ry; Ev-er this the war-cry, Vic-to-ry;

Write it on your ban-ners, Waft it on the breeze, Vic-to-ry, vic-to-ry, vic-to-ry!

(WORK AND WARFARE.)

STAND UP FOR JESUS.

ASA HULL.

R. TORREY, Jr.

From "Casket No. 1," by per.

1. Stand up for Je - sus, Christian, stand! Firm as a rock on o-cean's strand! Beat back the waves of
2. Stand up for Je - sus, Christian, stand! Sound forth His name o'er sea and land! Spread ye His glo-rious
3. Stand up for Je - sus, Christian, stand! Lift high the cross with steadfast hand! Till heathen lands with
4. Stand up for Je - sus, Christian, stand! Soon with the blest im-mor - tal band We'll dwell for a ye, life's

CHORUS.

sin that roll, Like rag - ing floods, a-round thy soul. Stand up for Je - sus, no - bly stand!
word a - broad, Till all the world shall own Him Lord!
wond'ring eye, Its ris - ing glo - ry shall des - cry.
jour - ney o'er, In realms of light on Heaven's bright shore.

Firm as a rock on ocean's strand! Stand up, His righteous cause defend; Stand up for Jesus your best Friend.

(WORK AND WARFARE.)

HOLD THE FORT.

P. P. BLISS.

By per. John Church & Co.

P. P. BLISS.

1. Ho! my comrades, see the sig-nal, Wav-ing in the sky! Re - inforcements
2. See the might-y host ad-vanc-ing, Sa - tan lead-ing on; Might-y men a-
3. See the glorious ban - ner wav-ing, Hear the bu-gle blow; In our Lead-er's
4. Fierce and long the bat - tle ra - ges, But our help is near; On - ward comes our

now ap-pear-ing, Vic - to-ry is nigh! "Hold the fort, for I am com-ing,"
round us fall - ing, Cour-age al-most gone.
name we'll tri - umph O - ver ev-ery foe.
Great Commander, Cheer, my comrades, cheer!

CHORUS.

Je - sus sig-nals still, Wave the answer back to heav-en, "By Thy grace we will."

(WORK AND WARFARE.)

LATTER DAY. 8s & 7s.

Rev. SAMUEL JOHNSON, 1860.

1. On - ward, Christian, tho' the re - gion Where thou art be drear and lone; God hath set a
2. By the thorn-road and none oth - er, Is the mount of vis - ion won; Tread it without

guardian le - gion Ve - ry near thee,—press thou on! Lis - ten, Christian, their Hosan-na
shrinking, broth-er, Je - sus trod it,—Press thou on! By thy trustful, calm en-deavor,

Roll - eth o'er thee, "God is love," Write up - on thy red-cross banner, "Upward ever, heaven's a-bove."
Guiding, cheering, like the sun, Earth-bound hearts thou shalt deliver, For their sake, O press thou on.

(WORK AND WARFARE.)

STRIKE! O STRIKE FOR VICTORY!

W. H. DOANE. 103

Mrs. MARY A. KIDDER.

From "Pure Gold," by per.

1. Strike! O strike for vic-t'ry Soldiers of the Lord, Hoping in His mer-cy, Trusting in His word;
2. Strike! O strike for vic-t'ry He-roes of the cross, Sac-ri-fic-ing pleasure, Glo-ry-ing in loss;
3. Hand to hand u-nit-ed, Heart to heart as one, Let us still keep marching Till our journey's done,

Lift the gos-pel ban-ner High a-bove the world; Let its folds of beau-ty Ev-er be un-furled.
Ev-er pressing on-ward, On-ward to the light, Till we reach the Jordan, With our home in sight.
Till we see the an-gels Come in glo-ry down, With the shining garments And the vic-tor's crown.

CHORUS.

Strike! strike for Vic-t'ry, He-roes bold; Strike! till the Vic-t'ry You be-hold;

Strike! strike for Vic-t'ry, Ne'er give o'er; Rest then in glo-ry Ev-er more.

(WORK AND WARFARE.

"MARCHING ON!"

WM. B. BRADBURY.

Rev. R. LOWRY.

From "Bradbury Trio." by per

D.C. 1. Marching on! marching on! glad as birds on the wing, Come the bright ranks of soldiers from near and from far;
2. Press-ing on! pressing on! to the din of the fray, With the firm tread of faith to the bat-tle we go;
3. Fight-ing on! fight-ing on! in the midst of the strife, At the call of our Cap-tain, we draw every sword;
4. Sing-ing on! sing-ing on! from the bat-tle we come, Ev-ery flag bears a wreath, ev-ery soldier re-nown;

Hap-py hearts, full of song, 'neath our banners we bring, We are soldiers of Zi-on, prepared for the war.
'Mid the cheering of an-gels, our ranks march away, With our flags pointing ev-er right on tow'rds the foe.
We are battling for God, we are struggling for life, Let us strike ev-ery rebel that fights 'gainst the Lord.
Heav'nly an-gels are wait-ing to welcome us home, And the Saviour will give us a robe and a crown.

Marching on!   marching on!

Marching on! marching on! marching on! marching on! Sound the battle-cry! sound the bat-tle-cry! Marching

(WORK AND WARFARE.)

D. C.

on! marching on!

on! marching on! marching on! marching on! Shout the vic-to-ry, the vic-to-ry, the vic-to-ry!

WE ARE LITTLE TRAVELERS. (Infant Class.)

WM. STEVENSON.

R. LOWRY. From "Royal Diadem," by per.

1. We are lit-tle trav'lers, Marching, marching, We are lit-tle trav'lers, Marching on; Walk-ing in the
2. We are lit-tle la-b'rers, Working, working, We are lit-tle la-b'rers, Working on; Nev-er id-ling
3. We are lit-tle sol-diers, Fighting, fighting, We are lit-tle sol-diers, Fighting on; War-ring 'gainst the
4. We are lit-tle pilgrims, Hoping, hoping, We are lit-tle pilgrims, Hoping on; For a coun-try

nar-row way, Shunning paths that lead a-stray, We are lit-tle trav'-lers, Marching on.
time a-way, Bus-y working ev-ery day, We are lit-tle la-b'rers, Work-ing on.
pow'r of sin, Foes with-out and foes with-in, We are lit-tle sol-diers, Fight-ing on.
bet-ter far, Where our crown and kingdom are, We are lit-tle pil-grims, Hoping on.

(WORK AND WARFARE.)

106 SOUND THE BATTLE CRY!

WM. F. SHERWIN.

WM. F. SHERWIN.
From "Bright Jewels," by per.

Vigorously, in march time.

1. Sound the bat - tle cry! See! the foe is nigh; Raise the standard high For the Lord; Gird your ar - mor on,

CHORUS. *ff*

Stand firm ev - ery one; Rest your cause upon His ho-ly word. Rouse then, soldiers! ral-ly round the banner!

Read - y, stead - y, pass the word a - long; On - ward, for - ward, shout a - loud Hosan - na!

Christ is Cap - tain of the might-y throng.

2 Strong to meet the foe,
  Marching on we go,
  While our cause we know
    Must prevail;
  Shield and banner bright
  Gleaming in the light;
  Battling for the right
    We ne'er can fail.

3 Oh! Thou God of all,
  Hear us when we call;
  Help us one and all
    By Thy grace;
  When the battle's done,
  And the vict'ry won,
  May we wear the crown
    Before Thy face.

(WORK AND WARFARE.)

CHRISTIAN SOLDIERS.

HENRY KIRKE WHITE, 1804.

Arr. by JOHN B. WILKES.

1. Oft in dan-ger, oft in woe, On-ward, Christian, on-ward go! Fight the fight, main-
2. On-ward, Christian, on-ward go! Join the war, and face the foe; Will ye flee in

tain the strife, Strengthened with the Bread of life.
dan-ger's hour? Know ye not your Captain's power?

3 Let your drooping hearts be glad;
  March, in heavenly armor clad;
  Fight, nor think the battle long,
  Vict'ry soon shall tune your song.

4 Onward, then, to battle move!
  More than conq'rors you shall prove;
  Though opposed by many a foe,
  Christian soldiers, onward go!

LOOK, LOOK TO JESUS!

Rev. E. P. HAMMOND, 1873.

From "Song Evangel," by per, HUBERT P. MAIN.

1. Look, look to Je-sus! Be-hold a fountain free Is o-pen there for thee! Look, look to Jesus!
2. Look, look to Je-sus! For thee He in-ter-cedes,—His blood for thee now pleads, Look, look to Jesus!
3. Look, look to Je-sus! He's calling now for thee; Poor sinner, look to Me,— Look, look to Jesus!
4. Look, look to Je-sus! If thou would'st live above Where all is peace and love, Look, look to Jesus!

(WORK AND WARFARE.)

BRIGHTLY GLEAMS OUR BANNER.

T. J. POTTER, 1870.

Arr. from ARTHUR S. SULLIVAN.

1. Brightly gleams our ban - ner, Pointing to the sky, Waving wanderers on - ward To their home on high;
2. Je - sus, Lord and Mas - ter, At Thy sa-cred feet, Here with hearts rejoic - ing See Thy children meet;
3. All our days di - rect us, In the way we go, Lead us on vic-to - rious O - ver ev - ery foe;
4. Then with Saints and An-gels May we join a - bove, Offering pray'rs and praises At Thy throne of love;

Journeying o'er the de - sert, Glad-ly thus we pray, And with hearts unit - ed, Take our heav'nward way.
Oft - en have we left Thee, Oft - en gone a - stray, Keep us, mighty Sav-iour, In the narrow way.
Bid Thine an-gels shield us, When the storm-clouds lower, Pardon Thou and save us In the last dread hour.
When the toil is o - ver, Then comes rest and peace,—Jesus, in His beau - ty;—Songs that never cease.

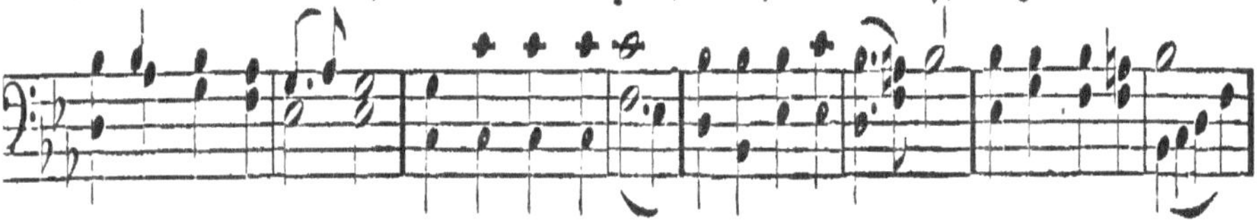

CHORUS.

Brightly gleams our ban - ner, Pointing to the sky, Waving wanderers on-ward To their home on high.

(WORK AND WARFARE.)

ONWARD, CHRISTIAN SOLDIERS.

Rev. SABINE BARING GOULD.   JOS. HAYDN, arr.

1. On-ward, Christian sol - diers, Marching as to war, With the Cross of Je - sus Go - ing on be-fore.
2. Like a might-y ar - my Moves the Church of God; Brothers, we are treading Where the saints have trod;
3. Crowns and thrones may perish, Kingdoms rise and wane, But the Church of Je - sus Constant will re-main;
4. On-ward, then, ye peo - ple, Join our hap-py throng, Blend with ours your voices In the triumph song;

Christ the Roy-al Mas-ter Leads a-gainst the foe, For-ward in - to bat - tle, See, His ban-ners go.
We are not di - vid - ed, All one bo - dy we ; One in hope, and doc-trine, One in char - i - ty.
Gates of hell can nev - er 'Gainst that Church prevail; We have Christ's own promise, And that cannot fail.
Glo - ry, laud, and hon-or, Un - to Christ the King, This thro' countless a - ges Men and An - gels sing.

CHORUS.

Onward Christian sol-diers, Marching as to war, With the Cross of Je - sus Go - ing on be-fore.

(WORK AND WARFARE.)

ONE MORE DAY'S WORK FOR JESUS.

Miss ANNA WARNER, 1864.   From "Bright Jewels," by per. Rev. R. LOWRY.

1. One more day's work for Je - sus, One less of life for me! But heav'n is nearer, And Christ is
2. One more day's work for Je - sus: How glo - rious is my King! 'Tis joy, not du - ty, To speak His
3. One more day's work for Je - sus; How sweet the work has been, To tell the sto - ry, To show the
4. One more day's work for Je - sus—Oh, yes, an earn-est day; For heav'n shines clearer And rest comes
5. Oh, bless - ed work for Je - sus; Oh, rest at Je - sus' feet! There toil seems pleasure, My wants are

dear - er Than yes - ter-day to me; His love and light Fill all my soul to-night. One more day's work for
beau - ty; My soul mounts on the wing At the mere tho't How Christ my life has bought.
glo - ry, Where Christ's flock enter in! How it did shine In this poor heart of mine!
near - er, At each step of the way; And Christ in all—Before His face I fall.
trea - sure, And pain for Him is sweet. Lord, if I may, I'll serve an - other day!

CHORUS.

Jesus,   One more day's work for Jesus, One more days work for Jesus,   One less of life for me.

(WORK AND WARFARE.)

NEVER BE AFRAID.

(178) Bradbury Trio, 272. Key F.

1 NEVER be afraid to speak for Jesus,
    Think how much a word can do;
Never be afraid to own your Saviour,
    He who loves and cares for you.
CHO.—||: Never be afraid,:||
        Never, never, never;
    Jesus is our loving Saviour,
        Therefore never be afraid.

2 Never be afraid to work for Jesus,
    In His vineyard day by day;
Labor with a kind and willing spirit,
    He will all your toil repay.

3 Never be afraid to die for Jesus;
    He, the Life, the Truth, the Way,
Gently in His arms of love will bear you
    To the realms of endless day.

DARE TO DO RIGHT.

(179) Bradbury Trio, 260. Key Eb.

1 DARE to do right! dare to be true!
You have a work that no other can do;
Do it so bravely, so kindly, so well,
Angels will hasten the story to tell.
CHO.—Dare, dare, dare to do right!
        Dare, dare, dare to be true!
    Dare to be true! dare to be true.

2 Dare to do right! dare to be true!
Other men's failures can never save you!
Stand by your conscience, your honor, your
    faith;
Stand like a hero, and battle till death.

3 Dare to do right! Dare to be true!
God, who created you, cares for you too;
Treasures the tears that His striving ones
    shed,
Counts and protects every hair of your head.

MARCHING ALONG.

(180) Christian Songs, 94. Key Bb.

1 THE children are gathering from near and
    from far,
The trumpet is sounding the call for the war;
The conflict is raging, 'twill be fearful and
    long,
We'll gird on our armor, and be marching
    along.
CHO.
Marching along, we are marching along,
Gird on the armor and be marching along,
The conflict is raging, 'twill be fearful and
    long,
Then gird on the armor and be marching
    along.

2 We've listed for life, and will camp on the
    field,   [yield;
With Christ as our Captain we never will
The "sword of the Spirit," both trusty and
    strong,
We'll hold in our hands as we're marching
    along.

3 Thro' conflicts and trials our crowns we
    must win,   [sin;
For here we contend 'gainst temptation and
But one thing assures us, we cannot go wrong
If trusting our Saviour while marching
    along.

THE OLD WAY.

(181) Pure Gold, 18. Key Bb.

1 WE are going forth with our staff in hand,
Thro' a desert wild in a stranger land;
But our faith is bright and our hope is strong,
And the Good Old Way is our pilgrim song.
CHO.
'Tis the Good Old Way, by our fathers trod;
'Tis the way of Life, and it leadeth unto God;
'Tis the only path to the realms of day;
We are going home in the Good Old Way.

2 There are foes without, there are foes within
They would turn us back to the path of sin;
We will stop our ears to the words they say,
While we onward press in the Good Old Way.

3 On the brink of time when we stand at last,
When our sun has set, and our work is past,
When we bid farewell to our mortal clay,
We will praise the Lord for the Good Old
    Way.

SOMETHING TO DO IN HEAVEN.

(182) Christian Songs, 44. Key Bb.

1 THERE'LL be something in heaven for chil-
    dren to do;
    None are idle in that blessed land.
There'll be love for the heart, there'll be
    thought for the mind,
    And employment for each little hand.
CHO.
|: There'll be something to do::||
There'll be something for children to do,
    On the bright shining shore, where there's
    joy evermore.
There'll be something for children to do.

2 There'll be lessons to learn of the wisdom
    of God,
As they wander the green meadows o'er;
And they'll have for their teachers in that
    blest abode,
All the good that have gone there before.

3 There'll be errands of love from the man-
    sions above,
To the dear ones that linger below;
And it may be, our Father the children will
    send
To be angels of mercy in woe.

(WORK AND WARFARE.)

BATTLE SONG.

R. W. RAYMOND.

Arr. by J. R. HOWARD.

1. The God who spanned the heav'ns above, And spread the earth a-round us, Is He, whose pow'rful
2. Then fly our ban-ner o-ver-head, And let its mot-to glo-rious A-bove us ev-ery
3. The crown His faith-ful sol-diers win, Who would not proudly wear it! The praise, the Mas-ter's

arm of love From slav-'ry has un-bound us: And in His conqu'ring train we march, Not
where be spread, "In Christ we are vic-to-rious!" Lo! how the ranks of Sa-tan quake! And
"Welcome in!" Who would not die to share it! Then sound the trum-pets toward the foe! We'll

sul-len and des-pair-ing, But sword in hand at His command, For do-ing and for dar-ing.
thro' the bat-tle's frowning, See, Jesus stands, with outstretched hands, For blessing and for crown-ing.
show by our be-hav-iour, How free-men fight for God and right, Whose Captain is their Sav-iour.

(WORK AND WARFARE.)

WORK FOR THE NIGHT IS COMING.

(184) Bradbury Trio, 194. Key F.

1 WORK, for the night is coming,
Work thro' the morning hours;
Work, while the dew is sparkling,
Work 'mid springing flowers;
Work when the day grows brighter,
Work in the glowing sun;
Work, for the night is coming,
When man's work is done.

2 Work, for the night is coming;
Work through the sunny noon;
Fill brightest hours with labor,
Rest comes sure and soon;
Give every flying minute
Something to keep in store;
Work, for the night is coming;
When man works no more.

3 Work, for the night is coming,
Under the sunset skies,
While their bright tints are glowing,
Work, for daylight flies;
Work till the last beam fadeth,
Fadeth to shine no more:
Work, while the night is dark'ning,
When man's work is o'er.

ROTHWELL. L. M.

(185) Christian Songs, 201. Key Eb.

1 STAND up, my soul, shake off thy fears,
And gird the Gospel armor on;
March to the gates of endless joy,
Where Jesus, thy great Captain's gone.

2 Hell and thy sins resist thy course;
But hell and sin are vanquished foes,
Thy Saviour nailed them to the cross;
And sung the triumph when He rose.

3 Then let my soul march boldly on—
Press forward to the heavenly gate;
There peace and joy eternal reign,
And glittering robes for conquerors
wait.

4 There shall I wear a starry crown,
And triumph in almighty grace,
While all the armies of the skies
Join in my glorious Leader's praise.

LABAN. S. M.

(186) Bradbury Trio, 61. Key C.

1 MY soul, be on thy guard,
Ten thousand foes arise;
And hosts of sin are pressing hard
To draw thee from the skies.

2 O! watch, and fight, and pray'
The battle ne'er give o'er;
Renew it boldly every day,
And help divine implore.

3 Ne'er think the vict'ry won,
Nor lay thine armor down;
Thine arduous work will not be done,
Till thou obtain thy crown.

4 Fight on, my soul, till death
Shall bring thee to thy God;
He'll take thee at thy parting breath
To His divine abode.

(WORK AND WARFARE.

SUNDAY-SCHOOL ARMY.

(187) Bradbury Trio, 27. Key G.

1 ‖: O, do not be discouraged,
For Jesus is your Friend, :‖
‖: He will give you grace to conquer,‖
And keep you to the end.
CHO.—I am glad I'm in this army,
‖: Yes, I'm glad I'm in this army,:‖
And I'll battle for the Lord.

2 ‖: Fight on, ye little soldiers,
The battle you shall win,:‖
‖: For the Saviour is your Captain,:‖
And He has vanquished sin.

3 ‖And when the conflict's over,
Before Him you shall stand ;‖
‖: You shall sing His praise for ever,:‖
In Canaan's happy land.

WEBB. 7s, & 6s. D.

(188) Bradbury Trio, 104. Key Bb.

1 Go forward, Christian soldier,
Beneath His banner true:
The Lord Himself, thy Leader,
Shall all thy foes subdue.
Trust only Christ, thy Captain
Cease not to watch and pray;
Heed not the treach'rous voices
That lure thy soul astray.

2 Go forward, Christian soldier
Nor dream of peaceful rest,
Till Satan's host is vanquished,
And heaven is all possest;
Till Christ Himself shall call thee
To lay thine armor by,
And wear, in endless glory,
The crown of victory.

114. BEAUTEOUS DAY.

Rev. WM. O. CUSHING. GEO. F. ROOT 1866, by per. J. Church & C

1. We are watching, we are waiting, For the bright prophet-ic day: When the shadows, wea - ry shadows, From the world shall roll a-way.

CHORUS.

We are waiting for the morning, When the beauteous day is dawning; We are waiting for the morning, For the golden spires of day. Lo! He comes! see the King draw near; Zi - on, shout, the Lord is here.

2 We are watching, we are waiting,
  For the star that brings the day:
  When the night of sin shall vanish,
  And the shadows melt away.

3 We are watching, we are waiting,
  For the beauteous King of day:
  For the Chiefest of ten thousand,
  For the Light, the Truth, the Way.

(MISSIONARY.)

MISSIONARY HYMN.

(189) Bradbury Trio, 100. Key F.

1 From Greenland's icy mountains,
  From India's coral strand,
  Where Afric's sunny fountains
  Roll down their golden sand—
  From many an ancient river,
  From many a palmy plain
  They call us to deliver
  Their land from error's chain.

2 What though the spicy breezes
  Blow soft o'er Ceylon's isle;
  Though every prospect pleases,
  And only man is vile:
  In vain with lavish kindness
  The gifts of God are strewn;
  The heathen, in his blindness,
  Bows down to wood and stone.

3 Shall we, whose souls are lighted
  With wisdom from on high,
  Shall we to men benighted
  The lamp of life deny?
  Salvation, O salvation!
  The joyful sound proclaim,
  Till each remotest nation
  Has learned Messiah's name.

4 Waft, waft, ye winds, His story,
  And you, ye waters, roll,
  Till, like a sea of glory,
  It spreads from pole to pole—
  Till o'er our ransomed nature
  The Lamb for sinners slain,
  Redeemer, King, Creator,
  In bliss returns to reign.

WEBB. 7s & 6s.

(190) Bradbury Trio, 104. Key B♭.

1 The morning light is breaking,
  The darkness disappears;
  The sons of earth are waking
  To penitential tears:
  Each breeze that sweeps the ocean
  Brings tidings from afar,
  Of nations in commotion
  Prepared for Zion's war.

2 Rich dews of grace come o'er us
  In many a gentle shower,
  And brighter scenes before us
  Are opening every hour:
  Each cry to heaven going
  Abundant answer brings,
  And heavenly gales are blowing
  With peace upon their wings.

3 See heathen nations bending
  Before the God of love,
  And thousand hearts ascending
  In gratitude above:
  While sinners now confessing,
  The Gospel's call obey,
  And seek a Saviour's blessing,
  A nation in a day.

4 Blest river of salvation,
  Pursue thy onward way;
  Flow thou to every nation,
  Nor in thy richness stay:
  Stay not till all the lowly
  Triumphant reach their home,
  Stay not till all the holy
  Proclaim the Lord is come.

(MISSIONARY.)

THE HAPPY TIME.

(191) Christian Songs, 17. Key C.

1 O the happy time is coming
  When the Gospel trumpets sound,
  Shall be heard by every nation,
  To the earth's remotest bound;
  When the vale shall be exalted,
  And the verdant hills rejoice,
  And the ocean join the chorus,
  With a loud triumphant voice.
Cho.
  Lo! the morning light will break,
  And the day is drawing nigh,
  Yes, a glorious time is coming soon,
  We shall hail it by and by.

2 O the happy time is coming
  When the cry of war shall cease,
  And the standard of our Saviour,
  Be the olive branch of peace:
  Underneath our vine and fig-tree
  We will never be afraid,
  There is none will dare molest us,
  In their calm and quiet shade.

3 O the happy time is coming
  By our Fathers once foretold,
  It is promised in the Bible,
  It was sung by prophets old;
  They who sit in heathen darkness,
  Soon the morning light shall see,
  And the world, with songs of triumph,
  Hail the glorious jubilee.

ONWARD! ONWARD!

Mrs. L. H. SIGOURNEY, 1841.

From "Pure Gold," by per. A. J. POWELL.

1. On - ward! on - ward! men of hea - ven, Lift the gos - pel ban - ner high; Rest not, till its
2. Where the Arc - tic o - cean thunders, Where the tropics fierce-ly glow, Broadly spread the
3. Rude in speech, or grim in fea - ture, Dark in spir-it, though they be, Show that light to

light is giv-en, Star of ev - ery Pa-gan sky: Lift it where the pilgrim stranger Faints in Asia's
page of wonders, Bid its healing radiance flow: In - dia marks its lustre stealing; Shivering Greenland
ev - ery creature, Prince or vas-sal, bond or free. Lo! they haste to ev - ery na-tion; Host on host the

burn - ing ray; Bid the red-brow'd for - est ran-ger Hail it, ere it fades a - way.
feels its rays, Af-ric's sons, in de - serts kneeling, Pour at length their strains of praise.
ranks sup-ply: On - ward! Christ is your sal - va - tion, And your death is vic - to - ry.

(MISSIONARY.)

THE NINETY AND NINE.

ELIZABETH C. CLEPHANE. 1868.

IRA D. SANKEY.

1. There were ninety, and nine that safe - ly lay In the shel - ter of the fold, But one was
2. "Lord thou hast here thy ninety and nine ; Are they not e - nough for thee?" But the Shepherd made
3. But none of the ransomed ev - er knew How deep were the wa-ters crossed ; Nor how dark was the
4. And all thro' the mountains, thunder- riven, And up from the rock - y steep, There rose a

out on the hills a - way, Far off from the gates of gold— A - way on the moun - tains
an - swer: "This of mine Has wan-dered a - way from me ; And although the road be
night that the Lord passed thro', Ere he found his sheep that was lost ; Out in the des - ert he
cry to the gate of heaven, "Re - joice! I have found my sheep!" And the an - gels echoed a -

wild and bare, A - way from the ten - der Shepherd's care, A - way from the ten - der Shepherd's care."
rough and steep, I go to the desert to find my sheep, I go to the desert to find my sheep."
heard its cry—'Twas helpless and sick, and ready to die, 'Twas helpless and sick, and ready to die.
round the throne, "Rejoice, for the Lord brings back his own, Rejoice, for the Lord brings back his own."

(WARNING AND INVITATION.)

118

STILL UNDECIDED?

FANNY J. CROSBY. 1874.

R. LOWRY.

From "Brightest and Best," by per.

1. Still un-de-cid-ed? Look to thy heart; Grieve not the Spir-it, Lest He de-
2. Still un-de-cid-ed? Slight not the voice Breathing so kind-ly, "Make Me thy
3. Still un-de-cid-ed? Time flies a-pace; Je-sus en-treats thee; Spurn not His

part: Why wilt thou long-er wait? Come ere it be too late; Je-sus at
choice; Look at My hands and see I bore the nails for thee, I died to
grace; What if the word were passed, This night should be thy last? Where would thy

Mer-cy's gate Grace will im-part.
make thee free; Come and re-joice."
soul be cast? Where hide thy face?

4.
Still undecided?
What shall we say?
Still undecided?
Yet we will pray:
Oh, may the Spirit move!
Oh, may the God above
Melt thy poor heart to love—
Melt thee to-day !

(WARNING AND INVITATION.)

C. WESLEY, 1740.

BLUMENTHAL. 7s.

BLUMENTHAL.

Andante.

1. Depth of mer-cy, can there be   Mer-cy still re-served for me?   Can my God His wrath for-bear?
2. Kin-dled His re-lent-ings are;   Me, He now de-lights to spare;   Cries, how shall I give thee up?—

Me, the chief of   sin-ners, spare? I   have long withstood His grace, Long provoked Him to   His face,
Lets the lift-ed   thun-der drop. There for me the Saviour stands; Shows His wounds, and spreads His hands;

Would not hearken to His calls, Grieved Him by a thousand falls.
God is love! I know, I feel; Je-sus weeps and loves me still.

SECOND HYMN.

1 Come, my soul, thy suit prepare:
Jesus loves to answer prayer;
He Himself invites thee near,
Bids thee ask Him, waits to hear.
Lord, I come to Thee for rest;
Take possession of my breast;
There Thy blood-bought right maintain,
And without a rival reign.

2 While I am a pilgrim here,
Let Thy love my spirit cheer;
As my guide, my guard, my friend,
Lead me to my journey's end.

Show me what I have to do;
Every hour my strength renew·
Let me live a life of faith,—
Let me die Thy people's death.

John Newton, 1779.

(WARNING AND INVITATION.)

THE PRODIGAL CALL.

Mrs. CAROLINE DANA HOWE.

WM. H. DOANE.
From "Brightest and Best, by per.

1. O   Prodigal!   come, I am wait-ing,   Am wait-ing and watching for   thee;   Come, share in My
2. O   Prodigal!   wast-ing thy sub-stance,   And starving while plenty   is   near,   Why stay from the
3. Thy heart of its   sin   is re-pent-ing,   Thy com-ing a - far   I   be - hold;   I   hast-en to
4. O   Prodigal,   dead and yet liv - ing,   Wherev - er   on earth thou may'st be,   What ev - er thy

REFRAIN.

love and My bless - ing,   Till hun-ger for ev - er shall flee.   Come, come, re - turn to thy home,
arms of thy Fa - ther,   Thy Fa-ther to whom thou art   dear?
give thee My bless - ing,   My prodigal   child to en - fold.
sins and thy er - rors,   God still holds a blessing for   thee.

child of My care, There's bread and to spare; Come, come, return to thy home, Come, there's bread and to spare.

(WARNING AND INVITATION.)

THE PENITENT. 8s & 7s.

Rev. JOHN G. CHAFEE.

From "Bright Jewels," by per. CHESTER G. ALLEN.

1. Can my soul find rest from sor - row, Can my sins for - giv - en be, Must I wait un - til to -
2. Oh, the darkness, how it thickens, Like the brooding of de - spair! And my soul with - in me
3. Now He hears me, He will save me, I be - hold His shining face, Hear Him whisper He will

mor - row Ere my Sav - iour speaks to me? Will He speak in words of kind - ness? Will He
sick - ens—God, in mer - cy, hear my prayer! Give me but a hope to cher - ish, Give me
have me—Oh, the mir - a - cle of grace! I will joy to tell the sto - ry How He

wash a - way my sin? Will He lift this vail of blindness, And remove this dead - ly pain?
just one ray of light—Help me, save me, or I per - ish, Take a - way this aw - ful night!
com - eth from a - bove—Fills my soul, O, glo - ry, glo - ry! With the blessings of His love.

(WARNING AND INVITATION.)

GO BEAR THE JOYFUL TIDINGS.

THEO. F. SEWARD.

FANNY J. CROSBY. 1864.

From "New Golden Shower," by per.

1. Go bear the joy-ful tid-ings That first, on Ju-dah's plain, A-woke the wond'ring Shepherds
2. Go in your Master's vine-yard, And la-bor heart and hand; The word of life e-ter-nal P
3. Go tell the bro-ken spir-it That vainly sighs for rest, There is a home in glo-ry, A

praise Messiah's name; Exalt the King of glo-ry Who left His throne on high, And came on earth
claim to ev-ery land,— The sweet and precious promise To all who will be-lieve, Free grace and full
home for ev-er blest; Go bring the lost to Je-sus, His ten-der love to share; Go forth to ev-e

CHORUS.

ran-som, For guilt-y man to die, Go sound the gos-pel trumpet Be-yond the roll-i
va-tion, For all who will re-ceive.
na-tion, Im-mor-tal souls are there.

(WARNING AND INVITATION.)

sea, From chains of sin and dark-ness, To set the cap-tive free.

4 Haste on your work of mercy,
  The heavenly call obey;
Go in the strength of Jesus,
  The true and living way;
Go like the old disciples,
  And tread the path they trod;
Your duty lies before you,
  Go—leave the rest to God.
    Cho.—Go sound the, etc.

SAVED BY THE BLOOD.

WM. H. DOANE.

FANNY J. CROSBY. 1874.

From "Brightest and Best," by per.

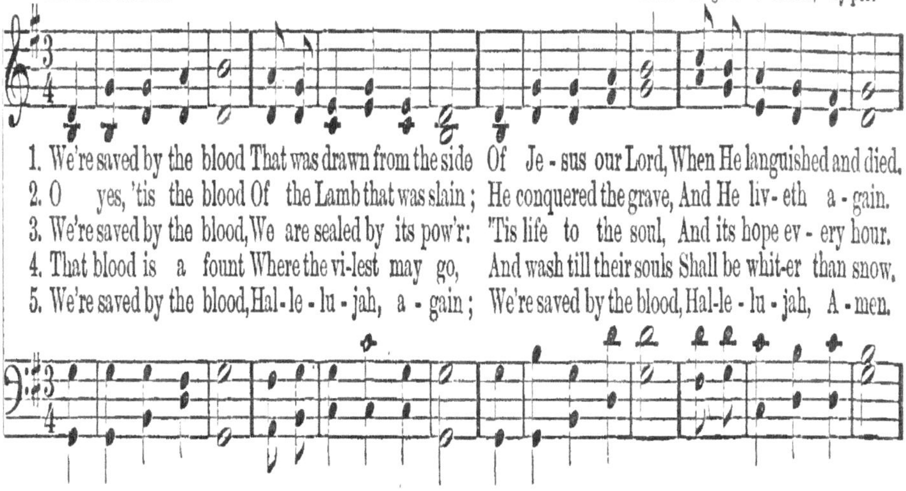

1. We're saved by the blood That was drawn from the side Of Je - sus our Lord, When He languished and died.
2. O   yes, 'tis the blood Of the Lamb that was slain ; He conquered the grave, And He liv- eth a - gain.
3. We're saved by the blood, We are sealed by its pow'r ; 'Tis life to the soul, And its hope ev - ery hour.
4. That blood is a fount Where the vi-lest may go, And wash till their souls Shall be whit-er than snow,
5. We're saved by the blood, Hal-le - lu - jah, a - gain ; We're saved by the blood, Hal-le - lu - jah, A - men.

REFRAIN.

Hal-le-lu-jah to God, For redemption so free ; Hal-le-lu-jah, Hal-le-lu - jah, Dear Sav-iour, to Thee.

(*WARNING AND INVITATION.*)

THE HEAVENLY DEW.

Mrs. LYDIA BAXTER. 1874.

HUBERT P. MAIN, 1874 by per.

1. The dews of heaven are fall - ing In si - lence all a - round; The Spir - it - voice is call - ing, Break
2. The cross is o - ver - shadowed By God's ma - jes - tic love; The way to heaven is o - pen, And
3. Come, give your life to Je - sus, In wis - dom make your choice; His lov - ing arms are o - pen, And

up the fal - low ground; Re - ceive the gold - en sun - light Of Je - sus' pre - cious love,
free the gifts a - bove; Like gen - tle mists de - scend - ing Up - on the opening day,
sweet His gracious voice; Thro' dew - y meads He'll lead you Up to His shin - ing throne,

To warm the soul for glo - ry, And ho - ly joys a - bove. O come while dew-drops
The voice of hope is blend - ing With faith to cheer the way. O come, &c.
And an - gels bid you wel - come To Heaven's e - ter - nal home. O come, &c.

lin - ger still A - round the foot of Zi - on's hill; Come, seek the love of Je - sus.

(WARNING AND INVITATION.)

MARTYN. 7s.

(198) Bradbury Trio, 14. Key F.

1 MARY to the Saviour's tomb
  Hasted at the early dawn,
Spice she brought, and sweet perfume,
  But the Lord she loved had gone.
For a while she lingering stood,
  Filled with sorrow and surprise,
Trembling, while a crystal flood
  Issued from her weeping eyes.

2 But her sorrows quickly fled
  When she heard His welcome voice:
Christ had risen from the dead,
  Now He bids her heart rejoice;
What a change His word can make,
  Turning darkness into day;
Ye who weep for Jesus' sake,
  He will wipe your tears away.

3 He who came to comfort her,
  When she thought her all was lost,
Will for your relief appear,
  Tho' you now are tempest-tossed:
On His word your burden cast,
  On His love your thoughts employ:
Weeping for a while may last
  But the morning brings the joy.

WOODWORTH. L. M.

(199) Bradbury Trio, 139. Key E♭.

1 O THAT my load of sin were gone;
  O that I could at last submit
At Jesus' feet to lay it down,
  To lay my soul at Jesus' feet!

2 Rest for my soul I long to find;
  Saviour of all, if mine Thou art
Give me Thy meek and lowly mind,
  And stamp Thine image on my heart.

3 Fain would I learn of Thee, my God;
  Thy light and easy burden prove;
The cross, all stained with hallow'd blood
  The labor of Thy dying love.

4 I would, but Thou must give the power,
  My heart from every sin release;
Bring near, bring near the joyful hour,
  And fill me with Thy perfect peace.

UTICA. 7s & 6s.

(200) Ply. Coll., 117. Key G.

1 DROOPING souls, no longer mourn,
  Jesus still is precious;
If to Him you now return,
  Heaven will be propitious.
Jesus now is passing by,
  Calling wanderers to Him;
Drooping souls, you need not die,
  Go to Him and hear Him.

2 He has pardons, full and free,
  Drooping souls to gladden;
Still He cries—"Come unto Me,
  Weary, heavy laden."
Though your sins like mountains high,
  Rise, and reach to heaven,
Soon as you on Him rely,
  All shall be forgiven.

3 Precious is the Saviour's name,
  Dear to all that love Him;
He to save the dying came;
  Go to Him and prove Him.
Wand'ring sinners, now return;
  Contrite souls, believe Him!
Jesus calls you, cease to mourn,
  Worship Him; receive Him,

THE GREAT PHYSICIAN.

(201) Gospel H. & S. S., 56. Key E♭.

1 THE great Physician now is near,
  The sympathizing Jesus:
He speaks the drooping heart to cheer,
  Oh, hear the voice of Jesus.
CHO. Sweetest note in seraph song,
  Sweetest name on mortal tongue,
Sweetest carol ever sung,
  Jesus, blessed Jesus.

2 Your many sins are all forgiven,
  Oh, hear the voice of Jesus;
Go on your way in peace to heaven,
  And wear a crown with Jesus.

3 All glory to the dying Lamb!
  I now believe in Jesus;
I love the blessed Saviour's name,
  I love the name of Jesus.

4 His name dispels my guilt and fear,
  No other name but Jesus;
Oh, how my soul delights to hear
  The precious name of Jesus.

5 And when to that bright world above,
  We rise to see our Jesus,
We'll sing around the throne of love
  His name, the name of Jesus.

(WARNING AND INVITATION.)

COME, COME TO JESUS!

Rev. GEO. B. PECK, 1864.

HUBERT P. MAIN, 1864, by per.

1. Come, come to Je - sus! He waits to welcome thee, O wand'rer, ea - ger-ly Come, come to Je - sus!
2. Come, come to Je - sus! He waits to ransom thee O slave! so willing-ly; Come, come to Je - sus!
3. Come, come to Je - sus! He waits to lighten thee, O burdened! trustingly Come, come to Je - sus!

4 Come, come to Jesus!
He waits to give to thee,
O blind! a vision free;
Come, come to Jesus!

5 Come, come to Jesus!
He waits to shelter thee,
O weary! blessedly
Come, come to Jesus!

6 Come, come to Jesus!
He waits to carry thee,
O lamb! so lovingly,
Come, come to Jesus!

SUBMISSION.

H. N. WHITNEY, by per.

1. Come to Je - sus erring one; Come to Jesus now; Humbly at His gracious throne, In submission bow.
2. At His feet confess your sin; Seek forgiveness there; For His blood can make you clean, — He will hear your prayer.
3. Seek His face without delay; Give Him now your heart; Tarry not, but while you may, Choose the better part.

(WARNING AND INVITATION.)

LET THE GOOD ANGELS.

(204)   Fresh Laurels, 122. Key F.

1 THEY hover around us, bright angels are near,
  To glory immortal they win;
Then gladly we'll open tho door of our hearts,
  And let the good angels come in.
How kindly our Father has sent them to keep
  A watch o'er His children below;
They're with us iu slumber, their eyes never sleep,
  They're with us wherever we go.

REF:—Let them come in, let them come in,
  Let the good angels come in, come in;
  Let them come in, let them come in,
  Let the good angels come in.
  ‖: Come in, come in, Good angels come in. ‖

2 To comfort the lonely, and strengthen the weak,
  Their mission of mercy and love;
And oft on their beautiful pinions of light
  They bear our petitions above.
O let them come in, they are holy and pure,
  Their presence how tenderly sweet;
They echo the song of the happy and blest,
  They learn at Immanuel's feet.

SCOTLAND. 12 S.

(205)   Coronation, 252. Key A.

1 THE voice of free grace cries,—escape to the mountain;
  For Adam's lost race Christ hath opened a fountain;
  For sin and uncleanness, and every transgression,
  His blood flows most freely in streams of salvation.

CHO. Hallelujah to the Lamb,
  Who has purchased our pardon,
  We will praise Him again,
  When we pass over Jordan.

2 Ye souls that are wounded O flee to the Saviour;
  He calls you in mercy—'t is infinite favor;
  Your sins are increasing,—escape to the mountain,—
  His blood can remove them,—it flows from the fountain.

3 O Jesus! ride onward, triumphantly glorious,
  O'er sin, death, and hell, Thou art more than victorious;
  Thy name is the theme of the great congregation,
  While angels and men raise the shout of salvation.

4 With joy shall we stand, when escaped to the shore;
  With harps in our hands, we'll praise Him the more;
  We'll range the sweet plains on the bank of the river,
  And sing of salvation for ever and ever!

GOOD ANGELS COME IN.

(206)   Fresh Laurels, 122. Key F.

1 MY Saviour stands waiting, and knocks at the door,
  Has knocked, and is knocking again;
I hear His kind voice; I'll reject Him no more,
  Nor let Him stand pleading in vain.
In infinite mercy He came from above
  To ransom, to cleanse me from sin;
I'll yield to the voice of His merciful love,
  And let my dear Saviour come in.

CHO. Saviour, come in; Cleanse me from sin;
  Jesus, my Saviour, come in, come in!
  Enter the door, Waiting no more
  Saviour, dear Saviour, come in.
  ‖: Come in, come in, dear Saviour, come in. ‖

2 O Saviour, my Ransom, Redeemer, and Friend,
  The Life, and the Truth, and the Way,
On Thy precious merit alone I depend;
  Dwell in me, and keep me, I pray.
Thy goodness hath opened the door of my heart;
  'Tis open in welcome to Thee;
Come in, blessed Saviour, and never depart;
  Come in, with Thy mercy, to me.

WARNING AND INVITATION.

COME TO CHRIST TO-DAY.

W. BENNETT.

W. B., 1875.

From "Brightest and Best," by per.

1. Come to Je-sus, pre-cious soul, Come to Je-sus, come to Je-sus; He will make the
2. Come to Je-sus, doubting heart, Come to Je-sus, come to Je-sus; Bid your un-be-
3. Come to Je-sus, don't de-lay, Come to Je-sus, come to Je-sus; Come to Je-sus

wounded whole, Come, O come to-day; He will wash you in His blood,—Free-ly flows the
lief de-part, Trust His word to-day; Faith is strong and must pre-vail— Come with faith, you
while you may, Come, O come to-day; Let His love your hearts constrain, Do not let Him

cleans-ing flood— He will take your sins a - way; Come, O come to Christ to-day.
can - not fail— All your doubts and fears shall fly; Faith tri - umph-ant mounts the sky.
plead in vain; He hath died up-on the tree, Shed His pre-cious blood for Thee.

(WARNING AND INVITATION.)

WONDROUS LOVE.

(208) Gospel H. & S. S., 31. Key E♭.

1 GOD loved the world of sinners lost
  And ruined by the fall;
  Salvation full, at highest cost,
  He offers free to all.

CHO.

  Oh, 'twas love, 'twas wondrous love!
    The love of God to me;
  It brought my Saviour from above,
    To die on Calvary.

2 E'en now by faith I claim Him mine,
  The risen Son of God;
  Redemption by His death I find,
  And cleansing through the blood.

3 Believing souls rejoicing go;
  There shall to you be given
  A glorious foretaste, here below,
  Of endless life in heaven.

4 Of victory now o'er Satan's power
  Let all the ransomed sing,
  And triumph in the dying hour
  Through Christ the Lord, our King.

ZEPHYR. L. M.

(209) Bradbury Trio, 263. Key C.

1 COME hither, all ye weary souls,
  Ye heavy-laden sinners, come;
  I'll give you rest from all your toils,
  And raise you to My heavenly home.

2 They shall find rest that learn of Me;
  I'm of a meek and lowly mind;
  But passion rages like the sea,
  And pride is restless as the wind.

HAMBURG. L. M.

(210) Bradbury Trio, 80. Key F.

1 BEHOLD a Stranger at the door!
  He gently knocks, has knocked before;
  Has waited long—is waiting still:
  You treat no other friend so ill.

2 Oh! lovely attitude—He stands
  With melting heart and loaded hands:
  Oh! matchless kindness—and He shows
  This matchless kindness to His foes!

3 But will He prove a friend indeed?
  He will—the very Friend you need;
  The Friend of sinners—yes, 'tis He,
  With garments dyed on Calvary.

4 Admit Him ere His anger burn,
  His feet, departed ne'er return;
  Admit Him, or, the hour's at hand,
  You'll at his door rejected stand.

WAITING SAVIOUR.

(211) Christian Songs, 82. Key A♭.

1 SEE Jesus standing at the door,
  O, hear Him pleading evermore,
  He waits for thee, O heart of sin,
  Wilt thou not let Him in?

2 He bore the cruel cross for thee,
  He died on rugged Calvary;
  Say, weary heart oppress'd with sin,
  Wilt thou not let Him in?

3 He'll bring thee joy from heaven above,
  He'll bring thee pardon, peace and love,
  And wash thy soul from every sin;
  O let the Saviour in!

4 O shall He plead with thee in vain?
  Remember all His grief and pain;
  His death atones for all thy sin,
  O rise, and let Him in.

JACOB'S PRAYER. 7 S.

(212) Christian Songs, 90. Key F.

1 ALL night long till break of day,
  Jacob wept his bitter pray'r,
  Till the angel on his way,
  Christ the Angel blest him there.
  I'm a needy sinner too,
  Torn with anguish, guilt and fears,
  I to Jesus too will go,
  Go and bathe His feet with tears.

2 Jesus, at Thy cross I lie
  All night long till break of day;
  Perish here, if I must die—
  Unforgiven, go not away.
  Saviour, wilt Thou take my heart?
  It is all I have to give,
  Sin defiled in every part,
  Such a gift wilt Thou receive?

3 Oh, how kindly Jesus spake:
  "Go in peace—all is forgiven,
  Wilt thou all for Me forsake,
  Love, and follow Me to heav'n?"
  Jesus, I Thy goodness bless,
  And with wondering love adore;
  Let me never love Thee less,
  Let me love Thee more and more.

(WARNING AND INVITATION.)

From "Jubilee Songs," by per.

REFRAIN.

1. Oh, the rocks and the mountains shall all flee a-way, And you shall have a new hid-ing-place that day.

1. Sin - ner, Sin - ner, give up your heart to God, And you shall have a new hid - ing-place that day.
2. Doubter, Doubter, give up your heart to God, And you shall have a new hid - ing-place that day.
3. Mourner, Mourner, give up your heart to God, And you shall have a new hid - ing-place that day.
4. Brother, Brother, give up your heart to God, And you shall have a new hid - ing-place that day.

Oh, the rocks and the mountains shall all flee a-way, And you shall have a new hid-ing-place that day.

(WARNING AND INVITATION.)

MERCY'S FREE!

(214) Christian Songs, 86. Key F.

1 By faith I view my Saviour dying,
‖: On the tree :‖
To every nation He is crying,
‖: Look to me. :‖
He bids the guilty now draw near,
Repent, believe, dismiss their fear;
Hark! hark! what precious words I
‖: Mercy's free! :‖   [hear,

2 Did Christ when I was sin pursuing,
‖: Pity me? :‖
And did He snatch my soul from ruin?
‖: Can it be? :‖
Oh, yes! He did salvation bring:
He is my Prophet, Priest, and King;
And now my happy soul can sing,
‖: Mercy's free! :‖

3 Jesus my weary soul refreshes;
‖: Mercy's free! :‖
And every moment Christ is precious
‖: Unto me :‖
None can describe the bliss I prove,
While thro' this wilderness I rove,
All may enjoy the Saviour's love,
‖: Mercy's free! :‖

4 Long as I live, I'll still be crying
‖: Mercy's free! :‖
And this shall be my theme when dying,
‖: Mercy's free! :‖
And when the vale of death I've passed,
When lodg'd above the stormy blast,
I'll sing, while endless ages last,
‖: Mercy's free! :‖

WHAT SHALL I DO TO BE SAVED?

(215) Christian Songs, 143. Key F.

1 O! what shall I do to be saved
From the sorrows that burden my
Like the cold, stormy deep   [soul?
When the dark billows sweep,
Chilling floods of distress o'er me roll.
What shall I do? What shall I do?
O! what shall I do to be saved?

2 O! what shall I do to be saved
When sickness my strength shall
Or the world in a day,   [subdue?
Like a cloud roll away,
And eternity opens to view?
What shall I do? What shall I do?
O! what shall I do to be saved?

3 O! Lord, look in mercy on me,
Come, O come and speak peace to
Unto whom shall I flee,   [my soul:
Dearest Lord, but to Thee,
Thou canst make my poor broken
heart whole.
That will I do! that will I do!
To Jesus I'll go and be saved.

COME YE SINNERS. 8s & 7s.

(216) Christian Songs, 173. Key A.

1 Come, ye sinners, poor and needy,
Weak and wounded, sick and sore;
Jesus ready stands to save you,
Full of pity, love, and power.

Cho.
Turn to the Lord and seek salvation,
Sound the praise of His dear name;
Glory, honor, and salvation,
Christ the Lord is come to reign.

2 Let not conscience make you linger,
Nor of fitness fondly dream;
All the fitness He requireth,
Is to feel your need of Him.

3 Come ye weary, heavy laden,
Bruised and mangled by the fall,
If you tarry till you're better,
You will never come at all.

COME YE SINNERS.

(217) Christian Songs, 173. Key A.

1 Now the Saviour standeth pleading
At the sinner's bolted heart;
Now in heaven He's interceding,
Taking there the sinner's part.

Cho.
Turn to the Lord, and seek salvation,
Sound the praise of His dear name;
Glory, honor, and salvation,
Christ the Lord is come to reign.

2 Now He's waiting to be gracious,
Now He stands and looks on thee;
See what kindness, love, and pity;
Shine around on you and me.

3 Come, for all things now are ready,
Yet there's room for many more:
O ye blind, ye lame and needy,
Come to wisdom's boundless store!

(WARNING AND INVITATION.)

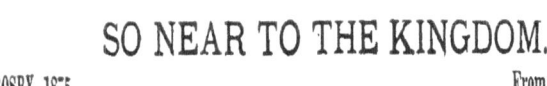

132

SO NEAR TO THE KINGDOM.

FANNY J. CROSBY, 1875.

R. LOWRY.

From "Brightest and Best," by per.

1. So near to the kingdom! yet what dost thou lack? So near to the kingdom! what keepeth thee
2. So near that thou hearest the songs that resound From those who be-liev-ing, a par-don have
3. O come, or thy sea-son of grace will be past, The door will be closed, and this call be thy
4. To die with no hope! hast thou counted the cost? To die out of Christ, and thy soul to be

back? Renounce ev-ery i-dol, tho' dear it may be, And come to the Saviour now pleading with thee.
found! So near, yet un-will-ing to give up thy sin, When Je-sus is waiting to welcome thee in!
last; O where wouldst thou turn if the light should depart That comes from the Spirit, and shines on thy heart.
lost! So near to the kingdom! O come, we implore, While Je-sus is pleading, come enter the door.

REFRAIN.

Plead - - -ing with thee,........ The Saviour is pleading, is pleading with thee.

Pleading with thee, pleading with thee,

(WARNING AND INVITATION.)

WINDHAM. L. M.

(219) Victory, 145. Key F.

1 STAY, thou insulted Spirit, stay,
Though I have done Thee such despite,
Nor cast the sinner quite away,
Nor take Thine everlasting flight.

2 Though I have most unfaithful been,
Of all who e'er Thy grace received;
Ten thousand times Thy goodness seen,
Ten thousand times Thy goodness
grieved;

3 Yet, O, the chief of sinners spare,
In honor of my great High-priest!
Nor in Thy righteous anger swear
I shall not see Thy people's rest.

4 E'en now my weary soul release,
And raise me by Thy gracious hand;
Guide me into Thy perfect peace,
And bring me to the promised land.

GANGES. C. P. M.

(220) Plym. Coll., 148. Key D.

1 AWAKED by Sinai's awful sound,
My soul in bonds of guilt I found,
And knew not where to go;
One solemn truth increased my pain
The sinner "must be born again,"
Or sink to endless woe.

2 I heard the law its thunders roll,
While guilt lay heavy on my soul—
A vast oppressive load;

All creature-aid I saw was vain;
The sinner "must be born again,"
Or drink the wrath of God.

3 The saints I heard with rapture tell—
How Jesus conquered death and hell,
To bring salvation near:
Yet still I found this truth remain—
The sinner "must be born again,"
Or sink in deep despair.

4 But while I thus in anguish lay,
The bleeding Saviour passed that way,
My bondage to remove;
The sinner, once by justice slain,
Now by His grace is born again,
And sings redeeming love.

WINDHAM. L. M.

(221) Victory, 145. Key F.

1 BROAD is the road that leads to death
And thousands walk together there;
But wisdom shows a narrow path,
With here and there a traveller.

2 "Deny thyself and take thy cross,"
Is the Redeemer's great command:
Nature must count her gold but dross,
If she would gain this heavenly land.

3 Lord! let not all my hopes be vain:
Create my heart entirely new:
There may Thy Holy Spirit reign,
And to Thy will my all subdue.

(WARNING AND INVITATION.)

WILLOWBY. C. P. M.

(222) Plym. Coll., 271. Key Ab.

1 OFT when the waves of passion rise,
And storms of life conceal the skies,
And o'er the ocean sweep,
Toss'd in the long tempestuous night,
We feel no ray of heavenly light,
To cheer the lonely deep.

2 But lo! in our extremity,
The Saviour walking on the sea!
E'en now He passes by!
He silences our clamorous fear,
And mildly says, "Be of good cheer,
Be not afraid, 'tis I."

3 Ah, Lord! if it be Thou indeed,
So near us in our time of need,
So good, so strong to save—
Speak the kind word of power to me,
Bid me believe, and come to Thee,
Swift-walking on the wave.

4 He bids me come! His voice I know,
And boldly on the waters go,
And brave the tempest's shock:
O'er rude temptations now I bound,
The billows yield a solid ground,
The wave is firm as rock!

5 Come in, come in, Thou Prince of peace,
And all the storms of sin shall cease,
And fall, no more to rise:
O, if Thy Spirit still remain,
Our rest on distant shores we gain,
Our haven in the skies!

WRECK AND RESCUE.

134

Rev. E. HOPPER, D. D.

C. C. CONVERSE, by per.

Moderato.

1. Wreck'd and struggling in mid o-cean, Clinging to a broken spar,—Darkness round me, billows o'er me,
2. All the e - vils of a life-time Bear-ing down on my dark path,—And I sinking,—Oh! I trem-ble,
3. Still my eyes grew dim thro' fainting, And the heavy storm and night Press'd me downwards, and the raging
4. Now a voice spoke to me cheerily, Spake as from that burning star,—With its blessed rays up-on me,

Not the glimmer of a star. Bil-lows o'er me, and no mer-cy, Gasping as I was for breath ;
Thinking of the night of wrath. Cast a-way, and lost, and sinking, Clinging to a broken spar ;
Billows quench'd that blessed light. Then a-gain its rays up-ris - ing, High-er than the highest wave ;
"Cling not to a broken spar." "Trust to Me, and I will save you !" Then I turned and saw such light ;

Night up-on me, and the com-ing Of the darker night of death.
Sud - den-ly a light from heaven Burst up-on me like a star.
Came with its bright arms outstretching, Raised me from a watery grave.
As if thousand suns were mingling All their glory on my sight.

5 Still the voice of love comes to me,
As I struggle on life's wave ;
Trials round me, sin within me,
Not a friend that's strong to save:
Trembling, yet believing, hoping,
To the Saviour I will call ;
He will help me, guide me, save me,
Be my present All in All.

(WARNING AND INVITATION.)

WATER OF LIFE.

(224) Fresh Laurels, 50. Key B♭.

1 Jesus the water of life will give
    Freely, freely, freely,
Jesus the water of life will give
    Freely to those who love Him:
Come to that fountain, O drink and live,
    Freely, freely, freely,
Come to that fountain, O drink and live,
    Flowing for those that love Him.

Duet.
The Spirit and the Bride say, come,
    Freely, freely, freely,
And he that is thirsty let him come
    And drink of the water of life.

Cho.
The fountain of life is flowing,
    Flowing, freely flowing,
The fountain of life is flowing,
    Is flowing for you and for me.

2 Jesus has promised a home in heaven,
    Freely, freely, freely,
Jesus has promised a home in heaven,
    Freely to those that love Him;
Treasures unfading will there be given,
    Freely, freely, freely,
Treasures unfading will there be given,
    Freely to those that love Him.

3 Jesus has promised a calm repose,
    Freely, freely, freely,
Jesus has promised a calm repose,
    Freely to those that love Him;
Come to the water of life that flows
    Freely, freely, freely,
Come to the water of life that flows
    Freely to all that love Him.

MERIBAH. C. P. M.

(225) Christian Songs, 198. Key E♭.

1 When Thou, my righteous Judge,
    shalt come,
To take Thy ransomed people home,
    Shall I among them stand?
Shall such a worthless worm as I,
Who sometimes am afraid to die,
    Be found at Thy right hand?

2 I love to meet Thy people now,
Before Thy feet with them to bow,
    Though vilest of them all;
But—can I bear the piercing thought—
What if my name should be left out,
    When Thou for them shalt call?

3 O Lord, prevent it by Thy grace—
Be Thou my only hiding-place,
    In this the accepted day;
Thy pardoning voice, O let me hear,
To still my unbelieving fear,
    Nor let me fall, I pray.

HARK! THOSE HAPPY VOICES. P. M.

(226)   Clariona, 20. Key E.

1 Hark those happy voices, saying,
    Yet there's room; Sinner come,
    ‖: Heaven's call obeying. :‖

2 Now the feast is spread before thee,
    Wait no more, Grace implore,
    ‖ Peace shall then come o'er thee. :‖

3 Bless the Lord of life for ever,
    O, my soul, Bountiful,
    ‖: Infinite His favor. :‖

4 Bless the Lord of Thy Salvation,
    Who in love From above,
    ‖: Heard thy supplication. :‖

5 Bless the Lord of earth and heaven;
    Through His blood That freely flow'd
    ‖ Are thy sins forgiven. :‖

6 Bless the Lord, whose love abounding,
    Fills Thy days With joy and praise,
    ‖: Songs of triumph sounding. :‖

SEEKING JESUS.

(227) Christian Songs, 45. Key F.

1 Thro' the world we daily roam,
    Seeking Jesus, Seeking Jesus;
None in vain for this have come,
    Seeking Jesus, Seeking Jesus;
In all places high or lowly,
    'Mid the sinful and the holy.

Duet. Seeking Jesus, Seeking Jesus,
Girls. We shall find Him,
Boys. We shall find Him,
All. We shall find Him, if we seek,
    He will hear us when we speak;
    He will answer us in love,
    Take us home to dwell above.

2 If our days on earth are spent
    Seeking Jesus, Seeking Jesus;
With all things we'll be content
    Seeking Jesus, Seeking Jesus;
Tho' our path be lone and dreary,
Tho' our steps be slow and weary;

3 Soon our life will all be o'er,
    Seeking Jesus, Seeking Jesus;
We shall reach the better shore,
    Seeking Jesus, Seeking Jesus;
In that land of peace and pleasure,
We've laid up our dearest treasure;

(WARNING AND INVITATION.)

YES, THERE IS PARDON FOR YOU.

FANNY J. CROSBY, 1874.

From "Brightest and Best," by per. HUBERT P. MAIN.

1. Oh, come to the Sav-iour, be-lieve in His name, And ask Him your heart to renew; He waits to be
2. The way of transgression that leads un-to death, Oh, why will you longer pursue? How can you re-
3. Be warn'd of your dan-ger; es-cape to the cross; Your on-ly sal-va-tion is there; Be-lieve, and that

Chorus.

gracious, O turn not a-way, For now there is pardon for you. Yes, there is pardon for you,....
ject the sweet message of love, That of-fers full pardon to you?
moment the Spir-it of grace Will answer your peni-tent pray'r.

for you,

Yes, there is pardon for you; For Je-sus has died to redeem you, And of-fers full pardon to you.

for you,

(WARNING AND INVITATION.)

EXPOSTULATION. IIS.

229)   Christian Songs, 199. Key A.

1 O TURN ye, O turn ye, for why will ye die?
   When God, in great mercy, is coming so nigh;
   Now Jesus invites you, the Spirit says come,
   And angels are waiting to welcome you home.

2 How vain the delusion, that while you delay,
   Your hearts may grow better by staying away;
   Come wretched, come starving, come just as you be,
   While streams of salvation are flowing so free.

3 And now Christ is ready your souls to receive,
   O how can you question, if you will believe?
   If sin is your burden, why will you not come?
   'Tis you He bids welcome; He bids you come home.

4 Come, give us your hand, and the Saviour your heart,
   And trusting in Heaven, we never shall part;
   O how can we leave you? why will you not come?
   We'll journey together, and soon be at home.

COME YE DISCONSOLATE.

(230)   Songs of Devotion, 102 Key D.

1 COME, ye disconsolate, where'er ye languish,
   Come, at the mercy-seat fervently kneel:
   Here bring your wounded hearts, here tell your anguish;
   Earth has no sorrow that heaven cannot heal.

2 Joy of the desolate, light of the straying,
   Hope of the penitent, fadeless and pure,
   Here speaks the Comforter, in mercy saying,
   Earth has no sorrow that heaven cannot cure.

3 Here see the Bread of Life; see waters flowing
   Forth from the throne of God, pure from above;
   Come to the feast of love—come, ever knowing,
   Earth has no sorrow but heaven can remove.

GO AND TELL JESUS.

(231)   Christian Songs, 53. Key A♭.

1 Go and tell Jesus, weary, sin-sick soul,
   He'll ease thee of thy burden, make thee whole;
   Look up to Him, He only can forgive,
   Believe on Him, and thou shalt surely live.

CHO.—Go and tell Jesus, He only can forgive,
      Go and tell Jesus, O turn to Him and live.
      Go and tell Jesus, Go and tell Jesus,
      Go and tell Jesus, He only can forgive.

2 Go and tell Jesus, when your sins arise
   Like mountains of deep guilt before your eyes:
   His blood was spilt, His precious life He gave,
   That mercy, peace and pardon you might have.

3 Go and tell Jesus, He'll dispel thy fears,
   Will calm thy doubts, and wipe away thy tears;
   He'll take thee in His arms, and on His breast
   Thou mayest be happy, and for ever rest.

ANGELS HOVERING ROUND. P. M.

(232)   Songs of Devotion, 50. Key G.

1 ‖:THERE are angels hovering round, :‖
   There are angels, angels hovering round.

2 To carry the tidings home
   To the new Jerusalem,
   There are angels &c.

3 Let him that heareth come,
   Oh, come, while yet there's room;
   There are angels &c.

(WARNING AND INVITATION.)

ALMOST PERSUADED.

P. P. BLISS.　　　　By per. John Church & Co.　　　　P. P. BLISS.

1. "Al - most per - suad - ed" now to be - lieve; "Al - most persuad - ed" Christ to re -
2. "Al - most per - suad - ed" come, come to - day; "Al - most persuad - ed," turn not a -

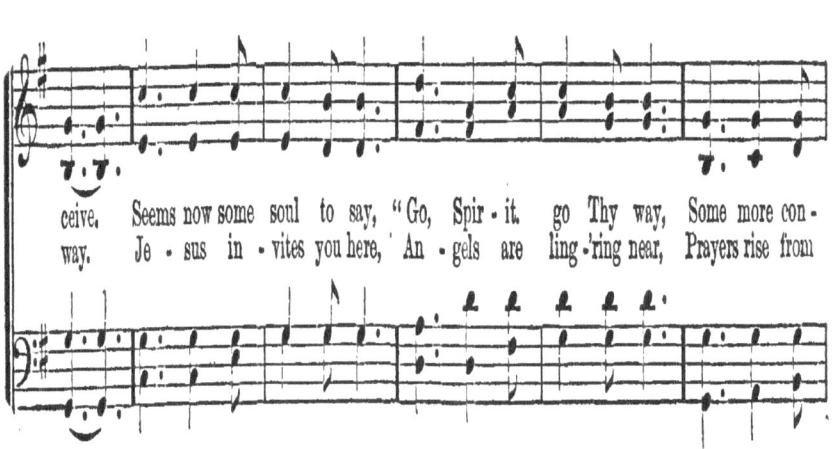

ceive.　Seems now some soul to say, "Go, Spir - it, go Thy way, Some more con -
way.　Je - sus in - vites you here, An - gels are ling - 'ring near, Prayers rise from

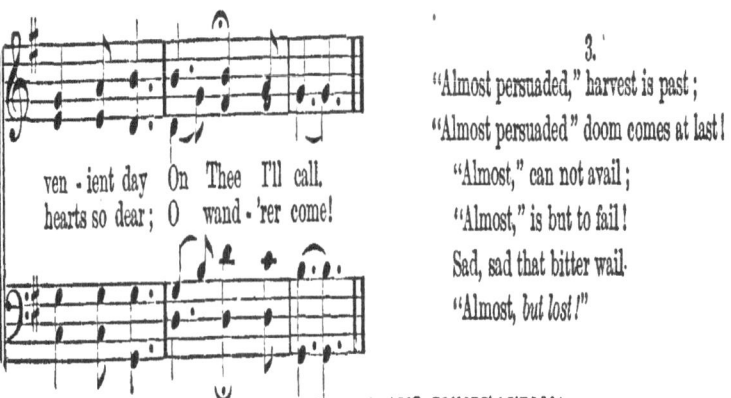

ven - ient day On Thee I'll call.
hearts so dear; O wand - 'rer come!

3.

"Almost persuaded," harvest is past ;
"Almost persuaded" doom comes at last !
　"Almost," can not avail ;
　"Almost," is but to fail !
Sad, sad that bitter wail·
　"Almost, *but lost !*"

(WARNING AND INVITATION.)

WHAT SHALL THE HARVEST BE ?

(233)Gospel H. & S. S., 76. Key C.

1 SOWING the seed by the daylight fair,
Sowing the seed by the noonday glare,
Sowing the seed by the fading light,
Sowing the seed in the solemn night ;
||: Oh, what shall the harvest be ? :||
CHO. ||: Sown in the darkness or sown
in the light, :||
||: Sown in our weakness or sown
in our might, :||
Gathered in time or eternity,
Sure, ah, sure will the harvest be.

2 Sowing the seed by the wayside high,
Sowing the seed on the rocks to die,
Sowing the seed where the thorns will
spoil,
Sowing the seed in the fertile soil ;
||: Oh, what shall the harvest be ? :||

3 Sowing the seed of a lingering pain,
Sowing the seed of a maddened brain,
Sowing the seed of a tarnished name,
Sowing the seed of eternal shame ;
||: Oh, what shall the harvest be ? :||

4 Sowing the seed with an aching heart,
Sowing the seed while the tear-drops
start,
Sowing in hope till the reapers come,
Gladly to gather the harvest home ;
||: Oh, what shall the harvest be ? :||

NOTHING BUT LEAVES.

(234)Gospel H. & S. S., 94. Key Eb.

1 NOTHING but leaves ! The Spirit
O'er years of wasted life ; [grieves
O'er sins indulg'd while conscience slept,
O'er vows and promises unkept,
And reap from years of strife—
Nothing but leaves ! nothing but leaves !

2 Nothing but leaves ! no gathered
Of life's fair ripening grain ! [sheaves,
We sow our seeds ; lo ! tares and weeds,—
Words, *idle* words, for earnest deeds,—
Then reap, with toil and pain,
Nothing but leaves ! nothing but leaves !

3 Nothing but leaves, sad mem'ry
No veil to hide the past : [weaves,
And as we trace our weary way,
And count each lost and misspent day,
We sadly find at last—
Nothing but leaves ! nothing but leaves !

4 Ah ! who shall thus the Master meet,
And bring but withered leaves ?
Ah, who shall at the Saviour's feet,
Before the awful judgment-seat
Lay down for golden sheaves
Nothing but leaves ! nothing but leaves !

TO-DAY. 6s & 4s.

(235)Gospel H. & S. S., 55. Key F.

1 TO-DAY the Saviour calls :
Ye wanderers, come !
O ye benighted souls,
Why longer roam ?

2 To-day the Saviour calls :
O, hear Him now ;
Within these sacred walls
To Jesus bow.

3 To-day the Saviour calls ;
For refuge fly :
The storm of justice falls,
And death is nigh.

4 The Spirit calls to-day ;
Yield to His power ;
Oh, grieve Him not away !
'T is mercy's hour.

RETURN. C. M.

(236)   Plym. Coll., 104. Key Bb.

1 RETURN, O wand'rer, to thy home,
Thy Father calls for thee ;
No longer now an exile roam,
In guilt and misery ;
Return, return !

2 Return, O wand'rer, to thy home,
'Tis Jesus calls for thee,
The Spirit and the Bride say—come ;
Oh ! now for refuge flee.

3 Return, O wand'rer, to thy home,
'T is madness to delay ;
There are no pardons in the tomb,
And brief is mercy's day.

GREENVILLE. 8s, 7s & 4.

(237)Christian Songs, 200. Key F.

1 HEAR, O sinner ! mercy hails you ;
Now with sweetest voice she calls ;
Bids you haste to seek the Saviour,
Ere the hand of justice falls :
Hear, O sinner !
'T is the voice of mercy calls.

2 Haste, O sinner ! to the Saviour :
Seek His mercy while you may ;
Soon the day of grace is over ;—
Soon your life will pass away ;
Haste, O sinner !
You must perish if you stay.

(*WARNING AND INVITATION.*)

THERE'S LIFE AT THE OPEN DOOR.

WM. H. DOANE.

FANNY J. CROSBY. 1875.

From "Brightest and Best, by per.

1. I have longed for the bliss of par-don, And sighed to be cleansed from sin; And I know if I come be-liev-ing, My Sav-iour will let me in; For the door of His love is o-pen, He wait-eth for those who seek; But I trem-ble with fear and doubting; O why is my faith so weak?

2. I have clung to the hopes that per-ish, And now in my hour of need, How they die in my heart, and leave me As frail as a brok-en reed; I have hard-ly the strength or cour-age, But O I will try once more; There is life if my faith can reach it, There's life at the o-pen door.

3. I will trust tho' I walk in dark-ness, And pray till the light I see; For the blood that has cleansed the vil-est, Will sure-ly a-vail for me; I have on-ly this plea to of-fer, That Je-sus for me has died; And with on-ly my heart to give Him, I haste to His bleeding side.

4. I have longed for the bliss of par-don, And sighed to be cleansed from sin; And I knock at the door, be-liev-ing That Je-sus will let me in; O the faith in my soul grows stronger, I trem-ble with fear no more; 'Tis my Saviour that bids me wel-come: I en-ter the o-pen door.

(WARNING AND INVITATION.)

REFRAIN.

O pre-cious Sav-iour! I know I have slighted Thy mer-cy; It comes, It comes, It

It comes to me more, It comes,

comes to me more and more; But soft-ly Thy Spir-it whispers to me, There's life at the o-pen door.

STEPHANOS.

Rev. JOHN MASON NEALE, 1851.

Rev. Sir HENRY WILLIAM BAKER, 1860.

1. Art thou weary, art thou languid? Art thou sore distress'd? "Come to Me," saith One, and coming, Be at rest."
2. Hath He marks to lead me to Him, If He be my guide? "In His feet and hands are wound-prints, And His side."
3. If I find Him, if I follow, What my future here? "Many a sorrow, many a la-bor, Many a tear."
4. If I still hold closely to Him, What hath He at last? "Sor-row vanquish'd, labor ended, Jordan past."
5. If I ask Him to receive me, Will He say me nay? "Not till earth and not till heaven Pass a-way,"

(WARNING AND INVITATION.)

I AM TRUSTING LORD, IN THEE.

Rev. WM. McDONALD. 1869.

WM. G. FISCHER, 1869. by per.

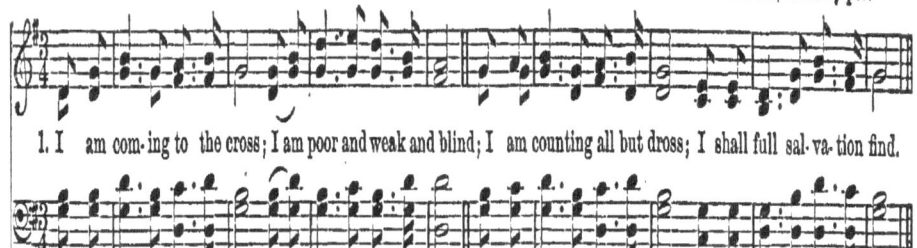

1. I am com-ing to the cross; I am poor and weak and blind; I am counting all but dross; I shall full sal-va-tion find.

CHO.—I am trusting, Lord, in Thee, Dear Lamb of Cal-va-ry; Humbly at Thy cross I bow, Save me Je-sus, save me now.

2 Long my heart has sighed for Thee;
   Long has evil reigned within;
' Jesus sweetly speaks to me,
   I will cleanse you from all sin.

3 In Thy promises I trust;
   Now I feel the blood applied;
   I am prostrate in the dust;
   I with Christ am crucified.

RATHBUN. 8s & 7s.

Sir JOHN BOWRING. 1825.

ITHAMAR CONKEY. 1850.

1. In the cross of Christ I glo-ry, Towering o'er the wrecks of time; All the light of sa-cred
2. When the woes of life o'er-take me, Hopes deceive and fears an-noy, Nev-er shall the Cross for-

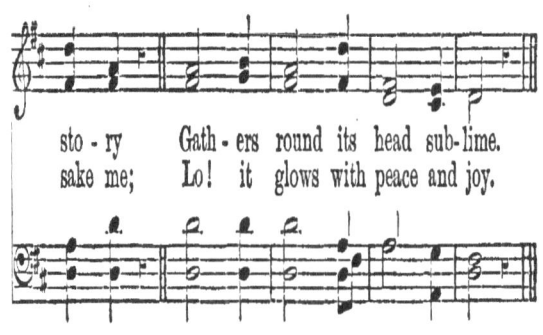

sto-ry   Gath-ers round its head sub-lime.
sake me;   Lo! it glows with peace and joy.

3 When the sun of bliss is beaming
   Light and love upon my way,
   From the cross the radiance streaming
   Adds more lustre to the day.

4 Bane and blessing, pain and pleasure,
   By the cross are sanctified;
   Peace is there that knows no measure,
   Joys that through all times abide.

(CONSECRATION.)

THE LORD IS MY SHEPHERD.

JAMES MONTGOMERY, 1822, alt.   HUBERT P. MAIN, 1872, by per.

1. The Lord is my Shepherd, no want shall I know; I feed in green pastures, safe folded I rest;

2. The Lord is my Shepherd, no e - vil I fear,— His rod will defend me and comfort me still;

3. He spreadeth my ta - ble, my cup runneth o'er; With goodness and mercy my days shall be crowned;

BOYS.   GIRLS.   BOYS.   GIRLS.

He lead - eth my soul where the still waters flow; He lead - eth my soul where the still waters flow;

The sha - dow and vale, my Re - deemer will cheer, The sha - dow and vale, my Re-deem - er will cheer,

My soul, from the grave will my Shepherd restore, My soul, from the grave will my Shepherd re-store,

ALL.

Restores me when wand'ring, redeems when oppressed; Restores me when wand'ring, redeems when oppressed.

The light of His presence, my spir - it shall fill; The light of His presence, my spir - it shall fill.

And I, in His dwelling for-ev - er be found; And I, in His dwelling for - ev - er be found.

(CONSECRATION.)

SWEET, SWEET PEACE.

WM. H. DOANE.

FANNY J. CROSBY, 1874.

From "Brightest and Best," by per.

1. Sweet peace in be-liev-ing, Je-sus, my Sav-iour, in Thee; Sweet rest in Thy king-dom,
2. In Thee I am trust-ing, All to Thy will I re-sign; I cling to Thy prom-ise,
3. To Thee I am pray-ing, Ask-ing, from day un-to day, The light of Thy Spir-it,

Thou hast pro-vid-ed for me. Sweet, sweet peace, Precious, en-dur-ing for ev-er:
Rest-ing on mer-cy di-vine.
Ev-er the guide of my way.

Sweet, sweet peace, Ev-er a-bide with me.

4.

On Thee I am leaning,
  Waiting and hoping in love ;
Soon, soon to be gathered
  Home with the dear ones above.
    Sweet, sweet peace, etc,

(CONSECRATION.)

Mrs. LYDIA BAXTER. 1872.

HUBERT P. MAIN, by per.

1. In the fadeless spring-time, on the heav'nly shore, Kindred spir-its wait us, who have gone be-fore;
2. In the mist-y gloaming, death awaits us all; Si-lent is his coming, sure the Master's call;
3. Trusting in the Saviour, may we hum-bly wait, Till the ho-ly an-gels ope tne pearl-y gate;

There no flow-ers with-er, and no pleasures cloy, In that land of beau-ty, in that home of joy.
And the an-gel foot-steps mark the up-ward way, Till the twi-light merges in-to heavenly day.
And the lov-ing Fa-ther, from His gracious throne, Smiling bids us welcome to our heavenly home.

CHORUS.

ritard.

By the gate they'll meet us, 'neath that golden sky, Meet us at the por-tal—Meet us by-and-by.

(CONSECRATION.)

LORD, IN THIS THY MERCY'S DAY.

ISAAC WILLIAMS, 1840.

W. H. MONK.

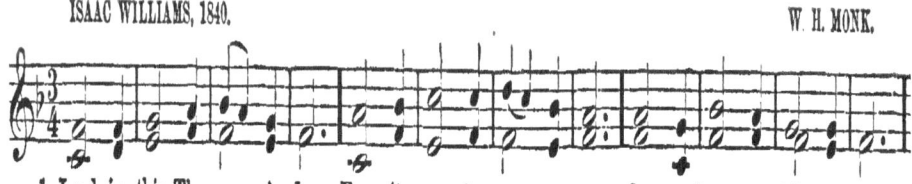

1. Lord, in this Thy mer-cy's day, Ere it pass for aye a-way, On our knees we fall and pray,
2. Ho-ly Je-sus, grant us tears, Fill us with heart-searching fears Ere that aw-ful doom ap-pears.
3. Lord, on us Thy spir-it pour, Kneeling low-ly at the door Ere it close for ev-er-more.

4 By Thy night of agony,
  By Thy supplicating cry,
  By Thy willingness to die.

5 By Thy tear of bitter woe
  For Jerusalem below,
  Let us not Thy love forego.

6 Grant us 'neath Thy wings a place,
  Lest we lose this day of grace—
  Ere we shall behold Thy face.

EVEN ME.

Mrs. ELIZABETH CODNER, 1860.

WM. B. BRADBURY, 1862.
From "The Golden Shower," by per.

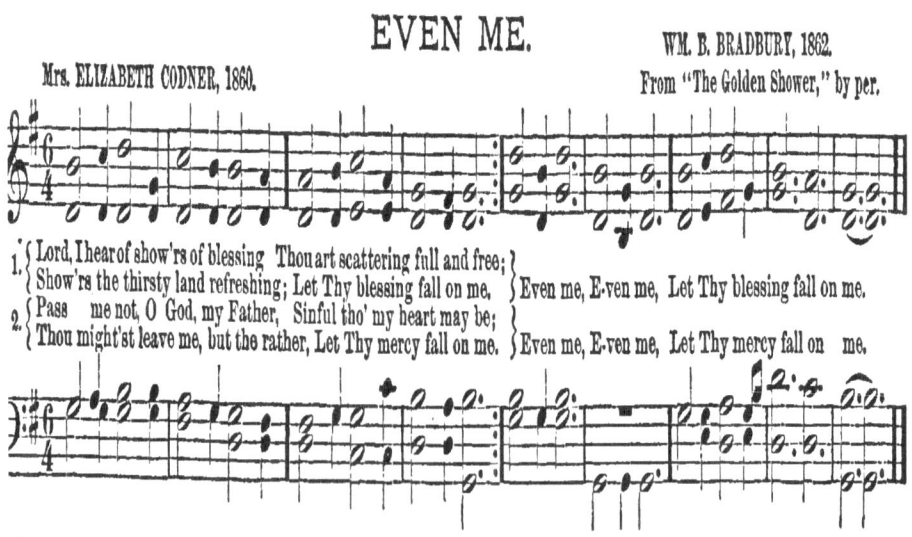

1. { Lord, I hear of show'rs of blessing Thou art scattering full and free; }
  { Show'rs the thirsty land refreshing; Let Thy blessing fall on me. } Even me, E-ven me, Let Thy blessing fall on me.
2. { Pass me not, O God, my Father, Sinful tho' my heart may be; }
  { Thou might'st leave me, but the rather, Let Thy mercy fall on me. } Even me, E-ven me, Let Thy mercy fall on me.

3 Pass me not, O gracious Saviour,
  Let me live and cling to Thee:
  Fain I'm longing for Thy favor;
  Whilst Thou'rt calling, call for me.—Even me.

4 Pass me not, Thy lost one bringing;
  Bind my heart, O Lord, to Thee;
  Whilst the streams of life are springing,
  Blessing others, O, bless me,—Even me.

(CONSECRATION.)

NEAR THE CROSS.

W. H. DOANE.
From "Bright Jewels," by per.

147

FANNY J. CROSBY, 1869.

1. Je - sus keep me near the cross, There a precious foun - tain, Free to all, a healing stream

2. Near the Cross, a trembling soul, Love and mer - cy found me; There the bright and morning star

CHORUS.

Flows from Calvary's mountain.   In the Cross, In the Cross, Be my glo - ry ev - er;

Shed its beams a - round me.

Till my raptured soul shall find Rest be - yond the riv - er.

3 Near the Cross! oh, Lamb of God
   Bring its scenes before me;
   Help me walk from day to day
   With its shadow o'er me.

4 Near the Cross I'll watch and wait
   Hoping, trusting ever,
   Till I reach the heavenly land,
   Just beyond the river.

(CONSECRATION.)

HALLELUJAH, 'TIS DONE!

By per. John Church & Co.

P. P. BLISS.

Allegro.

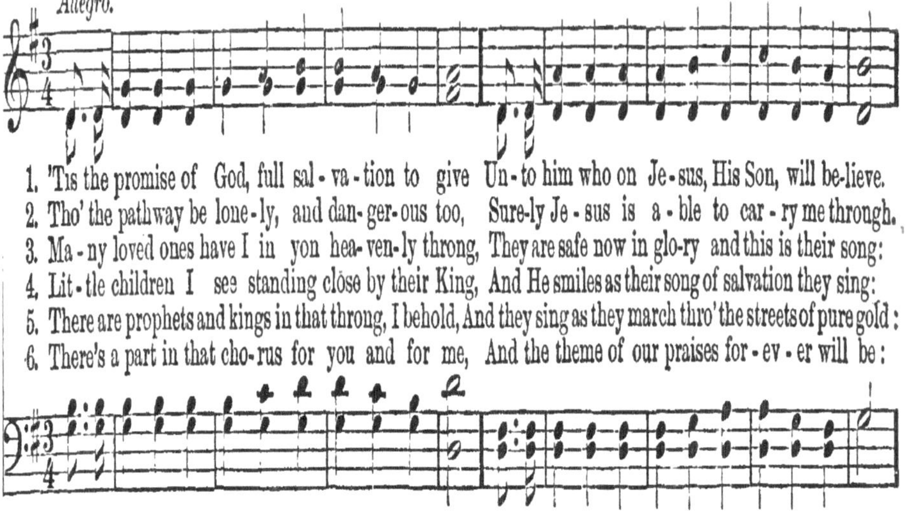

1. 'Tis the promise of God, full sal-va-tion to give Un-to him who on Je-sus, His Son, will be-lieve.
2. Tho' the pathway be lone-ly, and dan-ger-ous too, Sure-ly Je-sus is a-ble to car-ry me through.
3. Ma-ny loved ones have I in yon hea-ven-ly throng, They are safe now in glo-ry and this is their song:
4. Lit-tle children I see standing close by their King, And He smiles as their song of salvation they sing:
5. There are prophets and kings in that throng, I behold, And they sing as they march thro' the streets of pure gold:
6. There's a part in that cho-rus for you and for me, And the theme of our praises for-ev-er will be:

Hal-le-lu-jah, 'tis done! I be-lieve on the Son; I am saved by the blood of the cru-ci-fied One;

Hal-le-lu-jah, 'tis! done! I be-lieve on the Son; I am saved by the blood of the cru-ci-fied One.

(CONSECRATION.)

O MY SAVIOUR, HEAR ME.

149

FANNY J. CROSBY, 1875.   From "Brightest and Best," by per.   HUBERT P. MAIN.

1. O my Sav-iour, hear me, Draw me close to Thee; Thou hast paid my ran-som,
2. O my Sav-iour, bless me, Bless me while I pray; Grant Thy grace to help me,
3. O my Sav-iour, love me, Make me all Thine own; Leave me not to wan-der

Thou hast died for me; Now by sim-ple faith I claim Par-don thro' Thy gra-cious name;
Take my fear a - way; I be-lieve Thy prom-ise, Lord; I will trust Thy ho-ly word;
In this world a - lone; Bless my way with light di-vine, Let Thy glo-ry round me shine;

Thou, my ark of safe-ty, Let me fly to Thee.
Thou, my soul's Re-deem-er, Bless me while I pray.
Thou, my Rock, my Ref-uge, Make me all Thine own.

4.

O my Saviour, guard me,
    Keep me ever more;
Bless me, love and guide me,
    Till my work is o'er,
May I then, with glad surprise,
    Chant Thy praise beyond the skies;
There with Thee, my Saviour,
    Dwell for ever more.

(CONSECRATION.)

FROM THE FIRST DAWN. C. M.

Rev. JOHN B. DYKES.

1. From the first dawn of in - fant life   Thy goodness we   have shared, And still we live
2. To   seek Thy grace, to do   Thy will,   O Lord, our hearts in - cline; And o'er the paths

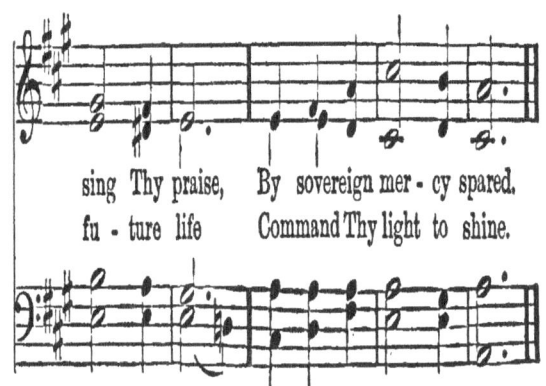

sing Thy praise,   By sovereign mer - cy spared.
fu - ture life   Command Thy light to shine.

3 While taught to read the word of truth
  May we that word receive ;
And when we hear of Jesus' name,
  In that blest Name believe.

4 Let not our feet incline to tread
  Sin's broad destructive road ;
But trace those holy paths which lead
  To glory and to God.

Gospel H. & S. Songs, 30. Key F.

JESUS OUR FRIEND.

1 WHAT a Friend we have in Jesus,
  All our sins and griefs to bear;
What a privilege to carry
  Everything to God in prayer.
Oh, what peace we often forfeit,
  Oh, what needless pain we bear—
All because we do not carry
  Everything to God in prayer.

2 Have we trials and temptations ?
  Is there trouble anywhere ?
We should never be discouraged,
  Take it to the Lord in prayer.

Can we find a Friend so faithful,
  Who will all our sorrows share ?
Jesus knows our every weakness,
  Take it to the Lord in prayer.

3 Are we weak and heavy laden,
  Cumbered with a load of care?
Precious Saviour, still our refuge,—
  Take it to the Lord in prayer.
Do thy friends despise, forsake thee?
  Take it to the Lord in prayer,
In His arms He'll take and shield thee
  Thou wilt find a solace there.

(CONSECRATION.)

Rev. H. Bonar.

KITTREDGE.

HORATIUS BONAR, D. D., 1850.

FRANZ ABT. Arr. by H. P. M.

SOLO OR DUET. GIRLS. SOLO OR DUET.

1. I heard the voice of Je-sus say, Come, un-to Me and rest; Lay down, thou weary one, lay down
2. I heard the voice of Je-sus say, Be - hold, I free-ly give The liv - ing wa - ter; thirs-ty one,
3. I heard the voice of Je-sus say, I   am this dark world's light; Look un-to Me, thy morn shall rise,

BOYS. FULL CHORUS.

Thy head up - on My breast. I came to Je - sus as   I   was, Wea-ry, and worn, and
Stoop down and drink, and live. I came to Je - sus, and I   drank Of that life - giv - ing
And all   thy day be bright. I looked to Je - sus, and I   found In Him my Star, my

sad,   I found in Him a rest - ing place, And He, and He has made me glad.
stream, My thirst was quenched, my soul re - vived, And now, and now I live   in Him.
Sun,   And in that light of life I'll walk, Till all, till all my days are done.

(CONSECRATION.)

I STOOD OUTSIDE THE GATE.

Miss. JOSEPHINE POLLARD, 1867.   HUBERT P. MAIN, by per.

1. I stood out-side the gate, A poor, way-far-ing child; With-in my heart there beat
2. Oh, "Mercy!" loud I cried, "Now give me rest from sin!" "I will," a voice re-plied;
3. In Mer-cy's guise I knew The Saviour long a-bused, Who of-ten sought my heart,

A tem-pest loud and wild; A fear oppressed my soul, That I might be *too late*;
And Mer-cy let me in; She bound my bleeding wounds, And soothed my heart, opprest;
And wept when I re-fused; Oh! what a blest re-turn For all my years of sin!

And oh, I trembled sore, And prayed outside the gate, And prayed out-side the gate.
She washed a-way my guilt And gave me peace and rest, And gave me peace and rest.
I stood out-side the gate, And Je-sus let me in, And Je-sus let me in.

(CONSECRATION.)

Words arranged.

B. M. M.

. There is a door that o - pens wide, And thro' it brightly gleaming, Come rays of love from
. Yes, Christ is made the door for all Who heavenly joys are seeking; Oh, that my heart would
. "I am the door,"—'tis Je - sus' word That points the way to heaven; Oh, cleanse my heart, mos

CHORUS.

Je - sus' side, His mer - cy still re - veal - ing. Oh, wondrous mer - cy! Can it be, That
heed His call, While kindly He is speak-ing.
precious Lord, And show my sins for - giv - en.

Christ is made the door for me, For me, for me, Christ is the door for me.

(CONSECRATION.)

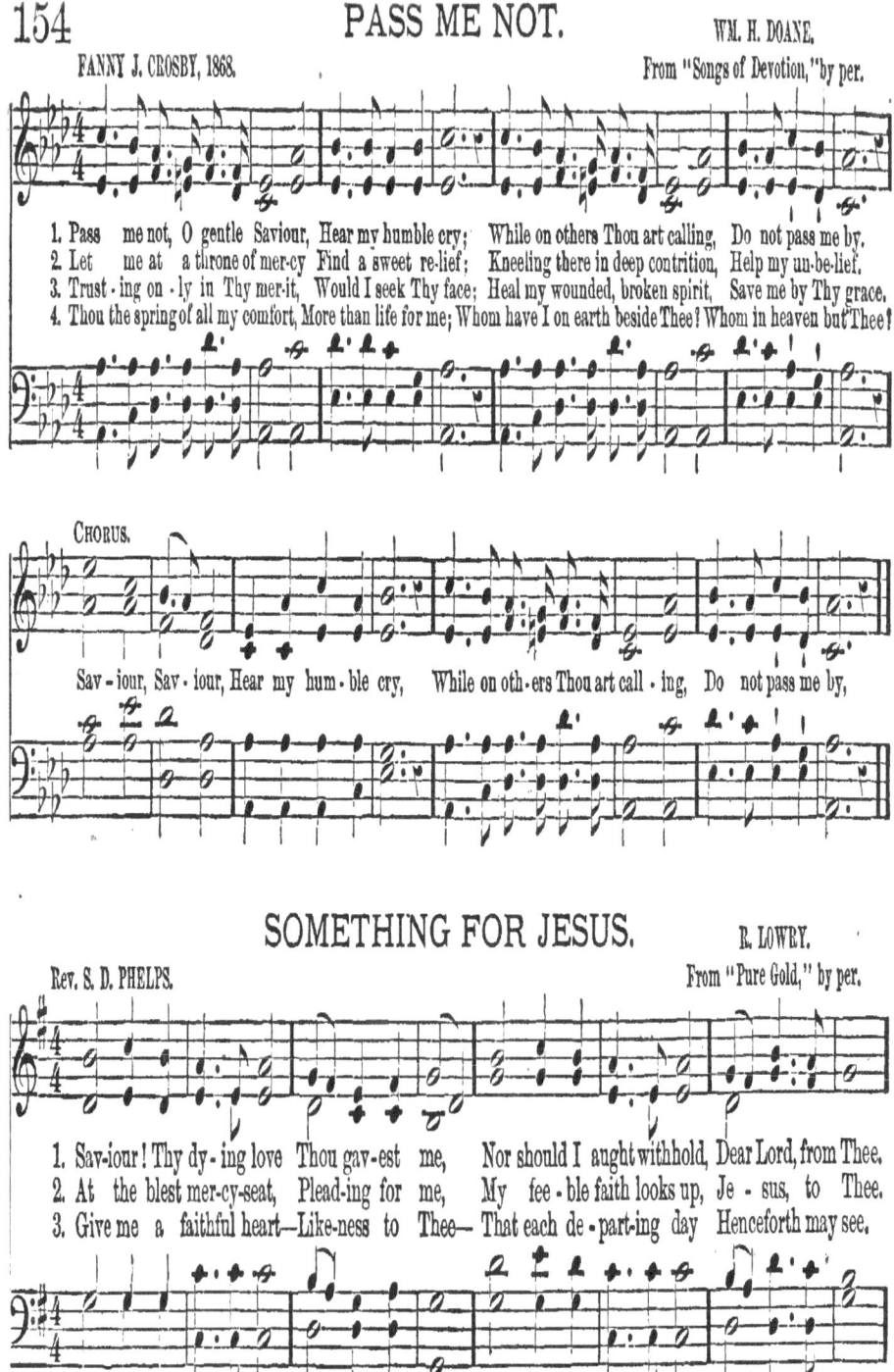

154

PASS ME NOT.

FANNY J. CROSBY, 1868.

WM. H. DOANE,
From "Songs of Devotion," by per.

1. Pass me not, O gentle Saviour, Hear my humble cry; While on others Thou art calling, Do not pass me by.
2. Let me at a throne of mer-cy Find a sweet re-lief; Kneeling there in deep contrition, Help my un-be-lief.
3. Trust-ing on-ly in Thy mer-it, Would I seek Thy face; Heal my wounded, broken spirit, Save me by Thy grace.
4. Thou the spring of all my comfort, More than life for me; Whom have I on earth beside Thee? Whom in heaven but Thee!

CHORUS.

Sav-iour, Sav-iour, Hear my hum-ble cry, While on oth-ers Thou art call-ing, Do not pass me by,

SOMETHING FOR JESUS.

Rev. S. D. PHELPS.

R. LOWRY.
From "Pure Gold," by per.

1. Sav-iour! Thy dy-ing love Thou gav-est me, Nor should I aught withhold, Dear Lord, from Thee.
2. At the blest mer-cy-seat, Plead-ing for me, My fee-ble faith looks up, Je-sus, to Thee.
3. Give me a faithful heart—Like-ness to Thee— That each de-part-ing day Henceforth may see.

(CONSECRATION.)

In love my soul would bow, My heart ful-fill its vow, Some off'ring bring Thee now, Something for Thee.
Help me the cross to bear, Thy wondrous love declare, Some song to raise, or pray'r, Something for Thee.
Some work of love be-gun, Some deed of kindness done, Some wand'rer sought and won, Something for Thee.

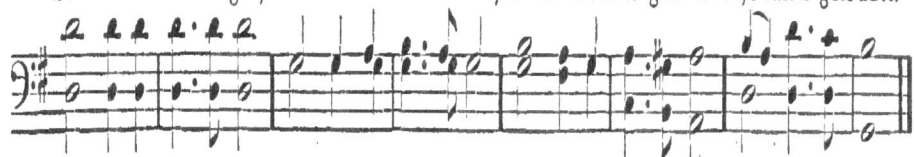

MORE LOVE TO THEE.

Mrs. E. PRENTISS.

WM. H. DOANE.
From "Songs of Devotion, by per.

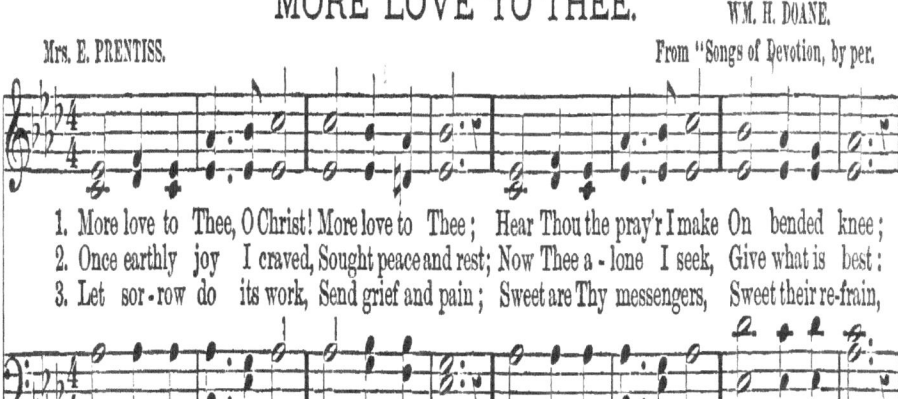

1. More love to Thee, O Christ! More love to Thee; Hear Thou the pray'r I make On bended knee;
2. Once earthly joy I craved, Sought peace and rest; Now Thee a-lone I seek, Give what is best:
3. Let sor-row do its work, Send grief and pain; Sweet are Thy messengers, Sweet their re-frain,

This is my earnest plea, More love, O Christ, to Thee, More love to Thee! More love to Thee!
This all my pray'r shall be, More love, O Christ, to Thee, More love to Thee! More love to Thee!
When they can sing with me,,—More love, O Christ, to Thee, More love to Thee! More love to Thee!

(CONSECRATION.)

JESUS, MY ALL.

FANNY J. CROSBY, 1865.   A. BOIELDIEU.

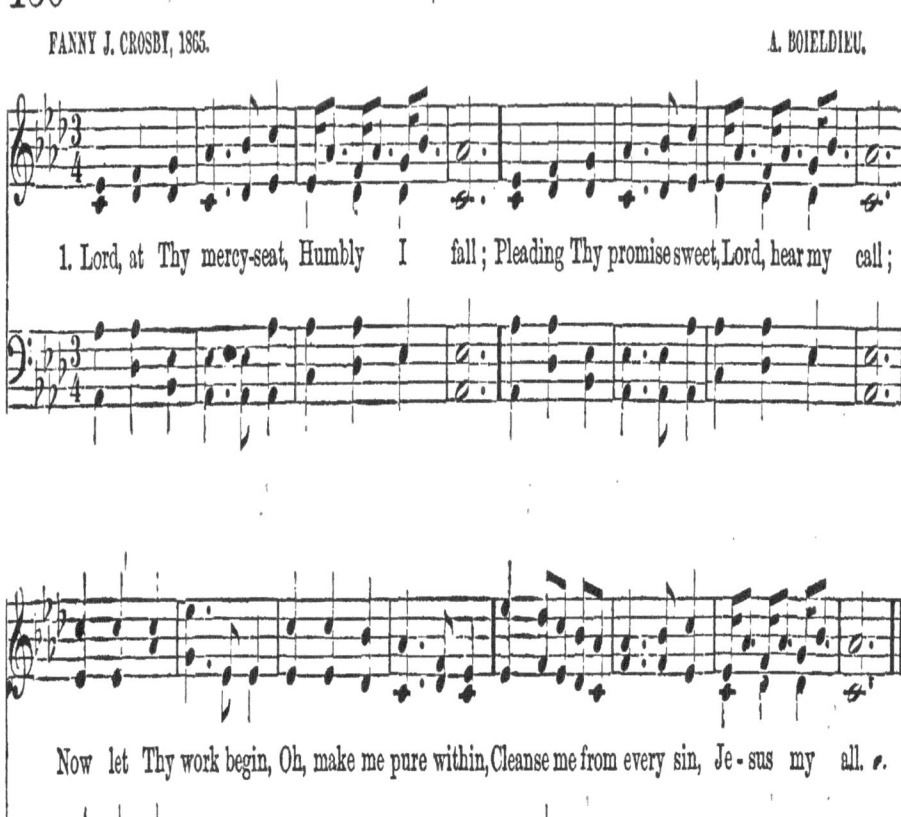

1. Lord, at Thy mercy-seat, Humbly I fall; Pleading Thy promise sweet, Lord, hear my call;

Now let Thy work begin, Oh, make me pure within, Cleanse me from every sin, Je-sus my all.

2 Tears of repentant grief
  Silently fall;
Help Thou my unbelief,
  Hear Thou my call.
Oh, how I pine for Thee!
'Tis all my hope, and plea:
Jesus has died for me,
  Jesus, my all.

3 Hark! how the words of love
  Tenderly fall,
Ere to the realms above,
  Heard is my call;
Now every doubt has flown,
Broken my heart of stone,
Lord, I am Thine alone.
  Jesus, my all.

4 Still at Thy mercy-seat
  Humbly I fall;
Pleading Thy promise sweet,
  Heard is my call.
Faith wings my soul to Thee;
This all my hope shall be,
Jesus has died for me,
  Jesus, my all.

(CONSECRATION.)

THE CROSS! THE CROSS! 8s & 7s.

Rev. J. H. S. Rev. J. H. STOCKTON, by per.

1. The cross! the cross! the blood-stained cross! The hallow'd cross I see! Reminding me of precious blood That
2. The cross! the cross! the heavy cross, The Saviour bore for me, Which bowed Him to the earth with grief, On

CHORUS. *Slow and soft.*

once was shed for me. Oh, the blood, the precious blood! That Jesus shed for me Up-on the cross, in
sad Mount Cal-va-ry.

rit.

crim-son flood, Just now by faith I see.

3 How light! how light! this precious cross,
Presented to my view:
And while, with care, I take it up,
Behold the crown my due.

4 The crown! the crown! the glorious crown!
The crown of victory!
The crown of life! it shall be mine
When Jesus I shall see.

SECOND HYMN. *(Sing music of chorus to second half of verses.)*

1 APPROACH, my soul! the mercy-seat,
Where Jesus answers prayer:
There humbly fall before His feet,
For none can perish there.
Thy promise is my only plea,
With this I venture nigh:
Thou callest burdened souls to Thee,
And such, O Lord! am I.

2 Be Thou my shield and hiding-place,
That, sheltered near Thy side,
I may my fierce accuser face,
And tell Him—"Thou hast died."
Oh! wondrous Love—to bleed and die,
To bear the cross and shame,
That guilty sinners, such as I,
Might plead Thy gracious name.

John Newton, 1779.

(CONSECRATION.)

TRUSTING IN THE WORD.

HARRY SANDERS.

J. C. MORGAN, M. D. 1874.

From "Brightest and Best," by per.

1. All my doubts I give to Je-sus, I've His gracious promise heard; I shall nev-er be con-
2. All my sin I lay on Je-sus, He doth wash me in His blood; He will keep me pure and

REFRAIN.

found-ed, I am trust-ing in His word. Trust-ing, trust-ing, trust-ing in His
ho-ly, He will bring me home to God.

word, Trust-ing, trust-ing, trust-ing in His word.

3 All my fears I give to Jesus,
  Rests my weary soul on Him;
Though my way be hid in darkness,
  Never can my light grow dim.

4 All in all I have in Jesus,
  Poor, yet rich as cherubim;
Ignorant and full of weakness,
  Heaven's own store I find in Him.

(CONSECRATION.)

COME THOU FOUNT.

(260) Christian Songs, 149. Key E. ♭.

1 COME, Thou Fount of every blessing,
Tune my heart to sing Thy grace;
Streams of mercy, never ceasing,
Call for songs of loudest praise.
CHO. I love Jesus, Hallelujah,
I love Jesus, yes, I do,
I do love Jesus, He's my Saviour,
Jesus smiles, and loves me too.

2 Teach me some melodious sonnet,
Sung by flaming tongues above;
Praise the mount, I'm fixed upon it;
Mount of Thy redeeming love.

3 Jesus sought me, when a stranger,
Wandering from the fold of God;
He, to rescue me from danger,
Interposed His precious blood.

4 Prone to wander,—Lord, I feel it,
Prone to leave the God I love;
Here's my heart—O, take and seal it,
Seal it for Thy courts above.

COME, THOU FOUNT.

(261) Christian Songs, 149. Key E. ♭.

1 "MERCY, O Thou Son of David!"
Thus the blind Bartimeus prayed,
"Others by the word are saved;
Now to me afford Thine aid."
Many for his crying chid him,
But he called the louder still;
Till the gracious Saviour bid him
"Come, and ask Me what you will."

2 Money was not what he wanted,
Though by begging used to live;
But he asked, and Jesus granted,
Alms which none but He could give.
"Lord, remove this grievous blindness,
Let my eyes behold the day!"
Straight he saw, and, won by kindness,
Followed Jesus in the way.

3 Oh! methinks I hear him praising,
Publishing to all around;
"Friends, is not my case amazing?
What a Saviour I have found!
O that all the blind but knew Him,
And would be advised by me!
Surely they would hasten to Him,
He would cause them all to see."

WE ARE COMING BLESSED SAVIOUR.

(262) Christian Songs, 91. Key D.

WE are coming, blessed Saviour,
We hear Thy gentle voice,
We would be Thine for ever,
And in Thy love rejoice.
CHO. We are coming, we are coming,
We are coming, blessed Saviour,
We are coming, we are coming,
We hear Thy gentle voice.

2 We are coming, blessed Saviour,
To meet that happy band,
And sing with them for ever,
And in Thy presence stand.

(CONSECRATION.)

3 We are coming, blessed Saviour,
Our Father's house we see—
A glorious mansion ever,
For souls from sin set free.

4 We are coming, blessed Saviour,
To crown our Jesus King,
And then with angels ever,
His praises we will sing.

I'M A PILGRIM GOING HOME.

(263) Christian Songs, 162. Key D.

1 CHRISTIANS, I am on my journey!
Ere I reach the narrow sea,
I would tell the wondrous story,
What the Lord has done for me.
CHO. Glory, glory, hallelujah,
Though a stranger here I roam,
I am on my way to Zion,
I'm a pilgrim going home.

2 I was lost, but Jesus found me,
Taught my heart to seek His face;
From a wild and lonely desert,
Brought me to His fold of grace.

3 Now my soul with rapture glowing,
Sings aloud His pard'ning love;
Looks beyond a world of sorrow,
To the pilgrim's home above.

4 I shall yet behold my Saviour,
When the day of life is o'er,
I shall cast my crown before Him,
I shall praise Him evermore.

SWEET THE MOMENTS. 8s & 7s.

WALTER SHIRLEY, 1771.

MOZART, arr.

1. Sweet the moments, rich in bless-ing, Which be - fore the cross I spend; Life, and health, and
2. Tru - ly bless-ed is this sta - tion. Low be - fore His cross to lie; While I see di -

peace pos-sess-ing, From the sin-ner's dy - ing Friend. Love and grief my heart di - vid-ing, With my
vine com-pas-sion Beaming in His gra-cious eye. Here I'll sit, for ev - er viewing, Mer - cy

tears His feet I'll bathe; Con-stant still, in faith a - bid-ing, Life de - riv - ing from His death.
streaming in His blood; Pre-cious drops my soul be - dew-ing, Plead, and claim my peace with God.

(CONSECRATION.)

ALL TO CHRIST I OWE.

(265) Christian Songs, 182. Key D.

1 I HEAR the Saviour say,
"Thy strength indeed is small;
O child of weakness, pray,
I am thine All in All."
Cho. Jesus paid it all;
All to Him I owe!
Sin had left a crimson stain;
He washed it white as snow.

2 Lord, now indeed I find
Thy word, and Thine alone,
Can change the leper's spots,
And melt the heart of stone.

3 But nothing good have I,
Whereby Thy grace to claim—
I'll wash me in the blood,
The blood of Calvary's Lamb.

4 When from my dying bed,
My ransomed soul shall rise,
Then "Jesus paid it all,"
I'll sing beyond the skies.

5 And when before the throne,
I stand in Him complete,
I'll lay my honors down,
All down, at Jesus' feet.

LEBANON. S. M.

(266) Christian Songs, 198. Key F.

1 I WAS a wandering sheep,
I did not love the fold:
I did not hear my Shepherd's voice,
I would not be controlled;

I was a wayward child,
I did not love my home,
I did not love my Father's voice,
I loved afar to roam.

2 The Shepherd sought His sheep,
The Father sought His child;
They followed me o'er vale and hill,
O'er deserts waste and wild.
They found me nigh to death,
Famished, and faint, and lone;
They bound me in the bands of love,
They saved the wandering one.

3 Jesus my Shepherd is,
'Twas He that loved my soul,
'Twas He that washed me in His blood
'Twas He that made me whole:
'Twas He that sought the lost,
That found the wandering sheep,
'Twas He that brought me to the fold—
'Tis He that still doth keep.

CROSS AND CROWN. C. M.

(267) Bradbury Trio, 85. Key B♭.

1 MUST Jesus bear the cross alone,
And all the world go free?
No, there's a cross for every one,
And there's a cross for me.

2 How happy are the saints above,
Who once went sorrowing here;
But now they taste unmingled love,
And joy without a tear.

3 The consecrated cross I'll bear,
Till death shall set me free,
(CONSECRATION.)

And then go home my crown to wear—
For there's a crown for me.

MARTYRDOM. C. M.

(268) Christian Songs, 201. Key A♭.

1 O THOU, whose tender mercy hears
Contrition's humble sigh;
Whose hand, indulgent, wipes the tears
From sorrow's weeping eye—

2 See, low before Thy throne of grace,
A wretched wanderer mourn;
Hast Thou not bid me seek Thy face?
Hast Thou not said—"Return?"

3 And shall my guilty fears prevail?
To drive me from Thy feet?
O let not this dear refuge fail,
This only safe retreat.

DENNIS. S. M.

(269) Bradbury Trio, 225. Key F.

1 How gentle God's commands!
How kind His precepts are!
Come, cast your burden on the Lord,
And trust His constant care.

2 Beneath His watchful eye,
His saints securely dwell;
That hand that bears all nature up,
Shall guard His children well.

3 His goodness stands approved,
Unchanged from day to day;
I'll drop my burden at His feet,
And bear a song away.

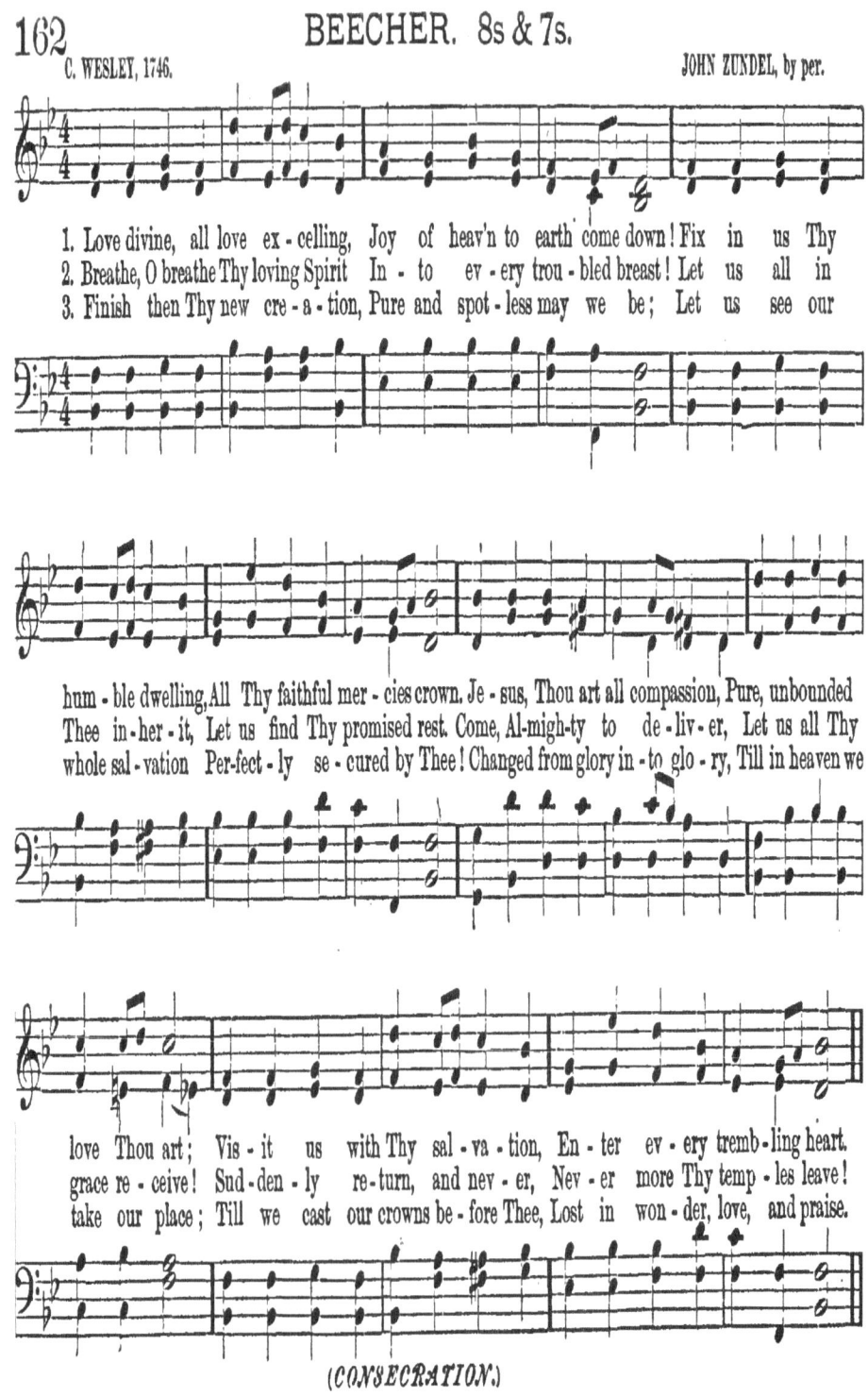

162 BEECHER. 8s & 7s.

C. WESLEY, 1746.

JOHN ZUNDEL, by per.

1. Love divine, all love ex - celling, Joy of heav'n to earth come down! Fix in us Thy
2. Breathe, O breathe Thy loving Spirit In - to ev - ery trou - bled breast! Let us all in
3. Finish then Thy new cre - a - tion, Pure and spot - less may we be; Let us see our

hum - ble dwelling, All Thy faithful mer - cies crown. Je - sus, Thou art all compassion, Pure, unbounded
Thee in - her - it, Let us find Thy promised rest. Come, Al - migh-ty to de - liv - er, Let us all Thy
whole sal - vation Per-fect - ly se - cured by Thee! Changed from glory in - to glo - ry, Till in heaven we

love Thou art; Vis - it us with Thy sal - va - tion, En - ter ev - ery tremb - ling heart.
grace re - ceive! Sud - den - ly re - turn, and nev - er, Nev - er more Thy temp - les leave!
take our place; Till we cast our crowns be - fore Thee, Lost in won - der, love, and praise.

(CONSECRATION.)

WOODWORTH. L. M.

(271) Bradbury Trio, 139. Key D.

1 JUST as I am—without one plea,
  But that Thy blood was shed for me,
  And that Thou bid'st me come to Thee,
    O Lamb of God, I come! I come!

2 Just as I am—and waiting not
  To rid my soul of one dark blot, [spot,
  To Thee whose blood can cleanse each
    O Lamb of God, I come! I come!

3 Just as I am—though tossed about
  With many a conflict, many a doubt,
  "Fightings and fears, within, without,"
    O Lamb of God, I come! I come!

4 Just as I am—poor, wretched, blind;
  Sight, riches, healing of the mind,
  Yea, all I need, in Thee to find,
    O Lamb of God, I come! I come!

5 Just as I am—Thou wilt receive;
  Wilt welcome, pardon, cleanse, relieve;
  Because Thy promise I believe,
    O Lamb of God, I come! I come!

6 Just as I am—Thy love unknown
  Has broken every barrier down;
  Now, to be Thine, yea, Thine alone,
    O Lamb of God, I come! I come!

HAPPINESS. 11s & 9s.

(272) Plym. Coll., 232. Key F.

1 OH! how happy are they
  Who the Saviour obey,
And have laid up their treasure above:
  Oh! what tongue can express
  The sweet comfort and peace
Of a soul in its earliest love?

2 It was heaven below
  My Redeemer to know,
And the angels could do nothing more
  Than to fall at His feet,
  And the story repeat,
And the Lover of sinners adore.

3 Jesus all the day long
  Was my joy and my song:
O that all His salvation may see;
  He hath loved me, I cried,
  He hath suffered and died,
To redeem even rebels like me.

———

NAOMI. C. M.

(273) Bradbury Trio, 145. Key D.

1 PROSTRATE, dear Jesus! at Thy feet
  A guilty rebel lies;
And upward to the mercy-seat
  Presumes to lift his eyes.

2 If tears of sorrow would suffice
  To pay the debt I owe,
Tears should from both my weeping eyes
  In ceaseless torrents flow.

(CONSECRATION.)

3 But no such sacrifice I plead
  To expiate my guilt;
No tears but those which Thou hast shed—
  No blood, but Thou hast spilt.

4 Think of Thy sorrows, dearest Lord!
  And all my sins forgive:
Justice will well approve the word
  That bids the sinner live.

———

THE SOLID ROCK. 8s.

(274) Bradbury Trio, 335. Key G.

1 My hope is built on nothing less
  Than Jesus' blood and righteousness;
  I dare not trust the sweetest frame,
  But wholly lean on Jesus' name:
    On Christ the Solid Rock, I stand;
    All other ground is sinking sand.

2 When darkness seems to veil His face,
  I rest on His unchanging grace;
  In every high and stormy gale,
  My anchor holds within the vail:
    On Christ, the Solid Rock, I stand;
    All other ground is sinking sand.

3 His oath, His covenant, and blood,
  Support me in the whelming flood:
  When all around my soul gives way,
  He then is all my hope and stay:
    On Christ, the Solid Rock, I stand;
    All other ground is sinking sand.

WHITER THAN SNOW.

JAMES NICHOLSON.   Wm. G. FISCHER, 1872, by per.

1. Dear Je - sus, I long to be per - fect - ly whole; I want Thee for - ev - er to live in my soul;
2. Dear Je - sus, come down from Thy throne in the skies, And help me to make a complete sac - ri - fice;
3. Dear Je - sus, for this I most humbly en - treat; I wait, blessed Lord, at Thy sac - ri - ficed feet,
4. The blessing by faith, I re - ceive from a - bove; O glo - ry! my soul is made perfect in love;

Break down ev-ery i - dol, cast out every foe; Now, wash me, and I shall be whiter than snow.
I give up my - self, and what-ev - er I know—Now wash me, and I shall be whiter than snow.
By faith, for my cleansing, I see the blood flow—Now wash me, and I shall be whiter than snow.
My pray'r has prevailed, and this moment I know—The blood is applied, I am whiter than snow.

CHORUS.

Whit - er than snow, yes, whit - er than snow; Now wash me, and I shall be whit - er than snow.

(CONSECRATION.)

DOVER. S. M.

(276) "Coronation," 178. Key E.

1 Give to the winds thy fears:
  Hope, and be undismay'd;
God hears thy sighs, and counts thy tears,
  God shall lift up thy head.

2 Through waves, through clouds and
  He gently clears thy way; [storms,
Wait thou His time: so shall this night
  Soon end in joyous day.

3 Far, far above thy thought
  His counsel shall appear,
When fully He the work hath wrought,
  That caused thy needless fear.

4 What though thou rulest not!
  Yet heaven, and earth, and hell,
Proclaim God sitteth on the throne,
  And ruleth all things well!

RETREAT. L. M.

(277) Christian Songs, 198. Key B♭.

1 From every stormy wind that blows,
From every swelling tide of woes,
There is a calm, a sure retreat,
'Tis found beneath the mercy-seat.

2 There is a place where Jesus sheds
The oil of gladness on our heads;
A place than all besides more sweet,
It is the blood-bought mercy-seat.

3 There is a scene where spirits blend,
Where friend holds fellowship with
  friend,
Though sundered far, by faith they meet
Around one common mercy-seat.

UXBRIDGE. L. M.

(278) Coronation, 129. Key F.

1 I send the joys of earth away;
  Away, ye tempters of the mind,
False as the smooth, deceitful sea,
  And empty as the whistling wind.

2 Your streams were floating me along,
  Down to the gulf of dark despair;
And while I listened to your song,
  Your streams had e'en conveyed me
    [there.

3 Lord, I adore Thy matchless grace,
  Which warned me of that dark abyss,
Which drew me from those treacherous
  And bade me seek superior bliss. [seas,

4 Now to the shining realms above,
  I stretch my hands and glance my eyes;
O for the pinions of a dove,
  To bear me to the upper skies!

MEROE. L. M.

(279) Bradbury Trio, 325, Key G.

1 Jesus! and shall it ever be,
A mortal man ashamed of Thee!
Ashamed of Thee, whom angels praise—
Whose glories shine thro' endless days?

2 Ashamed of Jesus! sooner far
Let evening blush to own a star:
He sheds the beams of light divine
O'er this benighted soul of mine.

3 Ashamed of Jesus! that dear Friend
On whom my hopes of heaven depend:
No: when I blush, be this my shame,
That I no more revere His name.

4 Ashamed of Jesus! Yes, I may,
When I've no guilt to wash away,—

No tear to wipe, no good to crave,
No fears to hush, no soul to save.

5 Till then—nor is my boasting vain—
Till then I boast a Saviour slain!
And O may this my glory be,
Jesus is not ashamed of me!

JESUS DEAR.

(280) Fresh Laurels, 31. Key A.

1 Jesus dear, I come to Thee,
  Thou hast said I may;
Tell me what my life should be,
  Take my sins away;
Jesus, dear, I learn of Thee
  In Thy word divine:
Ev'ry promise there I see,
  May I call it mine.

Cho. Jesus hear my humble song;
  I am weak, but Thou art strong;
  Gently lead my soul along;
  Help me come to Thee.

2 Jesus, dear, I long for Thee,
  Long Thy peace to know,
Grant those purer joys to me,
  Earth can ne'er bestow:
Jesus, dear, I cling to Thee;
  When my heart is sad,
Thou wilt kindly speak to me,
  Thou wilt make me glad.

3 Jesus, dear, I trust in Thee,
  Trust Thy tender love;
There's a happy home for me,
  With Thy saints above;
Jesus, I would come to Thee,
  Thou hast said I may;
Tell me what my life should be,
  Take my sins away.

(CONSECRATION).

JESUS, WE THY LAMBS WOULD BE.

Dr. C. A. MARVIN.

1. Je - sus, we Thy lambs would be, Hum-bly we would fol-low Thee, Wait-ing for the joy-ful day,
2. Now the field with grain is white, Now the day is dawning bright—Brighter far the sky will be,
3. May we wait, and watch, and pray, For the com-ing of that day, When the wheat shall sifted be,

CHORUS.

When all care will pass a - way. When the reap-ing time shall come, And an - gels shout the
When our Mas - ter we shall see.
And the chaff be driv'n from Thee,

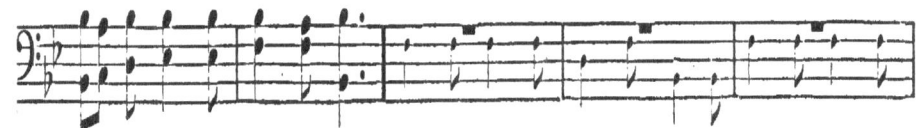

har - vest home, When the reap-ing time shall come, And An - gels shout the har - vest home.

(CONSECRATION.)

CHRISTMAS. C. M.

(283) Christian Songs, 200. Key E♭.

1 AWAKE, my soul, stretch every nerve,
    And press with vigor on :
    A heavenly race demands thy zeal,
    And an immortal crown.

2 A cloud of witnesses around
    Hold thee in full survey ;
    Forget the steps already trod,
    And onward urge thy way.

3 'Tis God's all animating voice,
    That calls thee from on high :
    'Tis His own hand presents the prize
    To thine aspiring eye.

4 Blest Saviour, introduced by Thee,
    Have I my race begun ;
    And, crowned with victory, at Thy feet
    I'll lay my honors down.

BALERMA. C. M.

(284) Bradbury Trio, 123. Key B♭.

1 AMAZING grace ; how sweet the sound
    That saved a wretch like me !
    I once was lost but now am found—
    Was blind, but now I see.

2 'Twas grace that taught my heart to
    And grace my fears relieved ;   [fear,
    How precious did that grace appear,
    The hour I first believed !

3 Thro' many dangers, toils, and snares,
    I have already come ;
    'Tis grace has brought me safe thus far,
    And grace will lead me home.

UXBRIDGE. L. M.

(285) Coronation, 129. Key F.

1 WHAT sinners value I resign ;
    Lord ! 'tis enough that Thou art mine ;
    I shall behold Thy blissful face,
    And stand complete in righteousness.

2 This life's a dream—an empty show ;
    But the bright world, to which I go,
    Hath joys substantial and sincere ;
    When shall I wake and find me there ?

3 Oh ! glorious hour !—oh ! blest abode,
    I shall be near, and like my God ;
    And flesh and sin no more control
    The sacred pleasures of the soul.

4 My flesh shall slumber in the ground,
    Till the last trumpet's joyful sound ;
    Then burst the chains with sweet surprise
    And in my Saviour's image rise.

HEBRON. L. M.

(286) Bradbury Trio, 19. Key B♭.

1 WE sing His love, who once was slain,
    Who soon o'er death revived again,
    That all His saints thro' Him might have
    Eternal conquests o'er the grave.

2 The saints who now with Jesus sleep,
    His own Almighty power shall keep
    Till dawns the bright illustrious day
    When death, itself shall die away.

3 When Jesus we in glory meet,
    Our utmost joys shall be complete ;
    When landed on that heavenly shore,
    Death and the curse will be no more.

(CONSECRATION.)

4 Hasten, dear Lord, the glorious day,
    And this delightful scene display
    When all Thy saints from death shall rise
    Raptured in bliss beyond the skies !

OLIVET. 6s. & 4s.

(287) Christian Songs, 200. Key F.

1 MY faith looks up to Thee
    Thou Lamb of Calvary,
        Saviour divine :
    Now hear me while I pray,
    Take all my guilt away,
    O let me from this day
        Be wholly Thine.

2 May Thy rich grace impart
    Strength to my fainting heart,
        My zeal inspire ;
    As Thou hast died for me,
    O may my love to Thee,
    Pure, warm, and changeless be,
        A living fire.

3 While life's dark maze I tread,
    And griefs around me spread,
        Be Thou my guide ;
    Bid darkness turn to day,
    Wipe sorrow's tears away
    Nor let me ever stray,
        From Thee aside.

4 When ends life's transient dream,
    When death's cold, sullen stream
        Shall o'er me roll ;
    Blest Saviour, then in love,
    Fear and distrust remove ;
    O, bear me safe above,
        A ransomed soul !

168

TO JESUS I WILL GO.

FANNY J. CROSBY, 1869.

W. H. DOANE.

From "Bright Jewels," by per.

1. There's a gen-tle voice within calls a-way, 'Tis a warning I have heard o'er and o'er;
But my heart is melt-ed now, I o-bey; From my Saviour I will wan-der no (Omit.) more.

2. He has promised all my sins to for-give, If I ask in sim-ple faith for His love;
In His ho-ly word I learn how to live, And to la-bor for His kingdom a-(Omit.) bove.

CHORUS.

Yes, I will go; yes, I will go; To Je-sus I will go and be saved; Yes, I will go;

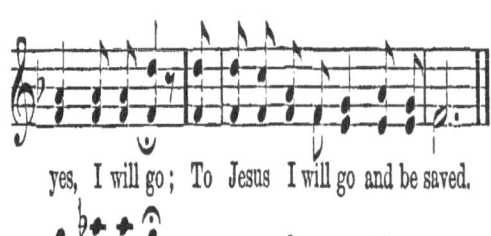

yes, I will go; To Jesus I will go and be saved.

3 I will try to bear the cross in my youth,
   And be faithful to its cause till I die;
If with cheerful step I walk in the truth,
   I shall wear a starry crown by and by.

4 Still the gentle voice within calls away,
   And its warning I have heard o'er and o'er;
But my heart is melted now, I obey;
   From my Saviour I will wander no more.

(CONSECRATION.)

THE RIFTED ROCK.

(289) Christian Songs, 61. Key G.

1 In the Rifted Rock I'm resting,
  Sure and safe from all alarm;
Storms and billows have united
  All in vain to do me harm;
In the Rifted Rock I'm resting,
  Surf is dashing at my feet,
Storm-clouds dark are o'er me hovering,
  Yet my rest is all complete.
    Cho. In the rifted Rock, &c.

2 Many a stormy sea I've traversed,
  Many a tempest-shock have known,
Have been driven, without anchor,
  On the barren shores, and lone;
Yet I now have found a haven,
  Never moved by tempest shock,
Where my soul is safe for ever,
  In the blessed Rifted Rock.

CLEANSING FOUNTAIN. C. M.

(290) Winnowed Hymns, 20. Key C.

1 There is a fountain filled with blood,
  Drawn from Immanuel's veins;
And sinners plunged beneath that flood
  Lose all their guilty stains.

2 The dying thief rejoiced to see
  That fountain in his day;
And there may I, though vile as he,
  Wash all my sins away.

3 Dear, dying Lamb, Thy precious blood
  Shall never lose its power

Till all the ransomed church of God
  Be saved to sin no more.

4 E'er since, by faith, I saw the stream
  Thy flowing wounds supply,
Redeeming love has been my theme,
  And shall be, till I die.

5 Then in a nobler, sweeter song,
  I'll sing Thy power to save,
When this poor lisping, stam'ring tongue
  Lies silent in the grave.

STATE STREET. S. M.

(291) Bradbury Trio, 71. Key B♮.

1 Blest be the tie that binds
  Our hearts in Christian love;
The fellowship of kindred minds
  Is like to that above.

2 Before our Father's throne,
  We pour our ardent prayers;
Our fears, our hopes, our aims are one—
  Our comforts and our cares.

3 We share our mutual woes;
  Our mutual burdens bear;
And often for each other flows
  The sympathizing tear.

4 When we asunder part,
  It gives us inward pain;
But we shall still be join'd in heart,
  And hope to meet again.

5 This glorious hope revives
  Our courage by the way;
While each in expectation lives,
  And longs to see the day.
    (CONSECRATION.)

MARTYRDOM. C. M.

(292) Christian Songs, 201. Key A♭.

1 O could I find from day to day,
  A nearness to my God,
Then would my hours glide sweet away,
  While leaning on His word.

2 Blest Jesus, come, and rule my heart,
  And make me wholly Thine,
That I may never more depart
  Nor grieve Thy love divine.

HAPPY DAY.

(293) Christian Songs, 198 Key G.

1 O happy day that fix'd my choice
  On Thee, my Saviour and my God!
Well may this glowing heart rejoice,
  And tell its raptures all abroad.
Cho.
Happy day, Happy day,
Here in Thy courts we'll gladly stay,
And at Thy footstool humbly pray
That Thou wouldst take our sins away;
Happy day, Happy day
When Christ shall wash our sins away.

2 O happy bond, that seals my vows
  To Him who merits all my love;
Let cheerful anthems fill His house,
  While to the sacred shrine I move.

3 Now rest, my long-divided heart,
  Fix'd on this blissful centre, rest;
Nor ever from Thy Lord depart,
  With Him of every good possessed.

THE OLD, OLD STORY.

170

Miss KATE HANKEY. 1867.

W. H. DOANE.

From "Songs of Devotion," by per.

1. Tell me the old, old sto-ry Of un-seen things a - bove, Of Je - sus and His glo - ry Of
2. Tell me the sto-ry slow-ly, That I may take it in— That won-der - ful re - demption, God's
3. Tell me the same old sto-ry, When you have cause to fear That this world's empty glo - ry Is

Je - sus and His love. Tell me the sto-ry sim-ply, As to a lit - tle child,
rem - e - dy for sin. Tell me the sto-ry of-ten, For I for-get so soon!
cost - ing me too dear. Yes, and when that world's glo-ry Is dawn-ing on my soul,

CHORUS.

For I am weak and wea-ry, And help-less and de - filed. Tell me the old, old sto-ry,
The "ear-ly dew" of morn-ing Has passed a - way at noon.
Tell me the old, old sto - ry: "Christ Je - sus makes thee whole."

Tell me the old, old sto-ry, Tell me the old, old sto - ry Of Je - sus and His love.

(CONSECRATION.)

I LOVE TO TELL THE STORY.

Miss KATE HANKEY. 1867.　　　　　　　　　　　　WM. G. FISCHER. 1869. by per.

1. I love to tell the sto - ry; Of unseen things above, Of Je - sus and His glo-ry Of Je - sus and His
2. I love to tell the sto - ry; More wonderful it seems Than all the golden fancies Of all our gold-en
3. I love to tell the sto - ry; 'Tis pleasant to re - peat What seems, each time I tell it, More wonder-ful-ly

love. I love to tell the sto - ry, Be - cause I know it's true; It sa - tis-fies my longings, As
dreams. I love to tell the sto - ry; It did so much for me! And that is just the rea - son I
sweet. I love to tell the sto - ry; For some have nev-er heard The message of sal - va-tion From

CHORUS.

noth-ing else can do. I love to tell the sto - ry, 'Twill be my theme in glo - ry, To
tell it now to thee.
God's own ho - ly word.

tell the old, old sto - ry Of Je - sus and His love.

4 I love to tell the story;
　For those who know it best
Seem hungering and thirsting
　To hear it like the rest.
And when, in scenes of glory,
　I sing the New, New Song,
'Twill be the Old, Old Story
　That I have loved so long!

(CONSECRATION.)

ANGRY WORDS.

H. R. PALMER, 1868, by per.

1. An - gry words! Oh let them nev - er From the tongue un - bri - dled slip; May the heart's best im - pulse
2. Love is much too pure and ho - ly; Friendship is too sa - cred far, For a moment's reckless
3. An - gry words are light - ly spo - ken; Bit - terest tho'ts are rash - ly stirred: Brightest links of life are

CHORUS.

ev - er Check them, e'er they soil the lip. "Love one an - oth - er," Thus saith the Sav-iour, Children o -
fol - ly Thus to des - o - late and mar.
bro - ken By a sin - gle an - gry word.

"Love each oth - er, Love each oth-er,"

bey thy Father's blest command; "Love one another," Thus saith the Saviour, Children obey His blest command.

'Tis thy Father's blest command: "Love each other, Love each other," 'Tis His blest command.

(CONSECRATION.)

YIELD NOT TO TEMPTATION.

H. R. PALMER 1868.

H. R. PALMER, by per.

1 Yield not to temptation, For weakness is sin, Each vict'ry will help us, Some other to win;
2. Shun e·vil companions, Bad language dis·dain, God's name hold in rev'rence, Nor take it in vain;
3. To him that o'er-cometh God giv·eth a crown, Thro' faith we shall conquer, Tho' often cast down;

Fight manful·ly on·ward, Dark passions sub·due, Look ever to Je·sus, He'll carry you through.
Be thoughtful and earnest, Kind-hearted and true, Look ever to Je·sus, He'll carry you through.
He who is the Saviour, Our strength will re·new, Look ever to Je·sus, He'll carry you through.

Chorus.

Ask the Saviour to help you, Comfort, strengthen and keep you, He is willing to aid you, He will carry you through.

(CONSECRATION.)

FANNY J. CROSBY, 1864.
From "Golden Shower." WM. B. BRADBURY, by per.

1. Thro' the new Je - ru - sa - lem, Lined with fair-est flow-ers, Flows a pure and crys-tal stream,
2. There are saints in robes of white, Who have gone be-fore us; With the an-gels they u - nite,
3. They who long the cross have borne Cast their crowns before Him; Mar-tyrs with their harps of gold,

Wat'ring the heavenly bow-ers; On its banks we hope to stand, Close by the beauti-ful riv - er,
Swelling the heavenly cho - rus; And with them we hope to stand, Close by the beauti-ful riv - er,
Sing-ing with joy, a - dore Him; Soon a-long the verdant banks, Close by the beauti-ful riv - er,

CHORUS.

There to join the ransomed band, Singing and praising for ev - er. Singing and praising for ev - er,
There to join the ransomed band, Singing and praising for ev - er.
We shall hail our Saviour King, Singing and praising for ev - er.

(HEAVEN.)

Close by the beau-ti - ful riv - er, There to join the ransomed band, Singing and praising for ev - er.

HEAR OUR PRAYER.

FANNY J. CROSBY, 1875.

From "Brightest and Best," by per. WM. H. DOANE.

Dear Fa . . . . ther,

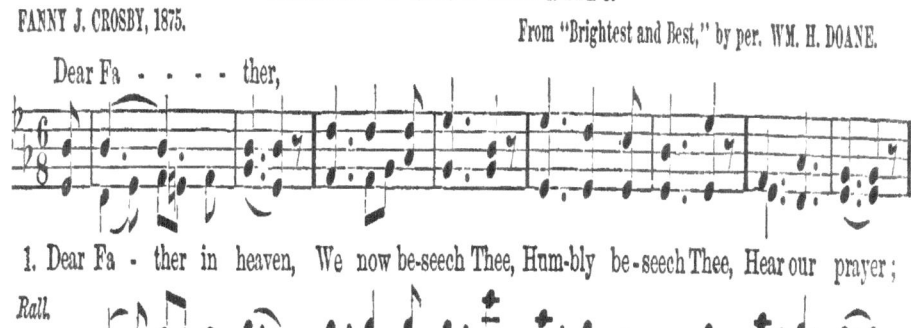

1. Dear Fa - ther in heaven, We now be-seech Thee, Hum-bly be-seech Thee, Hear our prayer;

Rall.

Hum-bly be-seech Thee, Hear our prayer, Hear our prayer.

2 O grant us Thy blessing,
   We now beseech Thee;
   Father, dear Father,
   Hear our prayer.

3 Behold us in mercy,
   Guide and defend us;
   Father, dear Father,
   Hear our prayer.

(HEAVEN.)

Rev. Ch. BEECHER, 1855.

MT. BLANC.

J. HUSBAND, 1798.

1. We are on our journey home, Where Christ our Lord is gone; We shall meet around His throne, When He
2. We can see that dis - tant home, Though clouds run dark between ; Faith views the radiant dome, And a

makes His peo - ple one In the new, in the new, In the new Je - ru - sa - lem.
lus - tre flash-es keen From the new, from the new, From the new Je - ru - sa - lem.

3 O glory shining far
   From the never-setting sun !
   O trembling morning star !
   Our journey's almost done
   To the new Jerusalem.

4 O holy, heavenly home !
   O, rest eternal there !
   When shall the exiles come,
   Where they cease from earthly
   In the new Jerusalem. [care,

5 Our hearts are breaking now,
   Those mansions fair to see ;
   O Lord ! Thy heavens bow,
   And raise us up with Thee
   To the new Jerusalem.

E. MILLS, 1829.

WE'LL WAIT TILL JESUS COMES.

Dr. Wm. MILLER, 1854.

1. O land of rest for thee I sigh, When will the moment come, When I shall lay my armor by, And dwell in peace at home.

(HEAVEN.)

CHORUS.

We'll wait till Jesus comes, We'll wait till Jesus comes, We'll wait till Jesus comes, And we'll be gather'd home.

We'll wait till Jesus comes, We'll wait till Jesus comes,

2 To Jesus Christ I'll flee for rest ;
  He bids me cease to roam,
  And lean for succor on His breast,
  Till He conducts me home.

3 I'll seek at once my Saviour's side,
  No more my steps shall roam ;
  With Him I'll brave life's stormy tide
  And reach my heavenly home.

Mrs. M. S. B. DANA, 1841.

I'M A PILGRIM.

"Buona Notte," ITALIAN MELODY.

FINE.

1. I'm a pil-grim, and I'm a stranger: I can tar-ry, I can tar-ry but a night. Do not de-tain me, for I am
D.C.—I'm a pil-grim, and I'm a stranger: I can tar-ry, I can tar-ry but a night. To where the streamlets, &c.

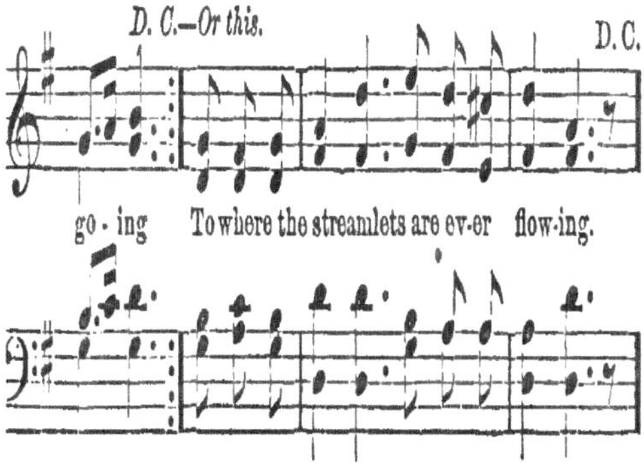

D. C.—Or this.

D. C.

go - ing   To where the streamlets are ev-er flow-ing.

2 There the sunbeams are ever shining,
  And I'm longing, I am longing for the sight ;
  Within a country, unknown and dreary,
  I have been wand'ring, forlorn and weary.

3 Of that country to which I'm going,
  My Redeemer, my Redeemer is the light :
  There is no sorrow, nor any sighing,
  Nor any sin there, nor any dying.

(HEAVEN.)

HARK! HARK, MY SOUL.

FRED W. FABER. 1863.

Rev. JOHN B. DYKES.

1. Hark! hark, my soul; An - gel - ic songs are swell-ing O'er earth's green fields, and ocean's wave-beat shore,
2. On - ward we go, for still we hear them sing-ing, "Come, wea-ry souls, for Je - sus bids you come:"
3. Far, far a - way, like bells at evening peal-ing, The voice of Je - sus sounds o'er land and sea,

How sweet the truth those blessed strains are tell - ing Of that new life when sin shall be no more.
And, through the dark its ech - oes sweet-ly ring-ing, The mu - sic of the Gos - pel leads us home.
And lad - en souls by thousands meekly steal-ing, Kind Shepherd, turn their wea-ry steps to Thee.

CHORUS.

An - gels of Je - sus, An - gels of light, Sing - ing to wel - come the pilgrims of the night,

Sing - ing to wel - come the pil - grims, the pil - grims of the night. A - men, A - men.

(HEAVEN.)

SWEET HOME.

Rev. DAVID DENHAM. 1826.   Sir HENRY ROWLEY BISHOP. 1829.

1. 'Mid scenes of con-fu-sion and creature complaints, How sweet to my soul is communion with saints;
2. Sweet bonds that u-nite all the children of peace! And thrice precious Je-sus, whose love cannot cease!

To find at the banquet of mer-cy there's room, And feel in the presence of Je-sus at
Tho' oft from Thy presence in sad-ness I roam, I long to be-hold Thee in glo-ry at

home. Home, home, sweet, sweet home, Pre-pare me, dear Sav-iour, for glo-ry, my home.
home, Home, home, sweet, sweet home, I long to be-hold Thee, in glo-ry, at home.

3 I sigh from this body of sin to be free,
  Which hinders my joy and communion with Thee;
  Though now my temptation like billows may foam,
  All, all will be peace, when I'm with Thee at home.

4 While here in the valley of conflict I stay,
  O give me submission, and strength as my day;
  In all my affliction to Thee would I come,
  Rejoicing in hope of my glorious home.

5 Whate'er Thou deniest, O give me Thy grace,
  The Spirit's sure witness,—the smiles of Thy face;
  Endue me with patience to wait at Thy throne,
  And find, even now, a sweet foretaste of home.

6 I long, dearest Lord, in Thy beauties to shine;
  No more as an exile in sorrow to pine;
  And in Thy dear image arise from the tomb,
  With glorified millions to praise Thee at home.

(HEAVEN.)

SAFE WITHIN THE VAIL.

JOHN M. EVANS. 1865.

Rev. E. ADAMS.

From "Bright Jewels," by per.

1. "Land a - head!" its fruits are waving O'er the hills of fadeless green ; And the liv - ing wa - ters
2. Onward, bark ! the cape I'm rounding; See the bless - ed wave their hands ; Hear the harps of God re -
3. There, let go the an - chor, rid - ing On this calm and sil - v'ry bay ; Sea - ward fast the tide is
4. Now we're safe from all tempta - tion, All the storms of life are past ; Praise the Rock of our sal -

CHORUS.

lav - ing Shores where heavenly forms are seen. Rocks and storms I'll fear no more, When on
sounding From the bright im - mor - tal bands.
glid - ing, Shores in sun - light stretch a - way.
va - tion, We are safe at home at last.

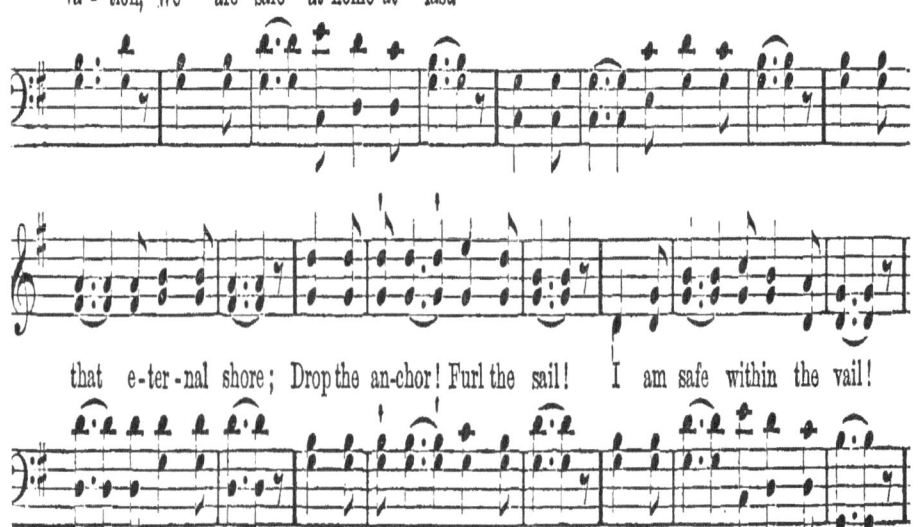

that e - ter - nal shore ; Drop the an - chor! Furl the sail ! I am safe within the vail !

(HEAVEN.)

Mrs. CECIL FRANCES ALEXANDER, 1848.

JOHN B. DYKES, 1868, arr.

1. Ev-'ry morn the ro-sy sun Ris-es warm and bright; But the evening cometh on And the

GIRLS.

BOYS.

dark, cold night: There's a bright land far a-way, Where is nev-er end-ing day

ALL.

2 Ev'ry spring the sweet young flowers
   Open fresh and gay ;
Till the chilly autumn hours
   Wither them away :
There's a land we have not seen,
Where the trees are always green !

3 Little birds sing songs of praise
   All the summer long ;
But in colder, shorter days
   They forget their song :
There's a place where angels sing
Ceaseless praises to their King.

4 Christ our Lord is ever near
   Those who follow Him !
But we cannot see Him here,
   For our eyes are dim :
There's a blissful happy place
Where men always see His face.

5 Who shall go to that bright land ?
   All who do the right :
Holy children there shall stand
   In their robes of white.
For that Heaven so bright and blest,
Is our everlasting rest.

(HEAVEN.)

IS THERE ONE FOR ME?

JOSEPH P. HOLBROOK, by per.

1. Mansions are pre-pared a-bove, By the gracious God of love; Man-y will those mansions see;—, Is there one pre-pared for me? Is there one pre-pared for me?

Is there one for me? Man-y will those mansions see; Is there one prepared for me?

2 Crowns that dazzle human eye,
Wait for those who reach the sky;
Many there, those crowns will see,
Is there one prepared for me?

3 Robes of spotless white are given,
By the glorious King of heaven;
All can have them, they are free,—
Is there one prepared for me?

4 Harps of joyful sound above,
Swell the praise of Jesus' love;
Oh! how sweet their strains will be,
Is there, Lord, a harp for me?

(HEAVEN.)

FANNY J. CROSBY, 1875.
From "Brightest and Best," by per. WM. H. DOANE.

1. When, my journey past, I am safe at last At the gate of life so fair, Who will take my hand,
2. Friends that left me here, Hearts that held me dear, Call me to their home of song; But, to find my rest,
3. To the golden shore, Thou wilt bear me o'er, I shall feel Thy ten-der care; Thou wilt take my hand,

REFRAIN.

In the spir-it land? Who will come to meet me there? When the morning bright Fills my soul with light,
Ev-er on Thy breast, Draws me with a love so strong.
In the spir-it land, Thou wilt bid me welcome there.

Je-sus, let me look on Thee; Lov-ing Saviour mine, Let Thy voice divine, Be the first to welcome me.

(HEAVEN.)

SHALL WE MEET IN HEAVEN.

WM. STEVENSON.

WM. STEVENSON.

From "Royal Diadem," by per.

1. Shall we meet in heaven, shall we meet in heaven, With the blest who have gone be - fore?
2. Will the an - gels bright, will the an - gels bright, Bear us on to that hap - py home?
3. Yes, we all may meet, yes, we all may meet, Where this life and its toils are o'er,

Will a crown be given, will a crown be given, When we stand on the oth - er shore?
With the saints in light, with the saints in light, Shall we stand round the great white throne?
And each oth - er greet, and each oth - er greet, In a land where we'll part no more.

REFRAIN.

We may all meet there, We may all meet there, If we

We may all meet there, meet there, We may all meet there, meet there,

love the Lord, and o - bey His word, We may all meet there.

meet there,

(HEAVEN.)

O PARADISE!

185

Rev. F. W. FABER, 1862.

JOSEPH BARNBY.

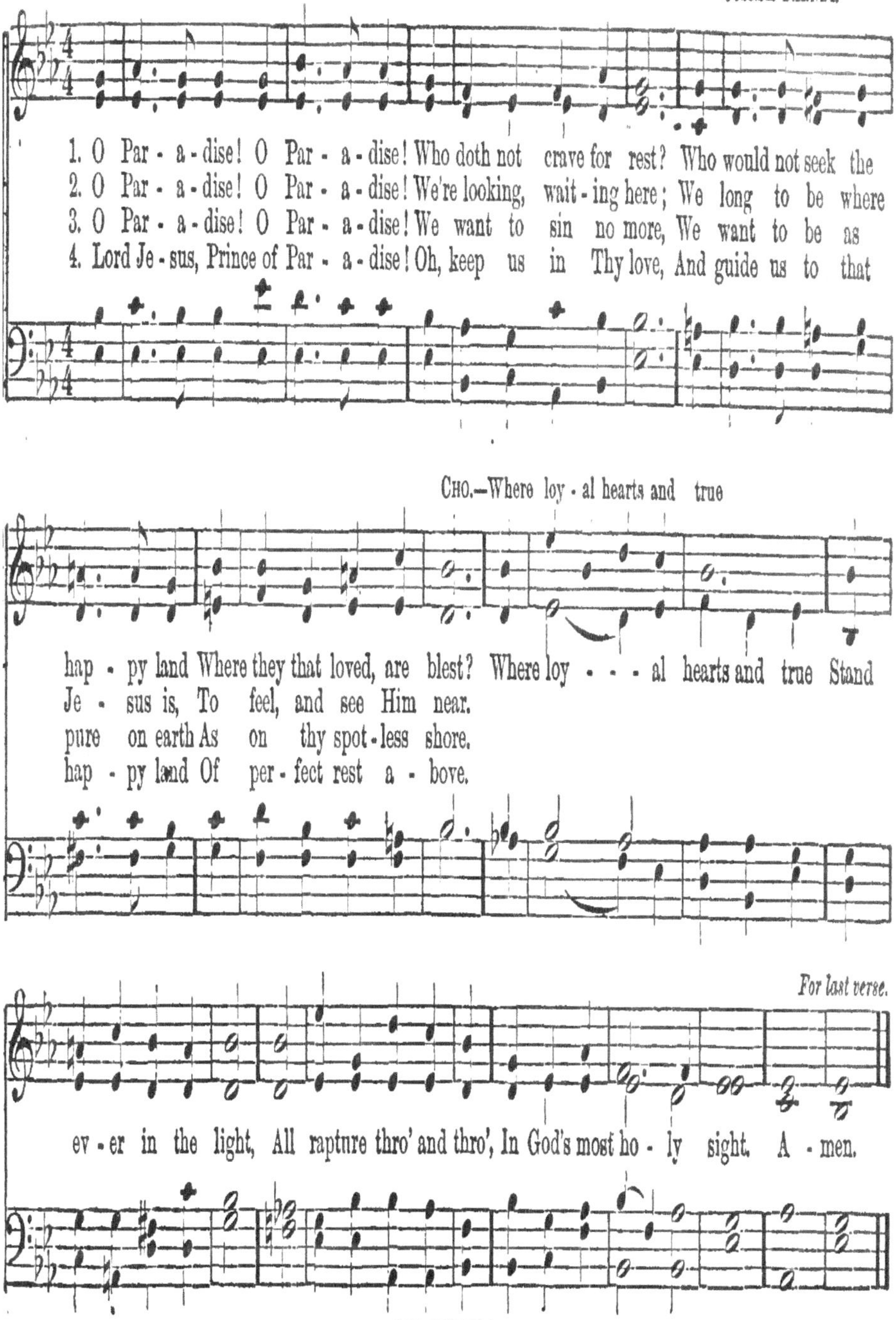

1. O Par - a - dise! O Par - a - dise! Who doth not crave for rest? Who would not seek the
2. O Par - a - dise! O Par - a - dise! We're looking, wait - ing here; We long to be where
3. O Par - a - dise! O Par - a - dise! We want to sin no more, We want to be as
4. Lord Je - sus, Prince of Par - a - dise! Oh, keep us in Thy love, And guide us to that

CHO.—Where loy - al hearts and true

hap - py land Where they that loved, are blest? Where loy - - - al hearts and true Stand
Je - sus is, To feel, and see Him near.
pure on earth As on thy spot - less shore.
hap - py land Of per - fect rest a - bove.

For last verse.

ev - er in the light, All rapture thro' and thro', In God's most ho - ly sight. A - men.

(HEAVEN.)

BEAUTIFUL RIVER.

Rev. R. LOWRY.
From "Bright Jewels," by per

Rev. R. LOWRY, 1864.

Cheerful.

1. Shall we gath-er at the riv - er Where bright angel feet have trod; With its crys-tal tide for
2. On the mar-gin of the riv - er, Wash-ing up its sil - ver spray; We will walk and worship
3. On the bo-som of the riv - er, Where the Saviour-king we own, We shall meet, and sorrow
4. Ere we reach the shining riv - er, Lay we ev - ery bur-den down; Grace our spir-its will de -

CHORUS.

p

ev - er Flowing by the throne of God? Yes, we'll gather at the riv - er, The beau-ti-ful, the
ev - er, All the hap-py, gold-en day.
nev - er, 'Neath the glo-ry of the throne.
liv - er, And provide a robe and crown.

beau-ti-ful riv - er— Gath-er with the saints at the riv - er That flows by the throne of God.

(HEAVEN.)

SWEET BY-AND-BY.

S. FILLMORE BENNETT.

JOS. P. WEBSTER, by per. arr.

1. There's a land that is fair-er than day, And by faith we can see it a-far;
For the Fa-ther waits o-ver the way, [Omit....................] } To prepare us a

2. We shall sing on that beauti-ful shore The mel-o-di-ous songs of the blest,
And our spir-its shall sorrow no more, [Omit....................] } Not a sigh for the

3. To our boun-ti-ful Fa-ther a-bove, We will of-fer our trib-ute of praise,
For the glo-ri-ous gift of His love, [Omit....................] } And the blessings that

CHORUS.

dwelling place there, In the sweet by-and-by, We shall meet on that beauti-ful
blessing of rest.
hal-low our days.

In the sweet by-and-by,

shore, In the sweet by-and-by, We shall meet on that beauti-ful shore.

by-and-by, by-and-by, In the sweet by-and-by,

(HEAVEN.)

FLEMMING.

F. F. FLEMMING, 1810.

1. Tranquil and peaceful is the path to heaven, Where now so man - y fresh from earth's ripe
2. There life is bliss - ful, shall the spir - it tremble? Bright heavenly an - gels wait to lead us
3. There our lost rose-buds in our hands shall open; Love, pure and ho - ly, in our bo - soms

vin - tage, So man-y hap - py, high and blessed spir - its, Wait to re - ceive us.
yon - der; There dwell the spir - its pu - ri - fied by suff'-ring, Blessing and bless - ed.
glow-ing, Flows from the Fa - ther, source of ev - ery bless-ing, Liv-ing and lov - ing.

Use slurs for second hymn.

SECOND HYMN.

Charlotte Elliott, 1834.

1 O holy Saviour! Friend unseen,
　Since on Thine arm Thou bidst me lean;
　Help me throughout life's changing scene,
　　By faith to cling to Thee!

2 What though the world deceitful prove,
　And earthly friends and hopes remove;
　With patient, uncomplaining love,
　　Still would I cling to Thee!

3 If e'er I seem to tread alone
　Life's weary waste, with thorns o'ergrown;
　Thy voice of love in gentlest tone,
　　Still whispers, "cling to Me!"

4 If faith and hope are often tried,
　I'll ask not, need not aught beside;
　So safe, so calm, so satisfied,
　　The soul that clings to Thee!

(*HEAVEN.*)

THE BRIGHT FOREVER.

FANNY J. CROSBY. 1871.   From "Pure Gold," by per. HUBERT P. MAIN. 1871.

1. Breaking thro' the clouds that gather O'er the christian's na-tal skies, Distant beams, like floods of glo-ry,
2. Yet   a lit - tle while we lin-ger, Ere we reach our journey's end; Yet   a lit - tle while of la - bor,
3. O   the bliss of life e-ter-nal! O   the long un-bro-ken rest! In   the gold-en fields of pleasure,

Fill the soul with glad surprise; And we al - most hear the e - cho Of   the pure and ho-ly throng,
Ere the evening shades descend; Then we'll lay us down to slumber, But   the night will soon be o'er;
In   the re-gion of   the blest; But, to see our dear Re-deem-er, And be-fore His throne to fall,

CHORUS.

In the bright, the bright for-ev - er,   In the summer-land of song. On the banks beyond the riv-er,
In the bright, the bright for-ev - er,   We shall wake, to weep no more.
There to hear His gracious welcome—Will be sweeter far than all.

ritard.

We shall meet, no more to sev-er; In the bright, the bright for-ev - er, In the summer-land of song.

(HEAVEN.)

RUTHERFORD. . 7s & 6s.

ANNIE ROSS COUSIN, 1857.

CHAS. D'URBAN, 1845.

1. The sands of time are wast . ing, The dawn of heav-en breaks, The sum-mer morn I've sighed for,
2. Oh! Christ He is   the foun-tain, The deep, sweet well of love; The streams of earth I've tast - ed,

The fair, sweet morn a - wakes. Oh, dark hath been the mid - night, But day-spring is   at hand,
More deep I'll drink a - bove, There to an o - cean ful - ness, His mer - cy doth ex - pand,

And glo - ry, glo - ry dwell-eth In Im - man-uel's land.
And glo - ry, glo - ry dwell-eth In Im - man-uel's land.

3 Oh! I am my Beloved's,
  And my Beloved's mine,
He brings a poor vile sinner,
  Into His house divine.
Upon the Rock of Ages,
  My soul redeemed shall stand,
Where glory, glory dwelleth
  In Immanuel's land.

(HEAVEN.)

ONLY TRUST HIM.

(317)Gospel H. & S. S., 92. Key G.

1 COME, every soul by sin oppressed
There's mercy with the Lord,
And he will surely give you rest,
By trusting in His word.

CHO. Only trust Him, only trust Him,
Only trust Him now;
He will save you, He will save you,
He will save you now.

2 For Jesus shed His precious blood
Rich blessings to bestow;
Plunge now into the crimson flood
That washes white as snow.

3 Yes, Jesus is the Truth, the Way,
That leads you into rest;
Believe in Him without delay,
And you are fully blest.

4 Come then, and join this holy band,
And on to glory go,
To dwell in that celestial land,
Where joys immortal flow.

VARINA. C. M.

(318)Christian Songs, 163. Key E♭.

1 THERE is a land of pure delight,
Where saints immortal reign;
Eternal day excludes the night,
And pleasures banish pain.

2 There everlasting spring abides,
And never-fading flowers:
Death, like a narrow sea, divides
This heavenly land from ours.

3 O, could we make our doubts remove,
Those gloomy doubts that rise,
And see the Canaan that we love,
With faith's illumined eyes ;—

4 Could we but climb where Moses stood,
And view the landscape o'er, [flood,
Not Jordan's stream, nor death's cold
Should fright us from the shore.

LAND BEYOND THE RIVER.

(319)Christian Songs, 178. Key D.

1 No mortal eye that land hath seen,
Beyond, beyond the river;
Its smiling valleys, hills so green,
Beyond, beyond the river.
Its shores are coming nearer,
The skies are growing clearer,
Each day it seemeth dearer,
That land beyond the river.
REF. ‖: We'll stand the storm, :‖
Its rage is almost over;
We'll anchor in the harbor soon,
In the land beyond the river.

2 That glorious day will ne'er be done,
Beyond, beyond the river; [won,
When we've the crown and kingdom
Beyond, beyond the river.
There is eternal pleasure,
And joys that none can measure,
For those who have their treasure
In the land beyond the river.

(*HEAVEN.*)

3 When shall we look from Zion's hill,
Beyond, beyond the river; [thrill,
With endless bliss our hearts shall
Beyond, beyond the river.
There angels bright are singing,
Where golden harps are ringing,
We ne'er shall cease our singing
In the land beyond the river.

THE GOLDEN SHORE.

(320)Christian Songs, 112. Key D.

1 WE are out on the ocean sailing,
Homeward bound we gently glide;
We are out on the ocean sailing,
To a home beyond the tide.
CHO.
All the storms will soon be over,
Then we'll anchor in the harbor.
‖: We are out on the ocean sailing,
To a home beyond the tide. :‖

2 Millions now are safely landed,
Over on the golden shore;
Millions more are on their journey,
Yet there's room for millions more.

3 Spread your sails, while heavenly
Gently waft our vessel on : [breezes
All on board are sweetly singing—
Free salvation is the song.

4 When we all are safely anchored,
We will shout—our trials o'er,
We will walk about the city,
And we'll sing for evermore.

BEAUTIFUL EDEN.

Mrs. MARY A. KIDDER. 1870.

From "Pure Gold," by per. W. H. DOANE.

DUET.

1. Beau-ti-ful E-den, re-fuge of peace, Home where the songs of the ransomed ne'er cease;
2. Beau-ti-ful E-den, sor-row or care Nev-er can with-er thy blossoms so fair;
3. Beau-ti-ful E-den, gar-den of grace, Where we may gaze on the Saviour's dear face;

Oh, how my spir-it when saddened by gloom, Longs to be-hold thee, thou gar-den of bloom!
Sin can-not blight them, and death cannot slay, Safe in the gar-den of prom-ise are they.
There we shall gath-er in gladness a-bove, Roam-ing the realms of an E-den of love.

CHORUS.

Beauti-ful E-den, beau-ti-ful E-den, Bright are thy flow-ers, gold-en thy fruits; Pure are thy

riv-ers, thy fountains how free! Beau-ti-ful E-den, my soul longs for thee.

(HEAVEN.)

(322) Christian Songs, 105. Key E♭.

1 SHALL we sing in heaven for ever—
  Shall we sing! Shall we sing!
Shall we sing in heaven forever,
  In that happy land?
REF.   [land,
Yes! oh, yes! in that land, that happy
They that meet shall sing for ever,
Far beyond the rolling river,
Meet to sing and love for ever,
  In that happy land.

2 Shall we know each other, ever,
  ‖: In that land? :‖
Shall we know each other, ever,
  In that happy land?   [land,
  Yes! oh, yes! in that land, that happy
They that meet shall know each other,
Far beyond the rolling river, &c.

3 Shall we rest from care and sorrow,
  : In that land? :‖
Shall we rest from care and sorrow,
  In that happy land?   [land,
  Yes! oh, yes! in that land, that happy
They that meet shall rest for ever,
Far beyond the rolling river, &c.

4 Shall we know our blessed Saviour
  ‖ :In that land? :‖
Shall we know our blessed Saviour
  In that happy land?   [land,
  Yes! oh, yes! in that land, that happy
We shall know our blessed Saviour,
Far beyond the rolling river,
Love and serve Him there for ever,
  In that happy land.

(323) Bradbury Trio, 36. Key C.

1 IN the Christian's home in glory
  There remains a land of rest;
There my Saviour's gone before me,
  To fulfil my soul's request.
CHO.
‖: There is rest for the weary, :‖
  There is rest for the weary,
    There is rest for you;
  On the other side of Jordan,
  In the sweet fields of Eden,
Where the tree of life is blooming,
  There is rest for you.

2 He is fitting up my mansion,
  Which eternally shall stand:
For my stay shall not be transient
  In that holy, happy land.

3 Sing, O sing, ye heirs of glory!
  Shout your triumphs as you go;
Zion's gates will open for you,
  You shall find an entrance through.

(324) Songs of Devotion, 214. Key A.

1 How pleasant thus to dwell below,
  In fellowship of love;
And though we part, 'tis bliss to know
  The good shall meet above.
CHO.
  O that will be joyful, joyful, joyful,
  O that will be joyful,
  ‖: To meet, to part no more :‖
    On Canaan's happy shore,
    And sing the everlasting song
  With those who've gone before.

2 Yes, happy thought! when we are free
  From earthly grief and pain,
In heav'n we shall each other see,
  And never part again.

3 Then let us each, in strength divine,
  Still walk in wisdom's ways:
That we, with those we love, may join
  In never-ending praise.

(325) Bradbury Trio, 83. Key G.

1 My days are gliding swiftly by,
  And I, a pilgrim stranger,
Would not detain them, as they fly,
  Those hours of toil and danger:
CHO.
  For, O we stand on Jordan's strand;
    Our friends are passing over;
  And just before, the shining shore
    We may almost discover.

2 We'll gird our loins, my brethren dear,
  Our distant home discerning;
Our absent Lord has left us word,
  "Let every lamp be burning:"

3 Should coming days be cold and dark,
  We need not cease our singing;
That perfect rest naught can molest,
  Where golden harps are ringing:

4 Let sorrow's rudest tempest blow,
  Each cord on earth to sever; [home,
OurKing says, "Come!" and there's our
  Forever, O for ever!

(HEAVEN.

REVIVE US AGAIN.

Tune on page 3. Key G.

1 REJOICE and be glad! the Redeemer has come!
Go look on His cradle, His cross and His tomb.

CHO.—Sound His praises, tell the Story
    Of Him who was slain;
    Sound His praises, tell with gladness,
    He liveth again.

2 Rejoice and be glad! it is sunshine at last!
The clouds have departed, the shadows are past.

3 Rejoice and be glad! for the blood hath been shed;
Redemption is finished, the price hath been paid.

4 Rejoice and be glad! now the pardon is free!
The Just for the unjust has died on the tree.

5 Rejoice and be glad! for the Lamb that was slain
O'er death is triumphant and liveth again.

6 Rejoice and be glad! for our King is on high,
He pleadeth for us on His throne in the sky.

7 Rejoice and be glad! for He cometh again;
He cometh in glory, the Lamb that was slain.

CHO.—Sound His praises, tell the Story
    Of Him who was slain;
    Sound His praises, tell with gladness,
    He cometh again.

I AM PRAYING FOR YOU.

Gospel H. & S. Songs, 13. Key G.

1 I HAVE a Saviour, He's pleading in glory,
    A dear, loving Saviour though earth-friends be few;
And now He is watching in tenderness o'er me,
    And oh, that my Saviour, were your Saviour too!

CHO.—For you I am praying, For you I am praying,
    For you I am praying, I'm praying for you.

2 I have a Father: to me He has given
    A hope for eternity, blessed and true;
And soon will He call me to meet Him in heaven,
    But oh, that He'd let me bring you with me too!

3 I have a robe: 'tis resplendent in whiteness,
    Awaiting in glory my wondering view;
Oh, when I receive it all shining in brightness,
    Dear friend, could I see you receiving one too!

4 When Christ has found you, tell others the story,
    That my loving Saviour is your Saviour too;
Then pray that your Saviour may bring them to glory,
    And prayer will be answered—'twas answered for you!

YET THERE IS ROOM.

Gospel H. & S. Songs, 79. Key F.

1 YET there is room! The Lamb's bright hall of song,
With its fair glory, beckons thee along:
Room, room, still room! oh, enter, enter now!

2 Day is declining, and the sun is low:
The shadows lengthen, light makes haste to go:
Room, room, still room! oh, enter, enter now!

3 The bridal hall is filling for the feast:
Pass in, pass in, and be the Bridegroom's guest:
Room, room, still room! oh, enter, enter now!

4 It fills, it fills, that hall of jubilee!
Make haste, make haste; 'tis not too full for thee:
Room, room, still room! oh, enter, enter now!

5 Yet there is room! still open stands the gate,
The gate of love; it is not yet too late:
Room, room, still room! oh, enter, enter now!

6 Pass in, pass in! that banquet is for thee;
That cup of everlasting love is free:
Room, room, still room! oh, enter, enter now!

7 All heaven is there, all joy! go in, go in;
The angels beckon thee the prize to win:
Room, room, still room! oh, enter, enter now!

8 Louder and sweeter sounds the loving call;
Come lingerer, come; enter that festal hall:
Room, room, still room! oh, enter, enter now!

9 Ere night that gate may close, and seal thy doom;
Then the last, low, long cry:—"No room, no room!"
No room, no room.—oh, woful cry, "No room!"

(HEAVEN.)

THE WELCOME HOME.

(327) Christian Songs, 147. Key C.

1 How sweet will be the welcome home,
When this short life is o'er,
When pain and sorrow, care and grief
Shall dwell with us no more.
When we that bright and heavenly land
With spirit eyes shall see,
And join the holy angel band,
In praise, dear Lord, of Thee.
Cho. ‖: The welcome home, :‖
The Christian's welcome home. :‖

2 Lord, grant my frail and wayward bark
May anchor sure and fast,
Beside the shining gates of pearl,
Where I may rest at last!
When once within, my soul shall know
No hunger, thirst or pain,
No sickness, sorrow, care or death
Shall visit me again!

3 Oh may I live while here below,
In view of that blest day,
When God's bright angels shall come
To bear my soul away!   [down,
When I shall walk the golden streets,
In garments white and pure;
And sing an endless song to Him,
Who made my soul secure!

THE BETTER LAND.

(328) Christian Songs, 113. Key D.

Boys. 1 Whither, pilgrims, are you going,
Going each with staff in hand?

Girls We are going on a journey.
Going at our King's command.
All. Over hills, and plains, and valleys;
‖: We are going to His palace, :‖
Going to the better land.
We are going to His palace,
Going to the better land.

B. 2 Tell me pilgrims what you hope for
In that far-off better land?
G. Spotless robes and crowns of glory
From a Saviour's loving hand.
A. We shall drink of life's clear river
‖: We shall dwell with God forever, :‖
In that bright, that better land.

B. 3 Pilgrims, may we travel with you
To that bright and better land?
G. ‖: Come and welcome. :‖
Welcome to our pilgrim band.
A. Come, O come and do not leave us,
‖: Christ is waiting to receive us, :‖
In that bright, that better land.

A LAND WITHOUT A STORM.

(329) Christian Songs, 137. Key G.
Boys.
1 Traveler, whither art thou going,
Heedless of the clouds that form?
Girls.
Nought to me the winds rough blowing,
Mine's a land without a storm.
All. ‖: And I'm going, yes, I'm going
To the land that has no storm. :‖

B. 2 Traveler art thou here a stranger,
Not to fear the tempest's power?
G. I have not a thought of danger,
Though the sky more darkly lower.

B. 3 Traveler, now a moment linger,
Soon the darkness will be o'er!
G. No! I see a beck'ning finger,
Guiding to a far off shore.

B. 4 Traveler, yonder narrow portal
Opens to receive thy form!
G. Yes! but I shall be immortal
In that Land without a storm.

THAT BEAUTIFUL LAND.

(330) Christian Songs, 135. Key B♭.

1 A beautiful land by faith I see,
A land of rest from sorrow free,   [fair,
The home of the ransomed, bright and
And beautiful angels too, are there.
Cho.   Will you go? Will you go?
Go to that beautiful land with me?
Will you go? Will you go?
Go to that beautiful land?

2 That beautiful land, the City of Light,
It ne'er has known the shades of night;
The glory of God, the light of day,
Hath driven the darkness far away.

3 The heav'nly throng arrayed in white,
In rapture range the plains of light;
And in one harmonious choir they praise
Their glorious Saviour's matchless grace.

(HEAVEN.)

GOING HOME.

WM. STEVENSON.

R. LOWRY.

From "Brightest and Best," by per.

1. Go-ing home, yes, go-ing home! Sweet words of comfort and of cheer; Go-ing home, soon go-ing
2. Go-ing home, yes, go-ing home! The chief of sin-ners saved by grace; Go-ing home, I'm go-ing
3. Go-ing home, yes, go-ing home! The pearl-y gates by faith I see; Go-ing home, I'm go-ing
4. Go-ing home, yes, go-ing home! My feet have almost reach'd the shore; Go-ing home, blest go-ing

REFRAIN.

home! My soul, the hoped for day is near. Go-ing home, sweet go-ing home To the
home To see my dear Re-deem-er's face.
home; My dear ones wait to wel-come me.
home, And there a-bide for ev-er more.

man-sions bright and fair; Go-ing home, sweet go-ing home! I shall dwell for ev-er there.

(HEAVEN.)

UNITY. 6s & 5s.

(332)   Key E♭.

1 WHEN shall we meet again,
    Meet ne'er to sever?
When will peace wreath her chain
    Round us for ever?
Our hearts will ne'er repose,
Safe from each blast that blows,
In this dark vale of woes,
    Never—no, never!

2 When shall love freely flow
    Pure as life's river?
When shall sweet friendship glow
    Changeless for ever?
Where joys celestial thrill,
Where bliss each heart shall fill,
And fears of parting chill
    Never—no, never!

3 Up to that world of light
    Take us, dear Saviour!
May we all there unite,
    Happy for ever;
Where kindred spirits dwell,
There may our music swell,
And time our joys dispel
    Never—no, never!

BRIGHT HOME ABOVE

(333)Christian Songs, 102. Key B♭.
1 WE are going, we are are going,
    To a home beyond the skies,
Where the fields are robed in beauty,
    And the sunlight never dies.

Where the fount of joy is flowing,
    In the valley green and fair,
We shall dwell in love together,
    There will be no parting there.
CHO.
We are going, we are going,
    To a home beyond the skies,
Where the fields are robed in beauty,
    And the sunlight never dies.

2 We are going, we are going,
    And the music we have heard
Like the echo of the woodland,
    Or the carol of a bird,
In the rosy light of morning,
    On the calm and fragrant air,
Still it murmurs, softly murmurs,
    There will be no parting there.

3 We are going, we are going,
    When the day of life is o'er—
To that pure and happy region
    Where our friends have gone before;
They are singing with the angels
    In that land so bright and fair;
We shall dwell with them forever,
    There will be no parting there.

BEAUTIFUL ZION.

(334)Christian Songs, 87. Key A♭.
1 BEAUTIFUL Zion built above,
    Beautiful city that I love,
Beautiful gates of pearly white,
    Beautiful temple—God its light;
He who was slain on Calvary,
    Opens those pearly gates to me.

(HEAVEN)

2 Beautiful crowns on every brow,
    Beautiful palms the conquerors show,
Beautiful robes the ransom'd wear,
    Beautiful all who enter there:
Thither I press with eager feet,
There shall my rest be long and sweet.

3 Beautiful throne of Christ our King,
    Beautiful songs the angels sing,
Beautiful rest, all wanderings cease,
    Beautiful home of perfect peace;
There shall my eyes the Saviour see;
Haste to this heav'nly home with me.

"RIVER OF LIFE."

(335) Page 59. Key E♭. By per.
1 GATHERED by the Crystal River,
    Toil and burden wholly past,
Life's dark mazes gone forever,
    We shall gain our home at last.
CHO.   [Throne!
O! pure flowing stream from golden
O! sweet song of host that Christ has won!
Joyous anthems to our King,
Through the heavens broad shall ring,
Hallelujahs to Him who rules alone.

2 Resting by the Crystal River,
    Filled with Jesus' love and light,
Dwelling in His presence ever,
    We shall know no clouds or night.

3 Chanting by the Crystal River,
    Songs Redeemed alone can sing,
We shall live and reign forever,
    One in Christ, our risen King.

THE DEAR ONES ALL AT HOME.

HORATIUS BONAR, D. D.　　　　　　　　　　　　From "New Golden Shower," by per. Wm. B. BRADBURY, 1864.

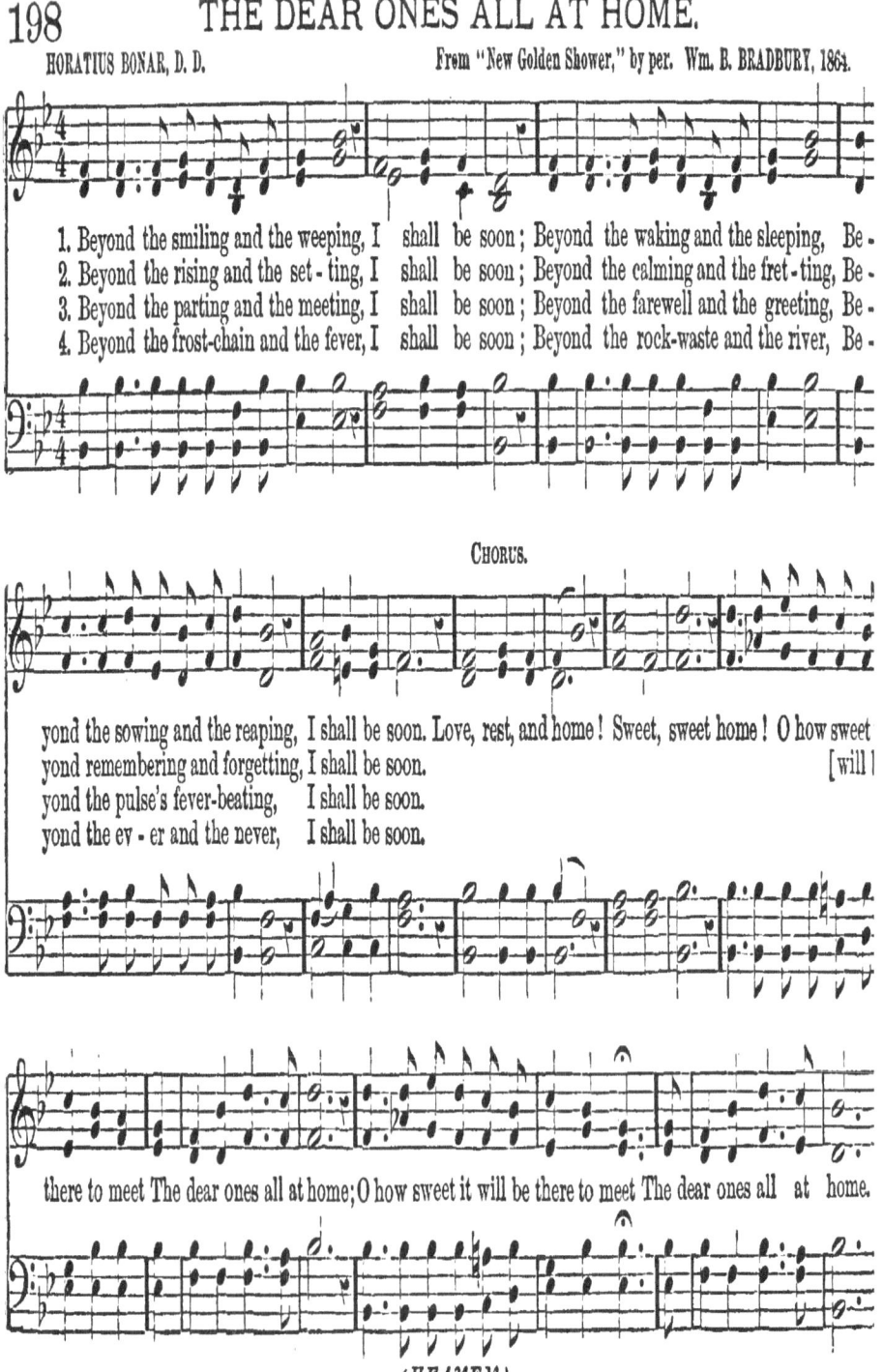

1. Beyond the smiling and the weeping, I shall be soon; Beyond the waking and the sleeping, Be-
2. Beyond the rising and the set-ting, I shall be soon; Beyond the calming and the fret-ting, Be-
3. Beyond the parting and the meeting, I shall be soon; Beyond the farewell and the greeting, Be-
4. Beyond the frost-chain and the fever, I shall be soon; Beyond the rock-waste and the river, Be-

CHORUS.

yond the sowing and the reaping, I shall be soon. Love, rest, and home! Sweet, sweet home! O how sweet
yond remembering and forgetting, I shall be soon.　　　　　　　　　　　　　　　　　　　[will]
yond the pulse's fever-beating, I shall be soon.
yond the ev-er and the never, I shall be soon.

there to meet The dear ones all at home; O how sweet it will be there to meet The dear ones all at home.

(HEAVEN.)

HOLY CITY. 7s & 6s.

(337) Plym. Coll., 406. Key G.

1 There is a holy city,
    A happy world above,
Beyond the starry regions,
    Built by the God of love,
An everlasting temple,
    And saints arrayed in white
There serve their great Redeemer,
    And dwell with Him in light.

2 The meanest child of glory
    Outshines the radiant sun;
But who can speak the splendor
    Of that eternal throne,
Where Jesus sits exalted,
    In godlike majesty!
The elders fall before Him,
    The angels bend the knee.

3 The hosts of saints around Him
    Proclaim His work of grace;
The patriarchs and prophets,
    And all the godly race,
Who speak of fiery trials
    And tortures on their way—
They came from tribulation
    To everlasting day.

4 And what shall be my journey,
    How long I'll stay below,
Or what shall be my trials,
    Are not for me to know;
In every day of trouble,
    I'll raise my thoughts on high;
I'll think of the bright temple,
    And crowns above the sky.

THE PRECIOUS NAME.

(338) Pure Gold, 13. Key A♭.

1 Take the name of Jesus with you,
    Child of sorrow and of woe—
It will joy and comfort give you,
    Take it, then, where'er you go.

Cho. ‖: Precious name, O how sweet,
    Hope of earth and joy of heaven.:‖

2 Take the name of Jesus ever,
    As a shield from every snare;
If temptations round you gather,
    Breathe that Holy Name in prayer.

3 Oh! the precious name of Jesus;
    How it thrills our souls with joy,
When His loving arms receive us,
    And His songs our tongues employ!

4 At the name of Jesus bowing,
    Falling prostrate at His feet,[Him,
King of kings in heaven we'll crown
    When our journey is complete.

THE HOME OVER THERE.

(339) Gospel H. & S. S., 90. Key A.

1 Oh, think of the home over there,
    By the side of the river of light,
Where the saints all immortal and fair,
    Are robed in their garments of white.

Ref. Over there, over there,
    Oh, think of the home over there.

2 Oh, think of the friends over there,
    Who before us the journey have trod,
Of the songs that they breathe on the air,
    In their home in the palace of God.

Ref. Over there, over there,
    Oh, think of the friends over there.

3 My Saviour is now over there, [rest;
    There my kindred and friends are at
Then away from my sorrow and care,
    Let me fly to the land of the blest.

Ref. Over there, over there,
    My Saviour is now over there.

4 I'll soon be at home over there,
    For the end of my journey I see;
Many dear to my heart over there,
    Are watching and waiting for me.

Ref. Over there, over there,
    I'll soon be at home over there.

THE WONDROUS GIFT.

(340) Gospel H. & S. S., 50. Key D.

1 Grace! 'tis a charming sound,
    Harmonious to the ear;
Heaven with the echo shall resound,
    And all the earth shall hear.

Ref. Saved by grace alone,
    This is all my plea;
Jesus died for all mankind,
    And Jesus died for me.

2 Grace first contrived a way
    To save rebellious man;
And all the steps that grace display,
    Which drew the wondrous plan.

3 Grace taught my roving feet
    To tread the heavenly road;
And new supplies each hour I meet,
    While pressing on to God.

4 Grace all the work shall crown,
    Through everlasting days;
It lays in heaven the topmost stone,
    And well deserves our praise.

(HEAVEN.)

JERUSALEM, THE GOLDEN!

BERNARD, 1140.

ALEX. EWING, (1830—) 1859.

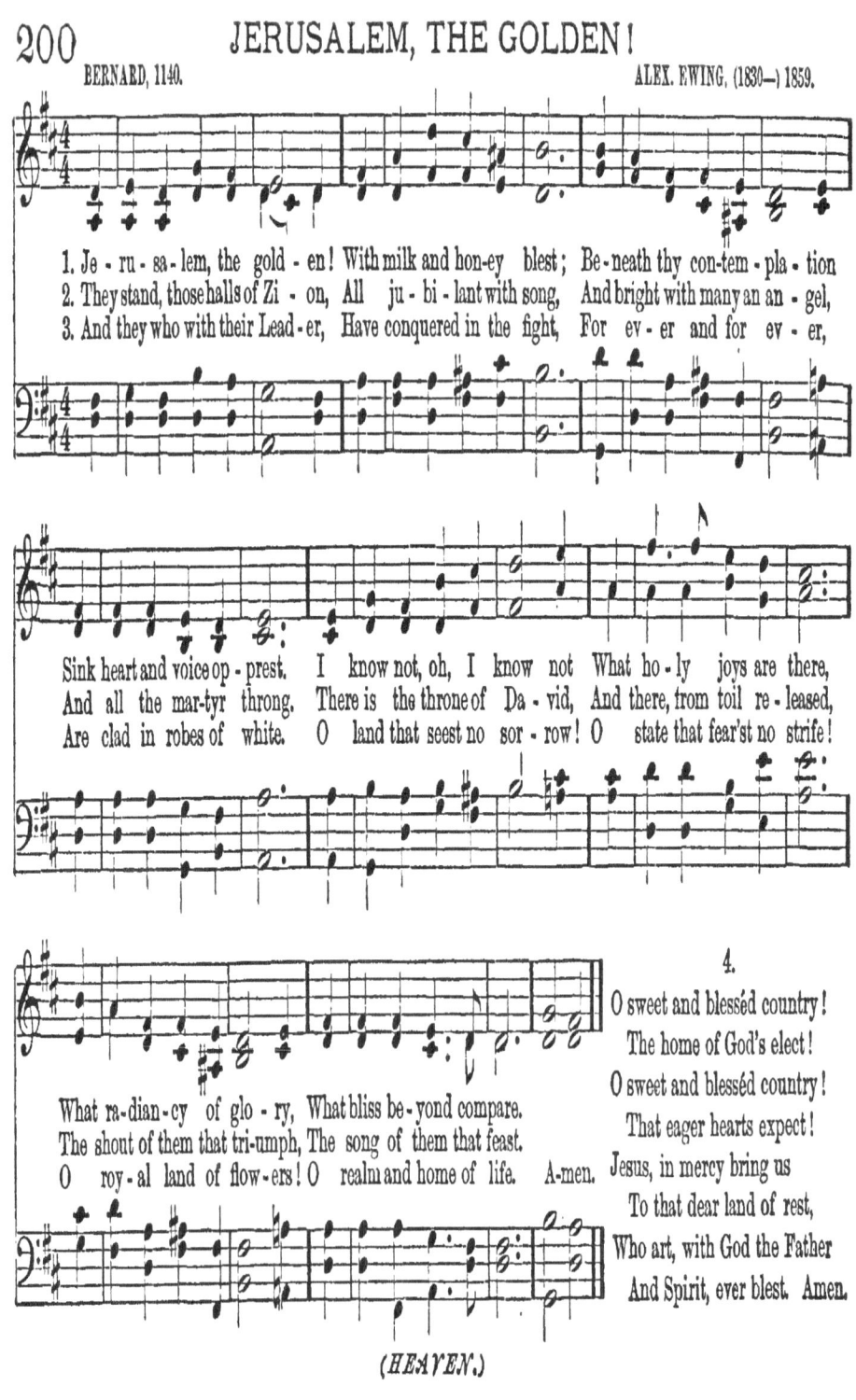

1. Je - ru - sa - lem, the gold - en! With milk and hon-ey blest; Be - neath thy con-tem - pla - tion
2. They stand, those halls of Zi - on, All ju - bi - lant with song, And bright with many an an - gel,
3. And they who with their Lead - er, Have conquered in the fight, For ev - er and for ev - er,

Sink heart and voice op - prest. I know not, oh, I know not What ho - ly joys are there,
And all the mar-tyr throng. There is the throne of Da - vid, And there, from toil re - leased,
Are clad in robes of white. O land that seest no sor - row! O state that fear'st no strife!

What ra-dian - cy of glo - ry, What bliss be - yond compare.
The shout of them that tri - umph, The song of them that feast.
O roy - al land of flow - ers! O realm and home of life. A-men.

4.
O sweet and blesséd country!
The home of God's elect!
O sweet and blesséd country!
That eager hearts expect!
Jesus, in mercy bring us
To that dear land of rest,
Who art, with God the Father
And Spirit, ever blest. Amen.

(HEAVEN.)

AROUND THE THRONE.

(342)　Clariona, 97.　Key G.

1 AROUND the throne of God in heaven,
　Thousands of children stand;
Children whose sins are all forgiven,
　A holy, happy band,
　Singing, Glory, Glory,
Glory be to God on high.

2 In flowing robes of spotless white,
　See every one arrayed;
Dwelling in everlasting light,
　And joys that never fade,
　Singing, Glory, Glory, etc.

3 What brought them to that world
　　　above—
That heaven so bright and fair,
Where all is peace, and joy, and love,
　How came those children there,
　Singing, Glory, Glory, etc.

4 Because the Saviour shed His blood
　To wash away their sin;
Bathed in that pure and precious flood,
　Behold them white and clean,
　Singing, Glory, Glory, etc.

EVENING SONG.

(343) Fresh Laurels, 10.　Key A♭.

1 'Tis sweet to think, as night comes on,
　‖: Dark and drear. :‖
Ere "stars come twinkling one by one,"
　‖: Earth to cheer. :‖
There is a world where comes no night,
It needs no sun or moon to light,
For Jesus' presence makes it bright—
　‖: No night there. :‖

2 'Tis sweet to think when round us lie,
　‖: Grief and care, :‖
Our Jesus hears the softest sigh,
　‖: Breath'd in pray'r; :‖
And if we love Him, we shall see,
That "land from sin and sorrow free,"
And oh! we know that there will be—
　‖: No tears there. :‖

FOR EVER WITH THE LORD.　S. M.

(344)　Clariona, 134.　Key A♭.

1 "FOR ever with the Lord!"
　Amen, so let it be!
Life from the dead is in that word,
　'Tis immortality.

CHO.
　Here in the body pent,
　　Absent from Him I roam;
　Yet nightly pitch my moving tent
　　A day's march nearer home;
　Nearer home, nearer home,
　　A day's march nearer home.

2 My Father's house on high,
　Home of my soul, how near
At times, to faith's foreseeing eye
　Thy golden gates appear.

3 "For ever with the Lord!"
　Father, if 't is Thy will,
The promise of that faithful word,
　E'en here to me fulfill.

BROWN.　C. M.

(345) Bradbury Trio, 97.　Key C.

1 WHEN I can read my title clear
　To mansions in the skies,
I 'll bid farewell to every fear,
　And wipe my weeping eyes.

2 Should earth against my soul engage,
　And fiery darts be hurled,
Then I can smile at Satan's rage
　And face a frowning world.

3 Let cares like a wild deluge come,
　And storms of sorrow fall;
May I but safely reach my home,
　My God, my heaven, my all.

4 There shall I bathe my weary soul
　In seas of heavenly rest,
And not a wave of trouble roll
　Across my peaceful breast.

NO SORROW THERE.

(346)Christian Songs. 198 Key G.

1 AND may I still get there?
　Still reach the heavenly shore?
The land forever bright and fair,
　Where sorrow reigns no more?

CHO.　There 'll be no sorrow there,
　There 'll be no sorrow there;
　In heaven above, where all is love,
　There 'll be no sorrow there.

2 Shall I, unworthy I,
　To fear and doubting given,
Mount up at last, and, happy, fly
　On angel's wings to heaven?

3 Hail, love divine, and pure,
　Hail, mercy from the skies!
My hopes are bright and now secure,
　Upborne by faith I rise.

(HEAVEN.)

SHALL WE ANCHOR.

JOSEPHINE POLLARD, 1863.

From "Bright Jewels," by per. WM. H. DOANE.

1. Shall we an-chor in the har - bor, When our journey's o'er; Shall we meet our blessed Sav - iour,
2. Shall we stem the surging bil - lows, And the heaving tide; Shall we reach that peaceful ha - ven,
3. O, the skies are nev-er cloud-ed, In that hap-py land; And a splendor gleams upon us,
4. We are sail-ing, we are sail - ing To that golden shore, And we'll an-chor in the har - bor,

CHORUS.

On that hap - py gold-en shore? Yes, we'll an-chor in the har - bor, When our tri - al days are
Where the ho - ly ones a - bide?
As we near the gold-en strand.
Where we'll rest for ev - er more.

o - ver; Yes, we'll an - chor in the har - bor, On that hap - py gold - en shore.

(HEAVEN.)

METROPOLIS. C. M. D.

(348) Christian Songs, 196. Key A.

1 YE weary, heavy-laden souls,
  Who are oppressed sore,
Ye travelers through the wilderness,
  To Canaan's peaceful shore;
Thro' chilling winds and beating rain,
  And waters deep and cold,
And enemies surrounding you,
  Take courage and be bold!

2 For Canaan's land is just before,
  Sweet spring is coming on,
A few more beating winds and rains,
  And winter will be gone.
Methinks I now begin to see
  The borders of that land;
The tree of life, with heavenly fruit,
  In beauteous order stand.

3 O what a glorious sight appears
  To my believing eyes;
Methinks I see Jerusalem,
  A city in the skies:
Bright angels whispering me away—
  "O come, my brother, come!"
And I am willing to be gone
  To my eternal home.

WILL YOU GO.

(349) Bradbury Trio, 61. Key F.

1 WE'RE trav'ling home to heaven above,
  Will you go? will you go?
To sing the Saviour's dying love,
  Will you go? will you go?

Millions have reached that blest abode,
Anointed kings and priests to God,
And millions now are on the road,
  Will you go? will you go?

2 We're going to see the bleeding Lamb,
  Will you go? will you go?
In rapturous strains to praise His name,
  Will you go? will you go?
The crown of life we there shall wear,
The conqueror's palms our hands shall
  bear,
And all the joys of heaven we'll share;
  Will you go? will you go?

3 Ye weary. heavy laden, come,
  Will you go? will you go?
In the blest house there still is room,
  Will you go? will you go?
The Lord is waiting to receive,
If thou wilt on Him now believe,
He'll give thy troubled conscience ease,
  Will you go? will you go?

NO SORROW THERE. S. M.

(350) Christian Songs, 198. Key G.

1 FAR from these scenes of night
  Unbounded glories rise,
And realms of joy and pure delight
  Unknown to mortal eyes.
CHO. There'll be no sorrow there,
  There'll be no sorrow there.
In heaven above, where all is love,
  There'll be no sorrow there.

2 Fair land! could mortal eyes
  But half its charms explore,
How would our spirits long to rise,
  And dwell on earth no more.

3 No cloud those regions know—
  Realms ever bright and fair;
For sin, the source of mortal woe,
  Can never enter there.

4 O may the prospect fire
  Our breasts with ardent love,
Till wings of faith and strong desire,
  Bear every thought above.

WOODLAND. C. M.

(351) Christian Songs, 196. Key G.

1 THERE is an hour of peaceful rest,
  To mourning wanderers giv'n;
There is a joy for souls distrest,
  A balm for every wounded breast,
  'T is found above, in heav'n.

2 There faith lifts up her cheerful eye,
  To brighter prospects giv'n;
And views the tempest passing by,
  The evening shadows quickly fly,
  And all serene in heav'n.

3 There fragrant flow'rs, immortal, bloom,
  And joys supreme are giv'n;
There, rays divine disperse the gloom:
  Beyond the confines of the tomb
  Appears the dawn of heav'n.

(HEAVEN.)

WE SHALL MEET BEYOND THE RIVER.

Rev. JNO. ATKINSON, 1867.

From "Bright Jewels," by per. HUBERT P. MAIN.

1. We shall meet be-yond the riv-er, By-and-by, by-and-by; And the
dark-ness will be o-ver, By-and-by, by-and-by; With the toil-some journey
done, And the glorious bat-tle won, We shall shine forth as the sun, By-and-by, by-and-by.

2 Done with all of earth's delusion,
  By-and-by, by-and-by ;
War, and strife, and sin's confusion,
  By-and-by, by-and-by.
We shall rest our pilgrim feet
On the shores where loved ones meet,
There to dwell in bliss complete,
  By-and-by, by-and-by.

3 We shall see and be like Jesus,
  By-and-by, by-and-by ;
He a crown of life will give us,
  By-and-by, by-and-by.
And the angels who fulfill
All the mandates of His will,
Shall attend and love us still,
  By-and by, by-and-by.

4 When with robes of snowy whiteness,
  By-and-by, by-and-by ;
And with crowns of dazzling brightness,
  By-and-by, by-and-by—
There our storms and perils passed,
And with glory ours at last,
We'll possess the kingdom vast,
  By-and-by, by-and-by.

(HEAVEN.)

METROPOLIS. C. M.

(353) Christian Songs, 196. Key A.

1 JERUSALEM, my happy home,
　　Name ever dear to me,
When shall my labors have an end
　　In joy and peace and thee?

2 When shall these eyes thy heaven-
　　And pearly gates behold? {built walls
Thy bulwarks with salvation strong,
　　And streets of shining gold?

3 There happier bow'rs than Eden bloom,
　　Nor sin nor sorrow know:
Blest seats, thro 'rude and stormy scenes,
　　I onward press to you.

4 Jerusalem, my happy home,
　　My soul still pants for thee:
Then shall my labors have an end
　　When I thy joys shall see.

NOW I HAVE FOUND. 6s & 4s.

(354) Bradbury Trio, 85. Key E.

1 THERE is a happy land,
　　Far, far away.
Where saints in glory stand
　　Bright, bright as day,
Oh, how they sweetly sing,
Worthy is our Saviour King,
Loud let His praises ring,
　　Praise, praise for aye!

2 Come to that happy land,
　　Come, come away;
Why will ye doubting stand?
　　Why still delay?

Oh, we shall happy be,
　　When, from sin and sorrow free,
Lord, we shall live with Thee,
　　Blest, blest for aye!

3 Bright, in that happy land,
　　Beams every eye;
Kept by a Father's hand,
　　Love cannot die.
Oh, then to glory run,
Be a crown and kingdom won;
And bright above the sun,
　　We reign for aye.

IVES or GREENWOOD. 7s.

(355) Coronation, 208. Key E♭.

1 WHO are these in bright array,
　　This innumerable throng,
Round the altar night and day,
　　Hymning one triumphant song?
"Worthy is the Lamb once slain,
　　Blessing, honor, glory, power,
Wisdom, riches to obtain,
　　New dominion every hour."

2 These through fiery trials trod;
　　These from great affliction came;
Now before the throne of God,
　　Sealed with His almighty name.
Clad in raiment pure and white,
　　Victor palms in every hand,
Through their dear Redeemer's might,
　　More than conquerors they stand.

3 Hunger, thirst, disease unknown,
　　On immortal fruits they feed;

Them. the Lamb amid the throne,
　　Shall to living fountains lead;
Joy and gladness banish sighs;
　　Perfect love dispels all fears,
And for ever from their eyes
　　God shall wipe away the tears.

6s & 4s.

(356) Winnowed Hymns, 116. Key G.

1 I'M but a stranger here,
　　Heaven is my home;
Earth is a desert drear,
　　Heaven is my home;
Danger and sorrow stand
Round me on every hand,
Heaven is my Fatherland,
　　Heaven is my home.

2 What though the tempest rage,
　　Heaven is my home;
Short is my pilgrimage;
　　Heaven is my home;
And time's wild, wintry blast
Soon will be over past,
I shall reach home at last;
　　Heaven is my home.

3 Therefore I murmur not,
　　Heaven is my home;
Whate'er my earthly lot,
　　Heaven is my home;
And I shall surely stand
There, at my Lord's right hand.
Heaven is my Fatherland,
　　Heaven is my home.

(HEAVEN.)

GOOD NIGHT.

Mrs. ANNIE S. HAWKS.   From "Brightest and Best," by per. R. LOWRY.

Very gently.

1. Good night, good night; it is morning now; Good night, I am go-ing home; I have kept the faith,
2. Good night, good night; I have wait-ed long In hope of the ear-liest ray Of a gold-en dawn
3. Good night, good night; let there be no tears; I'll wake with the an-gel band; And the songs of home
4. Good night, good night; you must tarry here, O ye who are tried and true; At the gates of pearl

REFRAIN. *p*

I have done my work, And the Mas-ter bids me come. Good night, good night, good
that shall break for me In-to full, vic-to-rious day.
we shall sing a-gain, When we reach the heavenly land.
I will stand and wait, When the Mas-ter calls for you.

Good night   good night;

night; I am go-ing home; Good night, good night; I am go-ing home.

Good night,   good night;
(DEATH.)

SECOND HYMN.

F. J. Crosby, 1875.

1 Good night, good night, I must leave you now,
    And go to my home so fair;
   I see the light of the morning break,
    I know I am almost there.

   Cho.—Good night, good night, good night,
     I am almost there;
    Good night, good night,
     I am almost there.

2 Good night, good night, I have heard a voice
   That said in a low, sweet tone:

"Fear not my child, for thy Saviour speaks,
    Look up, thou art not alone."

3 Good night, good night, it is sweet to die,
    And rest in His arms of love;
   To pass away when the heart is young,
    And live in His fold above.

4 Good night, good night, 'tis the angels' song,
    Rings out on the silent air;
   I've passed the waves of the narrow sea,
    Good night, I am safely there.

MARGARET MACKAY, 1832.

REST. L. M.

WM. B. BRADBURY, 1843, by per.

1. A-sleep in Je-sus! bless-ed sleep! From which none ev-er wake to weep; A calm and un-dis-turbed re-pose, Un-brok-en by the last of foes.

2. A-sleep in Je-sus! oh, how sweet To be for such a slum-ber meet; With ho-ly con-fi-dence to sing, That death has lost his venomed sting!

3 Asleep in Jesus! peaceful rest!
   Whose waking is supremely blest;
   No fear, no woe shall dim that hour,
   That manifests the Saviour's power.

4 Asleep in Jesus! oh, for me
   May such a blissful refuge be!
   Securely shall my ashes lie,
   And wait the summons from on high.

SECOND HYMN.

1 So fades the lovely, blooming flower,
   Frail, smiling solace of an hour;
   So soon our transient comforts fly,
   And pleasure only blooms to die.

2 Is there no kind, no healing art,
   To soothe the anguish of the heart?
   Divine Redeemer, be Thou nigh;
   Thy comforts were not made to die.

3 Now gentle patience smile on pain,
   And dying hope revive again;
   Hope wipe the tear from sorrow's eye,
   And faith point upward to the sky.

(DEATH.)

F. KRUMMACHER.   *In memory of Frank W. Howard.*   HORATIO C. KING.

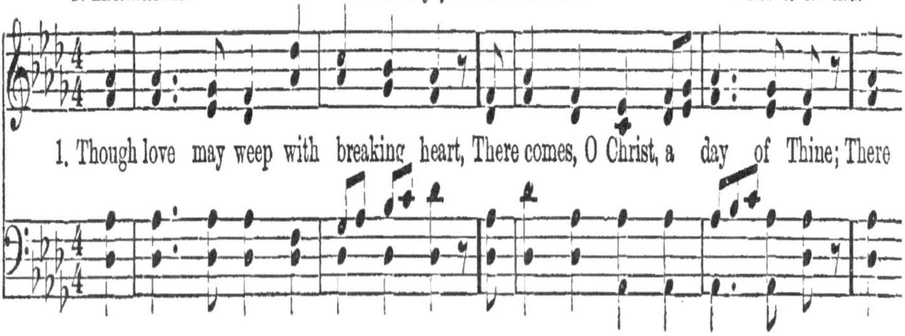

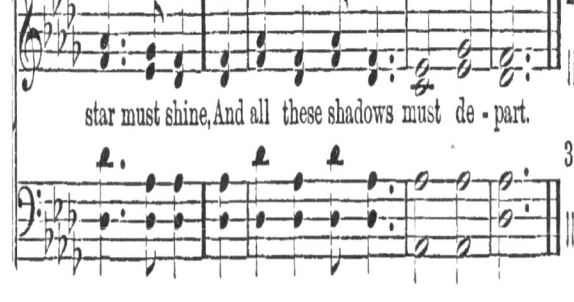

1, Though love may weep with breaking heart, There comes, O Christ, a day of Thine; There

is a morning star must shine, And all these shadows shall de - part; There is a morning

star must shine, And all these shadows must de - part.

2 Though faith may droop and tremble here,
    That day of light shall surely come,—
||: His path has led him safely home,—
    When twilight breaks the dawn is near. :||

3 Tho' hope seem to have hoped in vain,
    And Death seem King of all below;—
||: There yet shall come the morning glow,
    And wake our slumb'rers once again. :||

Plym. Coll. 104, Key of B♭.

RETURN.

Jno. G. Whittier.

1 Another hand is beckoning us,
    Another call is given;
    And glows once more with angel steps
    The path that leads to heaven.

2 Fold *her*, O Father, in Thine arms,
    And let *her* henceforth be
    A messenger of love between
    Our human hearts and Thee.

3 Still let *her* mild rebukings stand
    Between us and the wrong,
    And *her* dear memory serve to make
    Our faith in goodness strong.

(*DEATH.*)

EVENING SHADES.

C. C. COX, 1848.
Gently.

D. E. JONES, 1848. 209

1. Si - lent - ly the shades of evening, Gath-er round my lone-ly door; Si - lent-ly they bring be -
2. O, the lost, the un - for - got - ten, Tho' the world be oft for - got; O, the shrouded and the

fore me, Faces I shall see no more.
lone - ly, In our hearts they per - ish not.

3 Living in the silent hours,
   Where our spirits only blend ;
   They, unlinked with earthly trouble,—
   We still hoping for its end.

4 How such holy mem'ries cluster,
   Like the stars when storms are past ;
   Pointing up to that far heaven,
   We may hope to gain at last.

I'M THINKING OF MY SINS.

Rev. E. P. HAMMOND, 1864.

From "Song Evangel," by per. HUBERT P. MAIN, 1873.

1. I'm thinking of my sins, What wicked things I've done, How very sinful I have been, Although I am so young.
2. But Je-sus He has died For little ones like me; He on the cross was crucified, From sin to set me free.
3. With all my load of sin, I'll go to Jesus' feet, I'll tell Him then, how bad I've been, His mercy I'll entreat.
4. I know my prayer He'll hear, He'll fill my heart with love, He'll drive away my guilty fear, And take me home above.

(WORSHIP.)

MY SABBATH SONG.

Mrs. M. A. KIDDER, 1864.

From "Golden Censer," by per. WM. B. BRADBURY, 1864.

1. Strains of mu-sic oft-en greet me, As I join the busy throng, But there's nothing half so
2. 'Tis a song of love and mer-cy, Speaking peace to all man-kind, Tell-ing sin-ners poor and
3. While I live, O, may I ev-er Love the ho-ly Sab-bath song, And when death shall call me

CHORUS.

pleas-ant, As the ho-ly Sab-bath song. No fear of ill, no fear of wrong, While
need-y, Where the Sav-iour they may find.
home-ward, Join it with the blood-bought throng.

I can sing my Sabbath song: My Sabbath song, my Sabbath song: I love to sing my Sabbath song.

(WORSHIP.)

MY SABBATH HOME.

Dr. C. R. BLACKALL.

From "Pure Gold," by per. WM. H. DOANE.

1. Sweet Sabbath School! more dear to me Than fair-est pa-lace dome, My heart e'er turns with
2. Here to my will-ful, wand'ring heart, The way of life is shown; Here may I seek the
3. Here Je-sus stands with lov-ing voice, En-treating me to come And make of Him my

CHORUS.

joy to thee, My own dear Sabbath Home. Sabbath Home! Blessed Home! Sabbath
bet-ter part, And gain a Sabbath Home.
earn-est choice, In this dear Sabbath Home.

Sweet Home! Sweet Home!

Home! Blessed Home! My heart e'er turns with joy to thee, My own dear Sabbath Home.

Sweet Home! Sweet Home!

(WORSHIP.)

Bishop THOMAS KEN.

SAMUEL STANLEY.

Praise God, from whom all bless - ings flow; Praise Him, all creatures here be - low; Praise Him, all creatures

Praise God, from whom all blessings flow;   Praise Him, all creatures here below;

here be - low; Praise Him above,   Praise Him above,   Praise Him above,   ye heav'n-ly host;

Praise Him a-bove,   Praise Him a-bove,   Praise Him a-bove, ye heav'nly host;

Praise Him a-bove, Praise Him a-bove, Praise Him a - bove, ye heav'nly host; Praise Fa - ther, Son, and

Praise Father, Son,

(WORSHIP.)

Ho - ly Ghost, Praise Father, Son, and Ho - ly Ghost, Praise Father, Son, and Ho - ly Ghost.
and Ho-ly Ghost,

CHORUS, *ad lib.*

Hal - le - lu - jah, Hal - le - lu - jah, Hal - le - lu - jah, A - men, A - men, Hal - le - lu - jah.

SOLO.

Hal - le - lu - jah, Hal - le - lu - jah, Hal - le - lu - jah, Hal - le - lu - jah. Hal - le - lu - jah, Hal - le -

lu - jah, Hal - le - lu - jah, A - men, A - men, Hal - le - lu - jah, A - men, Hal - le - lu - jah, A - men.

(WORSHIP.)

THE PRAISE OF JESUS' NAME.

FANNY J. CROSBY. 1871.

CHESTER G. ALLEN, by per.

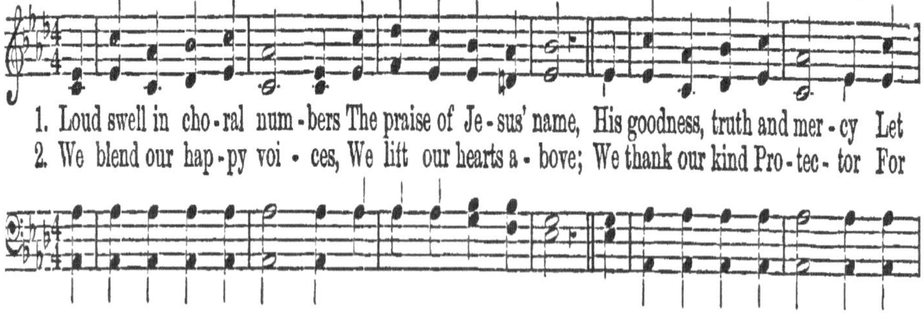

1. Loud swell in cho-ral num-bers The praise of Je-sus' name, His goodness, truth and mer-cy Let
2. We blend our hap-py voi-ces, We lift our hearts a-bove; We thank our kind Pro-tec-tor For

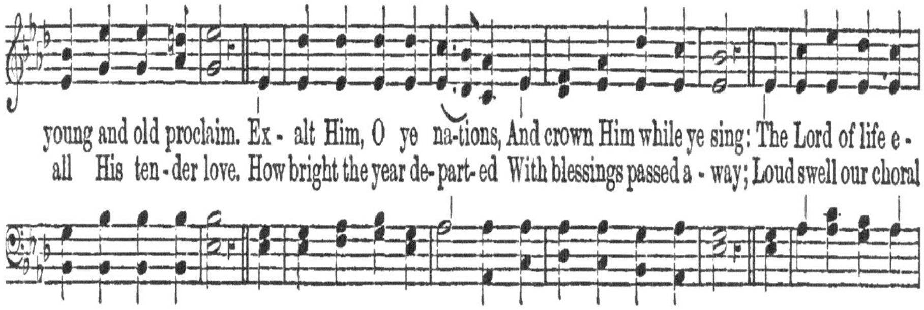

young and old proclaim. Ex-alt Him, O ye na-tions, And crown Him while ye sing: The Lord of life e-
all His ten-der love. How bright the year de-part-ed With blessings passed a-way; Loud swell our choral

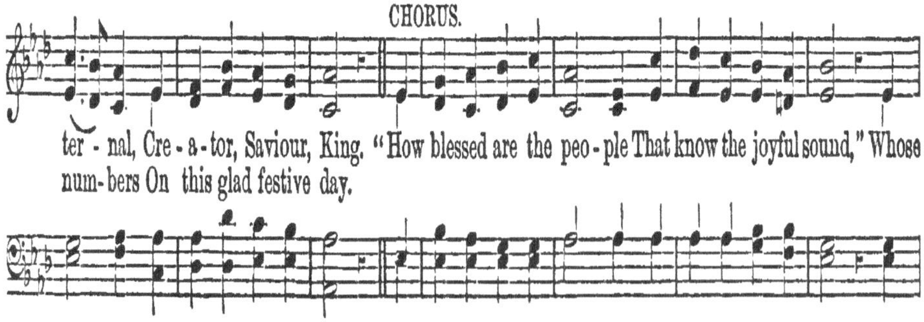

CHORUS.

ter-nal, Cre-a-tor, Saviour, King. "How blessed are the peo-ple That know the joyful sound," Whose
num-bers On this glad festive day.

strains shall yet be waft-ed To earth's re-motest bound.

3 Hosanna in the highest,
  Our grateful songs shall be;
Hosanna in the highest,
  Our Saviour God, to Thee:
And when, with all the ransomed,
  Around Thy throne we meet,
We'll cast our crowns before Thee,
  And worship at Thy feet.

(WORSHIP.)

WE ARE COMING.

FANNY J. CROSBY. 1875.   From "Brightest and Best," by per. HUBERT P. MAIN, 1875.

1. Com - ing, com - ing, we are com-ing To Thy temple, gracious Lord, To re - ceive the
2. Sing - ing, sing - ing, we are sing-ing How Thy wondrous love so free, Floweth on - ward
3. Pray - ing, pray - ing, we are pray-ing That Thy Spir-it, like a dove, May de - scend with

bless - ed teaching Of Thy pure and per - fect Word; Meek-ly would we learn our du - ty,
ev - er on-ward, Like a vast and might-y sea; And our souls mount up with gladness
gifts of mer - cy From Thy gra - cious hand a - bove; Lord we ask, that, by Thy watch-care,

Learn it kneeling at Thy feet, While a radiance from Thy glo - ry Cov - ers all the mercy-seat.
While we swell the loft - y strain, "Glo - ry, glo - ry, hal - le - lu - jah To the Lamb for sinners slain!"
We may all pro-tect - ed be, Ev - 'ry hand be quick to la - bor, And our hearts be stayed on Thee.

(WORSHIP.)

CHARLOTTE ELLIOTT, 1834.

Rev. J. B. DYKES.

1. My God! is a - ny hour so sweet, From blush of morn to eve - ning star, As that which
2. Blest is the tranquil hour of morn, And blest that sol - emn hour of eve, When, on the

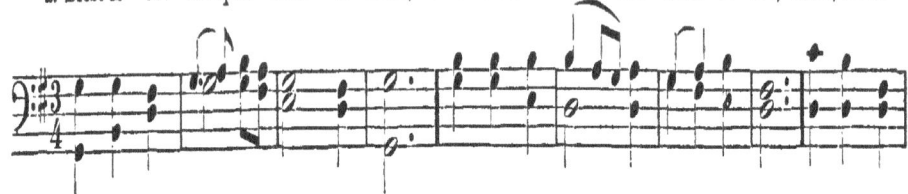

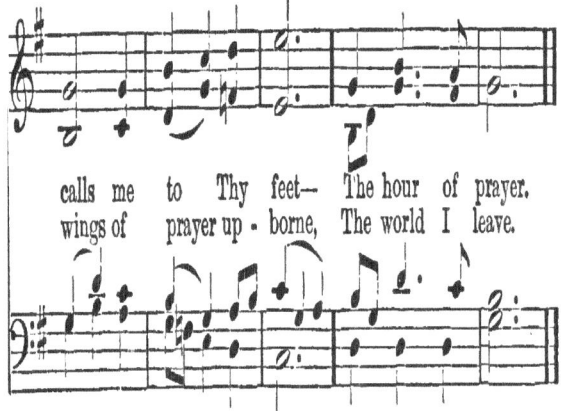

calls me to Thy feet— The hour of prayer.
wings of prayer up - borne, The world I leave.

3 Then is my strength by Thee renewed;
   Then are my sins by Thee forgiven;
   Then dost Thou cheer my solitude
     With hopes of heaven.

4 Lord! till I reach that blissful shore,
   No privilege so dear shall be,
   As thus my inmost soul to pour
     In prayer to Thee.

SWEET HOUR OF PRAYER. L. M. Double.

Bradbury Trio, 10, Key D.

1.

Sweet hour of prayer! sweet hour of prayer!
That calls me from a world of care,
And bids me at my Father's throne,
Make all my wants and wishes known:
In seasons of distress and grief,
My soul has often found relief,
And oft escaped the tempter's snare,
By thy return, sweet hour of prayer!

2.

Sweet hour of prayer! sweet hour of prayer!
Thy wings shall my petition bear,
To Him whose truth and faithfulness,
Engage the waiting soul to bless;
And since He bids me seek His face,
Believe His word, and seek His grace,
I'll cast on Him my every care,
And wait for thee, sweet hour of prayer!

3.

Sweet hour of prayer! sweet hour of prayer!
May I thy consolation share.
Till from Mount Pisgah's lofty height,
I view my home, and take my flight:
This robe of flesh I'll drop, and rise
To seize the everlasting prize;
And shout, while passing thro' the air,
Farewell, farewell, sweet hour of prayer!

(WORSHIP.)

Rev. W. W. Walford, 1846.

SAVIOUR, AGAIN. 10s.

Rev. JOHN ELLERTON, 1861.

E. J. HOPKINS, London, Eng.

1. Saviour, a - gain to Thy dear Name we raise With one ac - cord our parting hymn of praise;
2. Grant us Thy peace up - on our homeward way; With Thee be-gan, with Thee shall end the day;
3. Grant us Thy peace, Lord, thro' the coming night, Turn Thou for us its darkness in - to light;
4. Grant us Thy peace throughout our ear-ly life, Our balm in sor - row, and our stay in strife;

Organ.

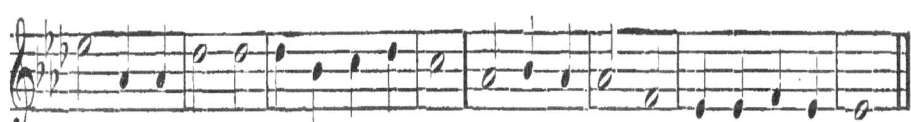

We stand to bless Thee ere our worship cease, Then, low-ly kneeling, wait Thy word of peace.
Guard Thou the lips from sin, the hearts from shame, That in this house have called upon Thy Name.
From harm and danger keep Thy children free, For dark and light are both a - like to Thee.
Then, when Thy voice shall bid our conflict cease, Call us, O Lord, to Thine e - ter - nal peace.

(WORSHIP.)

EVERY DAY AND HOUR.

218

FANNY J. CROSBY, 1874.

From "Brightest and Best," by per. W. H. DOANE.

Slowly.

1. Saviour, more than life to me, I am clinging, clinging close to Thee; Let Thy precious blood ap-
2. Thro' this changing world below, Lead me gently, gently as I go; Trusting Thee, I can-not
3. Let me love Thee more and more, Till this fleeting, fleeting life is o'er; Till my soul is lost in

REFRAIN.

plied, Keep me ever, ever near Thy side. Every-day, ev-ery day, Let me
stray, I can never, never lose my way. and hour, and hour,
love, In a brighter, brighter world above.

feel Thy cleansing power; May Thy ten-der love to me Bind me closer, closer, Lord, to Thee.

(TIMES AND SEASONS.)

DUKE STREET. L. M.

(374) 'Coronation,' 131, Key E♭.

1 Awake, my soul, and with the sun
Thy daily stage of duty run;
Shake off dull sloth, and joyful rise
To pay thy morning sacrifice.

2 Awake, lift up thyself, my heart,
And with the angels bear thy part,
Who all night long unwearied sing
High praises to th' eternal King.

3 All praise to Thee, who safe hast kept,
And hast refreshed me while I slept;
Grant Lord, when I from death shall
I may of endless life partake.   [wake,

4 Lord! I my vows to Thee renew;
Disperse my sins as morning dew;
Guard my first springs of tho't and will,
And with Thyself my spirit fill.

5 Direct, control, suggest, this day,
All I design, or do, or say;
That all my powers, with all their might,
In Thy sole glory may unite.

DOWNS. C. M.

(375) "Coronation," 158. Key E. ♭.

1 Lord! in the morning Thou shalt hear
My voice ascending high;
To Thee will I direct my prayer,
To Thee lift up mine eye:

2 Up to the hills where Christ is gone
To plead for all His saints,
Presenting at His Father's throne
Our songs and our complaints.

3 Oh! may Thy spirit guide my feet,
In ways of righteousness;
Make every path of duty straight,
And plain before my face.

SABBATH. 7s.

(376   Clariona, 89. Key G.

1 Safely thro' another week,
God has brought us on our way;
Let us now a blessing seek,
Waiting in His courts to-day·
Day of all the week the best
Emblem of eternal rest.

2 While we seek supplies of grace,
Thro' the dear Redeemer's name,
Show Thy reconciling face—
Take away our sin and shame;
From our worldly cares set free
May we rest this day in Thee.

3 Here we come Thy name to praise;
May we feel Thy presence near;
May Thy glory meet our eyes,
While we in Thy house appear;
Here afford us, Lord, a taste
Of our everlasting rest.

4 May the Gospel's joyful sound
Wake our minds to raptures new;
Let Thy victories abound—
Unrepenting souls subdue;
Thus may all our Sabbaths prove,
Till we rest in Thee above.

BEAUTEOUS DAY. 8s & 7s.

(377)   Page 114. Key G.

1 Blessed Saviour, watch us, guard us,
As we leave our Sabbath home;
Guide and keep us from all danger,
Till again to Thee we come.

Though we very often wander
In the paths of vice and sin,
‖: Yet we pray that Thou wouldst hear us,
Cleanse and make us pure within. :‖

2 Make each spirit meek and lowly,
Make us leave the ways of strife,
Lead us in the path of duty,
Lead us to the "better life."
Thus we'd serve Thee, blessed Saviour,
Till we've crossed life's stormy sea,
‖: And with each loved friend and teacher
All are gathered home to Thee. :‖

GREENVILLE. 8s & 7s.

(378) Christian Songs, 200. Key F.

1 Lord, dismiss us with Thy blessing,
Fill our hearts with joy and peace;
Let us each Thy love possessing,
Triumph in Redeeming grace;
Oh! refresh us,
Traveling through this wilderness!

2 Thanks we give, and adoration,
For Thy Gospel's joyful sound;
May the fruits of Thy salvation
In our hearts and lives abound!
May Thy presence
With us evermore be found.

3 So, whene'er the signal's given,
Us from earth to call away;
Borne on angel's wings to heaven,
Glad to leave our cumbrous clay,
May we, ready,
Rise and reign in endless day!

(TIMES AND SEASONS.)

PEACEFULLY REST. L. M.

WM. B. COLLYER, 1812.

From "Golden Chain," by per. WM. B. BRADBURY, 1861.

1. An-oth-er fleeting day is gone; Slow o'er the west the shadows rise; Swift the soft-stealing hours have flown.
2. An-oth-er fleeting day is gone; In solemn si-lence rest my soul! Bow down before His awful throne,

CHORUS.

And night's dark mantle veils the skies. Peacefully rest, Peacefully rest, Rest till the morning, Peacefully rest.
Who bids the morn and evening roll.

3 Soon shall a darker night descend,
And vail from me yon azure skies;
And soon shall death's oppressive hand
Lie heavy on these languid eyes.

4 Yet when beneath the dreadful shade,
I lay my weary frame to rest,
That night shall not make me afraid;
That bed the dying Saviour pressed.

5 Again emerging from the night,
I, like my risen Lord shall rise;
Again drink in the morning light,
Pure at its fount above the skies.

EVENING HYMN. L. M.
(380) Bradbury Trio, 291. Key G.

1 GLORY to Thee, my God, this night,
For all the blessings of the light;
Keep me, O keep me, King of kings,
Beneath the shadow of Thy wings.

2 Forgive me, Lord, for Thy dear Son,
The ill which I this day have done;
That with the world, myself, and Thee,
I, ere I sleep, at peace may be.

3 Be Thou my guardian, while I sleep,
Thy watchful station near me keep;
My heart with love celestial fill,
And guard me from th'approach of ill.

4 Teach me to live, that I may dread
The grave as little as my bed:
Teach me to die, that so I may
Rise glorious at Thy judgment-day.

HOLLEY. 7s.
(381) Christian Songs, 119. Key E♭.

1 SOFTLY now the light of day,
Fades upon my sight away;
Free from care, from labor free,
Lord, I would commune with Thee.

2 Soon for me the light of day
Shall for ever pass away;
Then from sin and sorrow free,
Take me Lord, to dwell with Thee.

(TIMES AND SEASONS.)

INDEX.

TITLES IN SMALL CAPS.—FIRST LINES IN ROMAN.

☞FOR INDEX OF SUBJECTS, SEE THE PREFACE.

CPSIA information can be obtained at www.ICGtesting.com
Printed in the USA
BVOW08s1141080714

358479BV00036B/1378/P